# BEYOND
## CONTEMPT

### THE INSIDE STORY OF THE
### PHONE HACKING TRIAL

## PETER JUKES

*This book is dedicated to Alastair Morgan, and the
quarter of a century he has spent pursuing justice for
his younger brother Daniel, murdered in 1987.*

# CONTENTS

# PREFACE
## THE UNTOLD STORY

'There has never been any trial like this,' a defence barrister told me during a smoking break outside the main doors of the Old Bailey – a place where a surprising number of journalists, lawyers and detectives congregated. He added: 'There will never be another trial like this.'

Weeks before the phone hacking trial began in October 2013 the *Daily Telegraph* commentator Peter Oborne billed it as 'the trial of the century.' Yet it had taken almost the whole of the century so far to arrive. Two years had already passed since the *News of the World* closed in 2011 and eleven years since the newspaper had hacked the mobile phone of the murdered teenager Milly Dowler.

In a sense it was, as one prosecutor described it, 'the trial nobody wanted.' In 2006, the Metropolitan Police had limited its inquiries into hacking to avoid a high-profile trial, partly to spare the Royal Family embarrassment. Neither the defendants nor their employer, News International (since re-branded News UK) wanted an Old Bailey showdown. And for all the glamour of some of the targets of hacking, compared to other famous murder or terrorism trials, the stakes could seem small: there were no dead bodies, no violent attacks against other individuals, or attempts to overturn the state.

Yet, the state was, somehow, at risk. Two of Britain's most senior police officers had resigned in the wake of the hacking scandal in 2011. Rebekah Brooks, former Murdoch protégé and not so long ago arguably the most powerful woman in Britain, had achieved the extraordinary feat of being friend to three successive prime ministers. Andy Coulson, her deputy and successor as *News of the World* editor, had been the Prime Minister's director of communications at Number 10. Meanwhile the *News of the World's* hacking victims ranged from actors and footballers to Cabinet ministers and princes. The tabloid had a reputation for exposing the private secrets of the rich and famous, without fear or favour; the trial promised to be as sensational as its front pages. When the judge, Mr Justice Saunders, warned in his opening remarks that not only the defendants but also 'British justice is on trial,' he might well have been concerned that intense media interest in such high-profile defendants could generate coverage that would improperly influence the jury.

The trial was unique in other ways. Normally the state in the form of the police and prosecutors holds the balance of power. Much of our legal system has evolved to help to redress that imbalance. But at the hacking trial the financial might of Rupert Murdoch's media companies News UK and News Corp reversed the situation. Privately funded criminal defences are rare: to have six of them (all the final defendants, bar Goodman) was unprecedented.

There are already several books about the phone hacking scandal. My publisher, Martin Hickman, co-wrote one, *Dial M for Murdoch*, exploring the origins of the scandal and the legal and political campaign in Parliament to expose it. Another, *Hack Attack*, tells of the long battle waged by the *Guardian's* Nick Davies to uncover the truth. Also published this summer was *The News Machine*, by the *Independent on Sunday's* deputy editor, James Hanning, with Glenn Mulcaire, the infamous private investigator whose notebooks provided the bulk of the trial evidence. There are therefore many things I won't cover in this book because they are or will be covered elsewhere: the role of Mulcaire and the origins of phone hacking at the *News of the World*. Or its cover-up. Or the cover-up of the cover-up. Or the role of media in politics. Or Rupert Murdoch's global empire. Or David Cameron's decision to appoint Andy Coulson as his press spokesman. Or Europe's largest planned media acquisition, the BSkyB takeover.

*Beyond Contempt* is not even primarily about the evidence heard at the Old Bailey. I'm not going to replicate what is already in the public domain; my crowd funding supporters could rightly claim their money back. This book is all about what couldn't be reported at the time: the documents and legal arguments embargoed till the verdict; behind the scenes activities by lawyers, police and journalists; and the backstage colour and comment which, given our stringent rules about prejudicing a jury, could have landed me in deep trouble if it had been expressed during the case.

This is partly a story about what it's like to report a long trial. While the reporters were sequestered in the Old Bailey, one gained a husband, another nearly lost his life (but in the end, only his appendix). There was friendship, hilarity, tension, and – in the last few weeks – some contention. There was also, as Brooks once alleged in an email to Will Lewis, suggestions of an 'old-fashioned *Guardian-BBC* hit job': but not against News International. A rather curt copper was rude to a female journalist in Court 12 when he tripped over her on the way to the evidence room. Two male reporters, from the Guardian and the BBC, stepped in to her defence. Voices were raised, but no blows traded.

No matter how objective I try to be about Court 12, this is also ultimately my story. Even on days when the evidence was dull and 'read' in the dry monotone of a barrister or detective, there was always something new to learn.

Court reporting is, as someone once described policing, 99 per cent boredom and 1 per cent terror. I was a completely inexperienced 'blogger' roaming around the legal minefields of the Old Bailey. Despite my lack of legal training, I knew that reporting any of the backstage drama, legal argument or comment described above could have been Contempt of Court (telling the jury things they were not supposed to hear), which is punishable by a large fine or imprisonment. One false move therefore could jeopardise the trial and lead straight to jail. Right at the end of the trial, when the jury retired, this book came up in Court 12 in a discussion on reporting restrictions. When I asked a defence barrister why I was singled out, he said: 'I don't want to have to visit you in Wandsworth Prison, Peter.'

I've also decided to use myself as a character in the drama, not because I want the attention but because my unfamiliarity with the law is a useful (and occasionally amusing) story-telling device for similarly baffled members of the public. Many people have also expressed an interest in how I stumbled into covering the case using social media.

Finally, too, I can answer the thousands of questions that so many people have had, which I could not answer for fear of falling foul of the contempt laws, or because I just didn't know. I was also constantly asked to comment on the evidence, what I thought of the guilt or innocence of the defendants and how I rated the various prosecution and defence arguments. Having refrained from anything but reporting for over 30 weeks now, at last I can speak out.

Yet in some ways I feel uncomfortable expressing an opinion. The glory of court reporting is this lack of comment. Going through the process of just saying who said what, when, has been completely refreshing. I see the phone hacking scandal and British journalism in a new light. I hope I've developed a more sceptical ear for commentary, a sharper eye for fact, and a willingness to present both sides of an argument and to let others come to their own conclusions. Our newspapers tend to mix fact and comment in a way that would perturb many American journalists. Often, many of our newspapers seem to more closely resemble vehicles for provocative comment than fact-finding enterprises. That said, Fleet Street arose in the vicinity of the Inns of Court in the discursive tumult of the early coffee shops, where opinionated lawyers argued the toss, scribes penned affidavits and pamphleteers sold scandalsheets. A search for disclosure and judgement in the shadow of the noose.

Clearly not all the public's interest in the criminal justice system is in the public interest. One telling of the hacking trial is that it was an old-fashioned witch-hunt disguised as a modern trial. There's undoubtedly a lot of prurience in trial coverage. Opposite the Old Bailey is the Magpie and Stump pub. Though housed in a bland modern building, it stands on the same place as an inn which sold special 'hanging breakfasts' to those who wanted a comfy upstairs room to watch someone swinging from a tree. In the same pub, court reporters carry on that tradition, discussing the demise of unpopular defendants. Indeed, before the *News of the World* focused on celebrity and sex, it was famous for court reporting, particularly salacious divorce and libel cases.

For serious and lurid reasons this book is called *Beyond Contempt*. The title was embargoed until the verdict because the resonance – an echo of 'beneath contempt' – could have been unfair to the defendants. As you'll see, that's not my intent. More importantly, the book explores some of the limitations of free speech and the law in a world of social media where every individual has become a publisher. In British law, the right to a fair trial outweighs the right to freedom of expression. As the Crown Prosecution Service notes:

> *Article 10 of the European Convention on Human Rights... **the right to freedom of expression, is a qualified right**, and interference of it in the form of restrictions may be appropriate where this is necessary and proportionate in pursuit of a legitimate aim such as the protection of the **rights of others to a fair trial*** (Article 6 ECHR), or to ***privacy (Article 8 ECHR).***

I suspect some journalists are rethinking this balance. Even Rebekah Brooks, a powerful newspaper editor who championed the rights of a free press, seemed to grasp the limitations of free expression when she protested about 'trial by media.' Before and throughout the trial, many defendants complained about media coverage. Andy Coulson was angered by the *Guardian*'s exclusive on his imminent arrest. Charlie Brooks, Rebekah's husband, explained that the intensive close protection of his wife (she texted her mother that she had more security than the Prime Minister) was partly because she feared a career-destroying photograph of her arrest. Defendants repeatedly ascribed their 'no comment' interviews to police to the fear that their answers would seep into print – an irony, perhaps, given that as journalists most had run stories from police leaks. During the trial this tension between disclosure, open justice and a fair trial was a nail-biting, moment by moment dilemma.

It's still something of a problem. Because of other pending related trials (there are at least 12 scheduled) this book does not quite contain everything the court heard in evidence or in legal argument. For the time being some names must be redacted to avoid prejudicing their trials, ongoing police investigations or charging decisions by the Crown Prosecution Service. But they are not in themselves deeply relevant to the 130 days the court sat.

Finally, this book has been written at speed, for publication as soon as possible after the verdicts, the mitigation pleas and sentencing. Because of that haste it might lack grace or contain a few typos, but should be solid on the facts. I can't claim to be exhaustive. The definitive work on all the trials, all the background, can only be written once all the criminal cases are over. But when it comes to the hacking trial, a window of public interest and legal opportunity has opened.

As I used to say to my producers when writing TV drama under the tight and expensive deadlines of a shooting schedule: 'Do you want it perfect? Or do you want it Tuesday?'

Hello Wednesday.

# CHARGES

## COUNT 1

*Conspiracy to intercept communications in the course of their transmission without lawful authority, contrary to section 1(1) of the Criminal Law Act 1977.*

*IAN EDMONDSON, REBEKAH BROOKS, ANDREW COULSON and STUART KUTTNER between 3 October 2000 and 9 August 2006 conspired together, and with Glenn Mulcaire, Clive Goodman, Greg Miskiw, Neville Thurlbeck, James Weatherup and persons unknown, to intercept, without lawful authority, communications in the course of their transmission by means of a public telecommunications system, namely mobile phone voicemail messages.*

**SUMMARY:** The phone hacking charge that dominated the trial. Four executives at the *News of the World* – including Rebekah Brooks and Andy Coulson – stood accused of approving its mass interception of voicemails between 2000 and 2006. On 8 August 2006, the hacking all but stopped when Scotland Yard anti-terrorism officers arrested the *News of the World* reporter, Clive Goodman and its private detective, Glenn Mulcaire, for hacking the Royal Family. In January 2007, Goodman and Mulcaire were jailed for hacking a total of eight victims. A cover-up by the paper's owner, News International, which claimed that Goodman had been the only reporter to hack phones, continued until 2011. One defendant, news editor Ian Edmondson, fell ill during the trial and was severed from proceedings on 12 December 2013. He may be re-tried.

## COUNT 2

*Conspiracy to commit Misconduct in Public Office, contrary to section 1(1) of the Criminal Law Act 1977.*

*CLIVE GOODMAN and ANDREW COULSON, between the 31st August 2002 and the 31st January 2003, conspired together and with persons unknown to commit misconduct in public office.*

**SUMMARY:** Andy Coulson, then editor of the *News of the World*, later David Cameron's director of communications, stood accused of conspiring with Clive Goodman to pay a Scotland Yard royal protection squad officer £1,750 for copies of two royal phone directories dated September and October 2002 (detectives had found the directories at Goodman's home in 2006 but taken no action then). The jury did not reach a verdict on this charge. There may be a re-trial.

## COUNT 3

*Conspiracy to commit Misconduct in Public Office, contrary to section 1(1) of the Criminal Law Act 1977.*

*CLIVE GOODMAN and ANDREW COULSON, between 31 January 2005 and 3 June 2005, conspired together and with persons unknown to commit misconduct in public office.*

**SUMMARY:** Similar to Count 2 but relating to the payment of £1,000 for a single royal phone directory dated February 2005. The jury did not reach a verdict on this charge.

## COUNT 4

**Conspiracy to commit Misconduct in Public Office, contrary to section 1(1) of the Criminal Law Act 1977.**

*REBEKAH BROOKS between 1 January 2004 and 31 January 2012, conspired with [other who cannot be named for legal reasons] and Bettina Jordan-Barber and persons unknown to commit misconduct in public office.*

**SUMMARY:** While editing the *Sun* Rebekah Brooks authorized a series of payments totalling £38,000 to a *Sun* reporter's 'number one military contact.' The contact was a public official, Ministry of Defence civil servant Bettina Jordan-Barber. Brooks denied knowing that the source (who was not named in the reporter's emails to her) was a public official.

## COUNT 5

**Conspiracy to commit Misconduct in Public Office, contrary to section 1(1) of the Criminal Law Act 1977.**

*REBEKAH BROOKS, between 9 February 2006 and 16 October 2008, conspired [other who cannot be named for legal reasons] and with persons unknown to commit misconduct in public office.*

**SUMMARY:** Again while editor of the *Sun*, in 2006, Rebekah Brooks was alleged to have authorized payment of £4,000 to a member of the Armed Services for a picture of Prince William in a bikini at a fancy dress party. The jury was discharged from entering a plea on this count on 20 February 2014.

## COUNT 6

*Conspiracy To Pervert The Course Of Justice, contrary to Section 1(1) Criminal Law Act 1977.*

*REBEKAH BROOKS and CHERYL CARTER between 6 July 2011 and 9 July 2011 conspired together to do a series of acts which had a tendency to and were intended to pervert the course of public justice, namely permanently to remove seven boxes of archived material from the archive of News International.*

**SUMMARY:** While chief executive of News International (now News UK), publisher of the *Sun* and the *News of the World*, Rebekah Brooks and her personal assistant, Cheryl Carter, stood accused of withdrawing seven boxes of Brooks' journalistic note-books from the company archives on 8 July 2011, in an attempt to frustrate the police inquiry into phone hacking. On that day Andy Coulson was arrested and the *News of the World* was preparing its final edition, four days after the *Guardian* revealed the paper had hacked the phone of Milly Dowler.

## COUNT 7

*Conspiracy To Pervert The Course Of Justice, contrary to Section 1(1) Criminal Law Act 1977.*

*REBEKAH BROOKS, CHARLES BROOKS and MARK HANNA, between the 15 July 2011 and the 19 July 2011 conspired together and with Lee Sandell, David Johnson, Daryl Jorsling, Paul Edwards and persons unknown to do an act or a series of acts which had a tendency to and were intended to pervert the course of justice, namely to conceal documents, computers, and other electronic equipment from officers of the Metropolitan Police Service who were investigating allegations of phone hacking and corruption of public officials in relation to the News of the World and the Sun newspapers.*

**SUMMARY:** By far the most complicated charge, Brooks, her husband Charlie and News International's head of security, Mark Hanna, were alleged to have plotted with security guards to hide evidence from the police. On 17 July 2011, Mrs Brooks, her husband and their guards drove from Enstone Manor in Oxfordshire, where they had been staying (they weren't at their home, Jubilee Barn) to London for her midday appointment at Lewisham police station. Minutes after Brooks was arrested, her husband hid a Jiffy bag containing pornography and a laptop computer behind a bin in the car park below their flat at Thames Quay, Chelsea Harbour.

Shortly afterwards, Hanna took that material to News International's headquarters in Wapping. Later that night a security guard returned two of Charlie's bags to Thames Quay and stashed them behind the bins in the underground car park. While he did so, the guard delivered a pizza to Charlie and a friend. The next morning a cleaner discovered the bags behind the bins and the police were alerted. Because this charge is so thicketed with detail it is dealt with only briefly in this book. Following the conclusion of the trial, the Crown offered no evidence against the security operatives who had been guarding the Brookses.

## FACTUAL NOTE

To avoid confusion, I have used Rebekah Brooks throughout, even when referring to the time when she was under her maiden name, Wade. Charlie Brooks is referred to as Charlie to avoid confusion with his wife. Likewise, to avoid confusion with Charlie's barrister Neil Saunders, I have referred to the judge throughout as Justice Saunders, omitting the formal 'Mr.' News International has since re-branded as News UK; most of the references here are to News International.

# LEGAL TEAMS

## PROSECUTION
*Andrew Edis QC, Mark Bryant-Heron QC, Don Ramble; Rebecca Chalkley; Polly Sprenger*

## REBEKAH BROOKS
*Jonathan Laidlaw QC, Clare Sibson*

## ANDREW COULSON
*Timothy Langdale QC, Alison Pople*

## STUART KUTTNER
*Jonathan Caplan QC, Nicholas Griffin QC*

## CLIVE GOODMAN
*David Spens QC, Benn Maguire*

## CHERYL CARTER
*Trevor Burke QC, Emma Collins*

## CHARLES BROOKS
*Neil Saunders*

## MARK HANNA
*William Clegg QC, Duncan Penny QC*

# NOT WAR AND PEACE

*Andrew Edis QC: These allegedly are criminals.*
*They do not wish to make their criminality clear to*
*every breakfast table on Sunday morning.*

There's nothing like a good courtroom drama – and the hacking trial at the Old Bailey was nothing like any courtroom drama I'd ever seen.

For a start, look at the venue. London's Central Criminal Court must rate with the Taj Mahal as one of the most photographed places on earth, but its exterior is completely untelegenic. From a distance, the Edwardian baroque dome, topped by a large brass statue of Justice wielding scales and sword, looks impressive. But from the street itself it's not grand. The main entrance that greets defendants, lawyers, witnesses and journalists is grim, with granitic buttresses, slotted windows and thick reinforced doors. It looks more like a fortress designed to prevent a bomb attack – which it is. In 1973 an IRA car bomb destroyed the original frontage, injuring 200 people. As a reminder, a piece of glass from the explosion has been left embedded in the ceiling above the main stairs.

Entering the building is forbidding. On my first visit for the pre-trial hearings and 'case management' of *Regina V Brooks & Others* in the summer of 2013, I was immediately accosted by a court guard who asked for a pass or witness summons. Having neither I was ushered out towards the public gallery, accessed via a dark tunnel to the right of the main entrance, where I queued with anxious relatives. Word passed down that phones and other electronic equipment were banned, and I was told that, other than turn back and go home, I could store my phone at a nearby travel agent for £1. When I finally made it in past the searches and up six flights of stairs, painted in dour institutional greens and greys, it felt like a punishment for something; a pre-amble for prison. The British legal system vaunts open justice – but it's not welcoming.

The Central Criminal Court is not a happy place. In cold war Berlin friends and relatives vanished to the other side of the Iron Curtain at a train station called the 'Palace of Tears.' At the Old Bailey tearful or fearful defendants, family or witnesses traipse through its doors every day. When high security suspects arrive, as with the two men who murdered an off-duty soldier in Woolwich, police cars blockade the street and the prison van enters via a fortified entrance to the north on Newgate Street (the Old Bailey occupies the site of the infamous Newgate Prison). The iron bars of incarceration are never far away.

Though one of the larger courtrooms at the Old Bailey, Court 12 is only marginally less functional than the public areas. The wood panelling and green carpet tiles recall a large classroom or small lecture hall. Behind three rows of desks are the barristers in gowns and horsehair wigs, precariously balancing laptops and legal bundles. Around them sit paralegals and police officers, dressed in dark suits. The only dash of colour comes from the judge's fur-trimmed scarlet robe and hood. Only when the usher announces 'Be upstanding in court' and all rise to greet the judge, is the space charged with solemnity. Otherwise it's studious and humdrum; bundles of paper and computer screens: the kind of place you'd sit an exam in, not fight for your freedom.

By Sunday 27 October 2013, the press and the defendants were preparing for that battle. But before the hacking trial could begin, a whole phoney war had taken place in Southwark Crown Court and the Old Bailey, hidden from public view by reporting restrictions.

At first the plan had been to hold the trial in September 2013, but the judge, Mr Justice John Saunders (hereafter Justice Saunders), agreed the trial could be about more than phone hacking. He ruled that two counts of conspiracy to commit misconduct in public office against Andy Coulson and Clive Goodman could be joined to the case – because the royal phone directories Goodman was accused of buying from a 'palace cop' could have been used for hacking. This spelled disaster for Brooks and Coulson's barristers. Brooks', John Kelsey-Fry, had to recuse himself because in 2007 he was counsel for Goodman, who, freshly joined to the trial, might call him as a witness. As Kelsey-Fry's eleventh-hour replacement, Jonathan Laidlaw, needed to read up on the case, the trial was delayed until October – which forced Coulson's QC, Clare Montgomery, to withdraw over a clash of timing. Timothy Langdale replaced her.

While I had covered many of the pre-trial hearings, I was only toying with attending part of the trial. I'd been writing journalistic pieces for a couple of years, mainly for the *Newsweek* and the *Daily Beast*. And though I'd written over 100 articles for those and other publications – not only on the phone hacking scandal but also Jimmy Savile, Hillsborough, LIBOR scandals and 'blue chip hacking' – I didn't see how reporting the trial could become a full time job. My boss Tina Brown had sold the *Daily Beast* that summer and announced she was leaving the website, taking my mentor, foreign editor Louise Roug with her. I was thinking I might pop into the Bailey to write the occasional piece and update my book, *The Fall of the House of Murdoch*. It was a complete accident that I managed to secure one of the sought-after press tickets.

I met the *Guardian* journalist Nick Davies outside court during one of these pre-trial hearings. He looked suspicious when I approached him. I told him I'd hung on every word of his reports since he exposed the hacking scandal at the *Guardian*; he said he'd 'flicked through' my book looking for things he might have missed. Despite that unpromising introduction, Davies was friendly and helpful – and regularly meeting him would be one of the unexpected benefits of the months ahead. Crucially, he told me I'd need a pass to get into the trial. He gave me his email address, and said he'd get his *Guardian* colleague Lisa O'Carroll to pass on contact details of Her Majesty's Courts and Tribunals Service so I could get myself on the list.

Weeks passed, nothing happened, and I almost forgot about the offer. Then sometime in late September I reminded Davies about providing a court contact. He got back to me a few days later and I whizzed off a request. The official at the end of the line told me they were allocating the seats that day and that they had been heavily oversubscribed. I explained I had been writing regularly on the phone hacking scandal for an American publication, but didn't hold up much hope. An hour or so later details of my press ticket arrived in my inbox. The media had been divided into two camps: those with 'gold' tickets that allowed them to claim one of the dozen or so tickets in Court 12 itself, and 'silver' tickets for Court 19, the 'press annex' where the proceedings would be watched on closed circuit television.

Two weeks later, when the trial began, I discovered I was even luckier than I thought. Many more experienced journalists had missed out on this allocation, including *Private Eye's* correspondent, Adam Macqueen, whose concise bi-weekly reports were written from the prison like conditions of the public gallery without access to any electronic equipment.

It wasn't until mid-October that I began to feel the build up to the 'Trial of the Century' – though it wasn't in the press. Given the massive attention senior newspaper figures such as Brooks and Coulson could generate in their own industry, the Attorney General, Dominic Grieve, had spent the summer sending out warning letters to the media about reporting restrictions and contempt of court. MPs had been briefed about the dangers of prejudicial comment or linking back to historic articles or interviews. I wrote a preparatory profile of Brooks for the *New Statesman* with nothing about the hacking or bribery allegations: its lawyers came back saying that nothing about her could be published.

On Sunday 27 October, after months of pre-trial hearings and delays, it looked like the trial would be delayed again. The weather forecasts were full of storm warnings – a major anticyclone was due to hit the South East of England overnight, felling trees and power lines and disrupting road and rail travel.

◆ ◆ ◆

Monday 28 October 2013. Though a blustery, wet autumn morning, the full media pack was braving wind and rain by the entrance of the Central Criminal Court; photographers on steps behind the crowd control barriers, media crews hooked up to terminals and ISDN lines. I took a quick snap of the paparazzi, and one snapped me back with a rapid fire telephoto lens – not because I was important, but to show he could outgun me anytime.

Through the main entrance, and into the queue through security. The guards were diligent about checking passes. One older guy never failed to stop me to inspect the expiry date of my NUJ pass for the next eight months. The queue for the airlock of the security felt like travelling back in time to airport security in the 1980s. Sometimes you could whiz through. At the wrong time, you had to join a queue of bewildered witnesses mixed with determined lawyers with suitcases and boxes brimming with legal papers. Despite always packing my keys, phone and wallet into the bag through the scanner, I never once failed to trigger the metal detector, and was 'wanded' two or three times a day for eight months.

After collecting my ticket I found myself in Court 19, the press overspill room, which had rows of chairs and two large flat screen TVs, a spaghetti of cables and a couple of small computer speakers. The screens switched between two camera angles – the witness box to the judge's left and the barristers in front of him. These wide-angle shots were wonky and ill-defined. Generally, only the prosecution team and some defence barristers on the right side of the courtroom were visible; Brooks and Coulson's QCs were not in the frame. In a blurry haze, you could just see the defendants in the glass box behind the wigs. Sound was variable. Sometimes the police controlling the feed down to the annex forgot to turn it on. At other times the barristers omitted to wear their radio mics, or left them too near mobile phones, causing interference. Early in the trial the sound system blew several times, leaving journalists in the annex belting up the eight flights of stairs to Court 12.

I found myself sat in front of James Doleman and behind Martin Hickman. Doleman was covering the trial for a media and marketing magazine called *The Drum* and Hickman was covering the trial for *Hacked Off*, the campaign group. The three of us unconsciously gravitated to the same section, quickly dubbed 'Bloggers Corner.'

Like the perfect storm that failed to materialise in the morning, the first day of the trial was an anti-climax. There was nothing to report. The court was taken up with jury empanelment, a typically British exercise. Unlike in the United States, there is no grilling about background, beliefs, attitudes or connections that could be favourable to the prosecution or defence. Instead, jurors have to complete questionnaires which are then argued about by counsel in their absence (along with all legal argument during the case; the jury never heard what went on when they were asked to leave the court). Two days were spent whittling away anyone with strong affiliations to journalism or the police. Potential jurors were challenged by the defence for following Lily Allen on Twitter, having excessive knowledge of Paul McCartney, or even being friends with someone who worked for the *Guardian*.

While this went on, the annex was a hotbed of gossip. The seven charges were serious and extensive, but they would also reveal life at News International and the lives of the men and women who made the news. Brooks, Coulson and a third *News of the World* executive – managing editor Stuart Kuttner - stood accused of approving phone hacking at the paper (Count 1). Separately, Coulson and Goodman faced two 'palace cop' corruption charges (Counts 2 & 3). Brooks, while editing the *Sun*, was accused of two other charges of conspiring to commit misconduct in a public office, by paying public officials (Counts 4 & 5).

Then came the conspiracy to pervert the course of justice charges. Brooks and her long-serving PA, Cheryl Carter, were charged with trying to hide Brooks' journalistic notebooks on 8 July 2011, two days before *News of the World*'s final edition (Count 6). Then there was a fantastically complicated charge claiming that Brooks, her husband Charlie and News International's head of security, Mark Hanna, tried to stash some bags from detectives on 17 July 2011 – the day of Rebekah Brooks' arrest (Count 7). Reporters knew that Charlie's defence was that he was only trying to hide some pornography. Inevitably, in the annex, the reporters had some questions. What kind of porn was on Charlie Brooks' laptop? Who had given Goodman a royal phone directory? Was Hanna angry with his former chief executive? And what had Brooks really said that in her love letter to Coulson…?

◆ ◆ ◆

The long running affair between the two principal defendants had been one of the worst kept secrets of 2013. It had come up in the pre-trial hearings. During a search of her London home, detectives had discovered an unsent letter from Brooks to Coulson on an old Hewlett Packard computer at the bottom of a cupboard. In pre-trial legal argument the love letter was dubbed 'the sensitive matter.' I don't know why the lawyers bothered with that euphemism. We all knew what they were discussing. A Fleet Street newspaper had dropped a heavy hint. On 1 June, a *Mail on Sunday* front-page, *No 10 Rocked by Secret Love Affair*, reported that the Prime Minister, David Cameron, had been 'stunned' by the disclosure of a secret, now-concluded affair between un-named 'middle-aged figures.' A No 10 source was quoted as saying: 'This revelation is dynamite. None of us could believe it when we first heard it. Then we just thought, 'What a complete mess'.' Guido Fawkes, the blogger, named the front-page graphic ACRB.PNG: the initials of Andy Coulson and Rebekah Brooks.

In the first of many ironies at the trial, Brooks and Coulson's barristers wanted the love letter excluded from the case because its disclosure would harm or breach their human rights, namely the right to privacy. Having lost that argument in pre-trial hearings, on Monday 28 October the barristers were now asking for the fact of the affair to be excluded from the opening prosecution argument. Jonathan Laidlaw, for Brooks, spoke about 'reducing the drama' by removing mention of the affair at the outset (the journalists in the annex groaned) because it would generate adverse publicity, which could impact on the jury and his client's right to a fair trial.

A former senior Treasury Counsel, and therefore one of the top prosecutors in the country, Laidlaw spoke with a forcefulness which combined steely logic with a sense of personal mission. While his vocal tone was light, polite and apologetic as he engaged in banter and practicalities with the judge, something would snap into place as soon as he moved onto his skeleton arguments: unyielding will combined with moral certainty. To Laidlaw, the prosecution had enough evidence of confidences shared by Brooks and Coulson in the phone call data, especially during the disappearance of Milly Dowler in 2002. The proximity of those calls to the disappearance of Dowler made mention of the affair superfluous, he said. 'My learned friend, Mr Edis,' Laidlaw said, referring to the Crown's prosecutor, Andrew Edis QC already had 'the professional relationship between deputy editor talking to editor.' By excluding mention of the affair during the opening, 'he does not lose very much if anything. '

◆ ◆ ◆

The courtly language of court conflict, spoken in the mellifluous tones of public school English, would fascinate me for months. I'm not sure any fictionalised version of modern legal dramas has quite caught its subtle inflections and barbed subtexts. Suffice to say there appeared to be an undertone of tension between Edis and Laidlaw, who practise at the same chambers. The simmering conflict between them would boil over in the months ahead.

The response of Justice Saunders (or to give him his full title, Sir John Henry Boulton Saunders) was just as sonorous and polite. To Laidlaw's contention that the prosecution already had enough evidence he observed: 'The argument 'You've got enough' is not attractive in this case,' he said. 'Not attractive' – the wry under-statement, typical of the court.

Trained as a chorister, and apparently still a keen singer, Justice Saunders had a lightness and clarity in his voice that cut through the bad acoustics of the court. As the trial went on, it would also become apparent he was a keen football supporter and an accomplished reciter of racy tabloid stories. Classy but also demotic, he often cut through the legal waffle with good humour and common sense. In reply to Laidlaw, he pointed out that he'd already made a 'concession' to exclude most of the letter to maintain the privacy of Brooks and Coulson – only including one paragraph that spoke of their close pro-fessional relationship, which was of 'real concern' to the case.

Laidlaw responded with a new argument. He reiterated that he was no longer defending Brooks' Article 8 Rights to privacy – even though the Brooks and Coulson teams had been fighting tooth and nail to keep the letter out of evidence on that basis for months. 'Her right to privacy has long gone, as we've all seen in the last couple of years,' Laidlaw said: 'Having held others to account, she has no issue about this matter being the subject of publicity in due course. She can't possibly complain about publicity of this sort. It would be hypocritical.' But though it was 'inevitable' the affair would come out in evidence, Laidlaw argued, it should not be 'opened' but should be deployed with 'circumspection' later.

This was the first sign of what I thought of as legal trench warfare – daily arguments over legal points and admissions, which would derail the whole process several times, and nearly turn the hacking trial into the 'Mistrial of the Century.' The trench warfare metaphor came to me early, but I was not alone in making the comparison. The prosecutor, Edis, later described the trial as being 'like World War One.'

As Laidlaw sat down, a second wave of attack was launched from the bench behind him, by Timothy Langdale QC, for Coulson. Another veteran criminal prosecutor, Langdale had been called to the Bar in 1968. He conveyed an air of familiarity with the law and casual personal authority. By strange coincidence, he was also the man who a decade earlier had prosecuted the killer of Sarah Payne, an eight-year-old whose abduction and murder initiated Rebekah Brooks' much discussed Sarah's Law campaign.

Instead of the moral rigour bordering on outrage of Laidlaw, Langdale's attitude was more relaxed, world-weary even – but no less lethal. He simply warned Justice Saunders they all had to be 'assured of the potential benefit, in relation to the alleged Milly Dowler conversation.' As would happen, time and time again, through weeks of legal argument ahead, Justice Saunders would note the forceful arguments down, and then defuse the combat with a brief and genuine-sounding 'Thank you. '

Now it was the turn of Edis, the lead prosecutor, to rise. Tall, slightly diffident and languorous, at first he most resembled a Latin schoolmaster from the era of *Mr Chips*: kindly, but too abstruse perhaps, or even vague or indecisive. Edis started slowly: the material had been 'considered very carefully' ever since 'it came to our attention in February this year.' He spoke quietly, as if circling around the issue. The affair was 'probative' since it provided 'direct evidence' of how much information Brooks and Coulson shared, how close their relationship was; how much they trusted each other.

Then, like a jazz player getting into a groove, Edis suddenly found his rhythm, and began to riff on the Count 1 conspiracy charge: phone hacking. 'The reality is that the true nature of the relationship of two people accused of conspiracy is essential to the case,' he argued, now clearer and swept up by the rightness of his thoughts. 'The true nature of the relationship is material for the jury to consider. There are a lot of Article 8 rights, not only of the defendants,' he added, pointing out that to prove the prosecution's case the lives of many phone hacking victims would be 'paraded in a public courtroom.' 'I can't take a different approach,' Edis said, in full flow now, the hesitance gone. 'We are not looking at any prejudicial effect… It is not my approach to inspire publicity. The reason I am keen to open it, is to make it clear to the jury why this matters.'

Publicity – again: the bane of the case. I had read a statement from Brooks' lawyers in the *Daily Telegraph* two years back saying she couldn't get a fair trial because of the volume of press coverage. Laidlaw underscored this by producing three huge ring binders for the judge which he said was just a 'selection' of the prejudicial press and social media comment against his client. Today, he had an even more recent article which was clearly in contempt of court. I gulped when I heard the source. *Newsweek,* the magazine I wrote for, had decided to post a piece on Brooks, complete with reference to her appearance before the Commons Committee on Culture, Media and Sport (hereafter, the Commons media committee) in 2003 when she admitted to paying police officers for information in the past. Since Parliament barred this evidence being used in the trial, Justice Saunders agreed to a 'take down' notice against the American website. Although I hadn't written the piece, I prayed nobody checked the name of the publication written on my annex ticket.

Returning home that evening I found these legal minefields exploding closer to my door. Steve Nott, a friend of Alastair Morgan (a campaigner for justice for his murdered brother Daniel) had been sent a letter by the Attorney General for contempt of court. Apparently this was over a tweet he'd sent in reply to me earlier that morning with a picture of Coulson outside the court, and an ill-considered remark about how 'guilty' he looked. I hadn't seen it on my timeline, preoccupied by the day's proceedings. But someone had, and reported him to the authorities. I put Nott in touch with a lawyer and thought nothing more about it. However, others online already seemed to know about his case before he informed anyone. A Twitter account named TabloidTroll was immediately blaming me, asking me why I hadn't reprimanded Nott for the tweet, adding I was the 'poster boy for such people.'

Unfortunately as the trial progressed there would be more to come in this proxy battle with TabloidTroll. But this was just a sideshow to the contempt arguments that raged in court the next day.

◆ ◆ ◆

*Private Eye* had decided to celebrate the opening of the hacking trial by picturing Rebekah Brooks on its front cover with the headline *Halloween Special: Horror Witch Costume Withdrawn from Shops.* The lawyers in Court 12 reacted as if this were cataclysmic. The prosecution was so concerned about the prejudicial effects that police officers were dispatched to seize some of the offending editions from a stall outside nearby Farringdon Station. The canny newspaper vendor told them to come back with a court order. But the comedy of that situation wasn't echoed in court.

For an hour or so, the trial looked on the verge of collapse. For Brooks' barrister, Laidlaw, this was more proof of what he'd been arguing all summer: there was a 'witch hunt' against his client. Laidlaw argued forcefully that the judge should stay the trial because justice for Brooks was 'impossible' given the 'campaign against her.' Justice Saunders looked cornered, and almost helplessly responded: 'What do you want me to do?' Langdale backed Laidlaw and added that – at the very least – the trial should be delayed for weeks so a new jury could be selected. *Private Eye* was referred to the Attorney General for contempt of court – who that afternoon ruled he would take no further action. Justice Saunders soothed the defence by promising to make specific directions to the jury about ignoring newspaper coverage and social media after they were sworn in. But already on that second day tempers were fraying, and lawyers seemingly gathering material for appeal against any unfavourable verdicts.

This trench warfare never stopped. Edis was keen to empanel the jury and start opening the prosecution case. But Laidlaw, wanting to dictate his own timetable, was resisting – breaking the Crown's momentum, dictating the pace. Laidlaw reproached Justice Saunders and Edis: 'You're both rushing it. You're rushing it!' Even Justice Saunders' equanimity was shaken by this suggestion. He blushed, and added that – given the three-month delay of the trial and over a year of legal argument – he could hardly be accused of 'rushing it.' However, Laidlaw won the tactical victory and delayed Edis' opening till the next day. So the jury were sworn in on Tuesday 29 October. As Saunders addressed them, I could start tweeting the 'Trial of the Century.'

# PASSION AND PREJUDICE

*Mr Justice Saunders: Don't believe
everything you read on Twitter.*

When it comes to live-tweeting the phone hacking trial, I was the happy beneficiary of three strokes of good fortune: I lucked out getting a pass to the annex; I lucked out getting a phone signal in the press annex; and more than anything, I lucked out with my judge.

I didn't know at the time, but Justice Saunders was a leading advocate of live coverage of criminal trials and 'open justice ': that justice has to be seen to be done to ensure it reflects the values of society. He'd pioneered this in 2011 during the trial of a Tory peer, Lord Taylor, for an expenses fraud. He did so despite a prejudicial comment by the entrepreneur Alan Sugar, whose tweet speculating whether the Tory would get as long a sentence as a Labour MP, David Chaytor, caused some stir in court. When he learnt of the peer's message, Justice Saunders cleared the court and said: 'Can someone contact Lord Sugar and get that removed.' Sugar duly complied and the threat to a fair trial evaporated.

The normal rule about coverage of trials is that journalists can use electronic devices in court, as long as they file through some intermediary editorial process. Live-tweeting from the courtroom itself was a novelty, though the *Guardian*'s Lisa O'Carroll pioneered reporting of judicial inquiries, and some other high profile cases had been covered on Twitter. Most old hands I'd spoken to thought it would be very unusual in such a complicated case, with so many reporting restrictions.

However, having checked and double-checked, my first tweet of the second day of the trial, Tuesday 29 October, was this:

> Left the courtroom and can confirm Judge has ordered we can live tweet prosecution argument in #hacking trial @DBanksy @nigelpauley

I'd 'live-blogged' before: mainly election coverage of presidential debates during the Obama campaign, and then the delivery of Lord Justice Leveson's report into the culture and ethics of the press in November 2012. After decades writing dialogue and drama, I could type quickly and had an ear for an arresting phrase. But as far as I knew, Justice Saunders would allow only the scripted opening speeches to be reported live. Tweeting a trial is different from newspaper reporting. For instance, my tweets on Justice Saunders' comments on the *Private Eye* cover were:

> Justice Saunders directs jury to ignore Private Eye cover. 'It is a joke which in the circumstance of today is in particularly bad taste.'

The longer phrase, noted down by the shorthand writers working for newspapers was:

*It's meant to be satire. You ignore it. It has no serious input and it's not relevant to your consideration. It's one of those things which you will have to ignore – a joke, that in the circumstances of today is a joke in especially bad taste. '*

I got the essence of his remarks – but the shorthand takers won on comprehensiveness. Mind you, my tweet was published within seconds of the judge speaking.

Next, Justice Saunders addressed the issue of media coverage. The full sentence went like this:

*'I'm going to give you some extremely important directions. They are always important, but they could not be more important than they are in this particular case. In this case in a way not only are the defendants on trial, but British justice is on trial... It is absolutely vital that you decide this case solely on the evidence and the arguments that you hear in court. '*

I tweeted:

Saunders on importance of phone hacking trial and related publicity 'Not only the defendants are on trial British justice is on trial'

There's no way you can tweet a whole speech in real time. Highly-skilled stenographers can record one with special keyboards, but I think I made the right decision in terms of the 'not only' line: that phrase has stuck ever since.

Justice Saunders went on, and even the shorthand takers went to précis. Though he wasn't going to order the jurors 'not to go on to Facebook or any social media for the duration of the trial. I urge you to consider whether you ought to.' He added they should avoid reading 'comment' or doing research, and avoid blogs by 'well-known actors, musicians, politicians and others' who might make comments on the internet. 'It is very much hoped that they will not do so during the trial…. and they may well be breaking the law if they do so. I hope appropriate action will be taken against them if they do.'

> In unusually long directions to jurors, Saunders told them not to comment or read comments about trial on social media, or google research

I think my next tweets got the gist:

> Well know actors, musicians and politicians may publish blogs and send tweets on… topics which they know very little

> Saunders to jurors: 'Do not look up back up editions of newspapers. Do not look up anything in search engines on Google or Yahoo'

> Justice Saunders warned jurors on pop stars, celebrities or politicians who may comment on the case 'Ignore what they say'

One advantage of live media is that you get immediate feedback. My snippets were retweeted by dozens of other people in real time, including by the Labour MP Tom Watson, who had more than 100,000 followers. Immediacy doesn't replace the qualities of the court reporter: a live account can never provide long detailed quotations, and the perspective of a daily record. But it can provide something else - some of the tempo of events, the cut and thrust of debate, in real time. Obviously cameras can do that, but they focus on the visual and the emotive: O J Simpson trying on gloves, Oscar Pistorious breaking down in court. Tweeting, because it's text-based, is about facts and evidence. And information has a half-life: the first time you hear something feels very different to every other time.

◆ ◆ ◆

On Wednesday 30 October yet more trench warfare delayed Edis' opening ( 'these things crop up,' Justice Saunders told the jury) so it wasn't till lunchtime that hard copies of Edis' opening speech were delivered to the annex. They were numbered, so if my version went astray, or found its way into the public domain before the prosecution finished, I could be traced.

To be frank, Edis sounded nervous as he began to outline the Crown's case. Given the force of the defence benches arrayed against him, and the media attention, it's no wonder. He spent the first part of his opening going through the eight defendants sitting in their order of indictments, before he remembered to introduce his prosecution team.

Racing through the warm photocopies, we now had confirmation of what would be coming: the affair (although the paragraphs from the love letter had been redacted), some deeply incriminating emails, and a mention of the porn in Charlie Brooks' bag. But the content couldn't be reported until Edis said it to the jury. And Edis, the classic improviser, was diverging wildly from the written text (the porn was never mentioned in the opening). So you just had to follow his points, beat by beat.

By the time Edis went back to the original phone hacking investigation in 2006, and Mulcaire's guilty plea, I could sense (partly through his pausing and logic) that some news was about to break. Anyone who had kept an eye on the court listing for the trial would have noticed the number of defendants had gone down from 12 to eight over the course of the year.

BREAKING: Edis: 'Mr Mulcaire has also pleaded guilty this year in these proceedings to three counts of phone hacking..'

BREAKING: 'Miskiw, Thurlbeck, Weatherup – News Editors have all pleaded guilty to count one' #hackingtrial

These pleas were highly significant. For four years after Goodman and Mulcaire had been convicted of phone hacking in 2007, News International had claimed phone hacking at the *News of the World* had been the fault of a 'rogue reporter' and a contracted private detective. Now the outside world knew that senior executives had admitted their part in a conspiracy to invade the privacy of thousands of individuals: Greg Miskiw, Neville Thurlbeck and James Weatherup had been news editors at the *News of the World*; the men who controlled the reporters, and reported to the editors. Mulcaire too had pleaded guilty to hacking Milly Dowler's phone.

To show just how the paper's hacking had worked, Edis gave the jury examples of Mulcaire's notes, a timeline of hacking 'narratives' by victims such as Louise Woodward, a friend of supermodel Kate Moss's brother; Tessa Jowell, the Labour minister; Lord Frederick Windsor; and *Mail on Sunday* reporters Sebastian Hamilton and Dennis Rice.

Edis' opening speech was 120 pages long. Connecting the hacking, alleged bribes to public officials (from two newspapers: the *News of the World* and the *Sun*) and two conspiracy to pervert the course of justice charges was a feat of narrative. As the clock ticked, it was clear Edis was unlikely to get to the 'sensitive matter' – the Brooks-Coulson affair – by 4.30pm, the end of that first court day proper. With a sense of occasion, and an eye for a memorable phrase, he concluded his first day with this peroration: 'Perhaps this evening I can leave you with a single thought... How much did the management know what was going on their newspapers? The *News of the World* was a Sunday paper. It was published once a week. It wasn't *War and Peace*. It wasn't an enormous document…. It was the management's job to know what was in the paper. '

When I got home, there were over 1000 interactions on my Twitter feed. As I tried to check through my *Daily Beast* piece I began to wonder if live-tweeting wasn't a more direct way of reporting the trial. In my career in radio and then television, I had had to listen to what other people told me the public wanted to watch or hear. Now I could ask them directly.

But there was a danger. I didn't have the protection of an in-house lawyer, and my timeline was stuffed with potentially prejudicial comments. After Steve Nott's experience, I decided to warn my Twitter followers about the perils of contempt of court. I would do this repeatedly in the months ahead – but it didn't stop my timeline becoming a resource for counsel arguing the defendants could not get a fair trial.

◆ ◆ ◆

By the second day of Edis' opening on Thursday 31 October, I was determined to be the first to break news of the 'sensitive matter'. As Edis moved onto the Milly Dowler evidence, where it would be raised, my fingers trembled as I typed.

> BREAKING: 'BROOKS AND COULSON having an affair that had been lasting at least six years'

I was so tense I forgot to release the caps key early enough.

My Twitter followers began to sky-rocket in a way which Head of UK Twitter News, Joanna Geary, later explained to me only happens on rare events or when users have bought followers. I was also told by someone that I beat Nick Davies by 20 seconds on tweeting out the affair – I was ridiculously pleased. As the news went viral, a number of commentators, many of whom had been employees of Brooks or Coulson, upbraided others over the alacrity with which they'd passed on the news: weren't they as guilty as any tabloid of invading privacy?

They had a point. But only up to a point. I felt for Brooks and Coulson who, because of the order of the charge sheet, had to sit next to each other in the dock as their private lives entered the public domain. I disagree with the argument that this was karma for two newspaper editors who made their careers with personal revelations of the lives of others. Even if the *News of the World* traded in public prurience, celebrating the embarrassment of its former editors just compounded the initial wrong. But these defendants were at least forewarned, forearmed, and the nature of their closeness was germane to the criminal allegations they faced.

◆ ◆ ◆

By now the trial had become blanketed in reporting restrictions, listing people whose existence couldn't be reported. A dozen or so names heard by the jury could not be reported to avoid prejudicing future trials. As the case went on, even the judge found it hard to keep track of the list of ever-changing embargoed names, which at one point rose to more than 30. Most of the live-tweeters got the names wrong at some point and had to delete what they had tweeted. Temporary holding names were agreed – 'senior Sunday Mirror executive,' 'senior NOTW journalist' – but even these were hotly contested regarding the possible levels of identification. Merely naming an article by a veteran journalist could identify him or her.

If live-tweeting carried these dangers of naming names, it had one advantage over traditional reporting – context. Since I nearly always phrased the statements as 'Edis says' or 'according to Laidlaw,' I could avoid the tiresome 'allegedlys' or 'the court was told' or 'the jury heard' which pepper full reports. My *Daily Beast* lawyers were particularly pedantic about adding 'according to the prosecution' to my articles. By the end of the second day I was tweeting some 5,000 or 6,000 words a day from court. A senior politician rang to tell me that most of the screens in Whitehall and the newsrooms he'd visited were watching my feed. The stakes were getting higher and any cock-up on my part would be monstrously visible.

Inevitably, social media reporting was becoming a part of Rebekah Brooks' defence. On the morning of Friday 1 November, her counsel was complaining there had been 4.7 million 'hits' on her name. A random Google search brought up 178 million, they claimed. None of the reporters present managed to replicate this: a Boolean search using quotation marks brought up 911,000 entries.

Most of the seasoned court reporters must have thought I was crazy to tweet as I did. Too kind to express it, they must have imagined I would burn out through exhaustion, or flame out on contempt. James Doleman, who has covered several trials in Scotland, told me later that he didn't think I'd survive more than a couple of weeks. Meanwhile, Harry Cole from the Guido Fawkes blog – one of my bigger re-tweeters – told me I'd better be there 'for the duration.' It sounded like a prison sentence.

◆ ◆ ◆

The weekend gave me space to gather my thoughts, and re-examine my financial situation, which was going from bad to dire. Without a retainer from the *Daily Beast* I couldn't afford to remain in court. Worse, a series of late payments and failed promised projects meant I was hitting my overdraft limit.

Ever since I'd written a piece about the poor state of British TV drama for *Prospect Magazine* five years ago my well paid (but often tedious and frustrating) TV drama writing career had dwindled. In some ways I wasn't unhappy about that, and writing about the problems of monopoly in a public broadcaster like the BBC gave me the courage to write about News Corp's tightening grip on newspapers and pay-TV. But like the Micawber equation for misery, my outgoings had exceeded my income for several years. I was now about to miss the first mortgage payment in my life.

Impending penury aside, I was still in demand for media appearances. A plush car took me to CNN's London studio, where I did a three-way interview with David Folkenflik, host of CNN's *Reliable Sources*, and the Columbia University academic, Emily Bell. They complimented me on my choice of shirt. I felt like a million dollars, but I was becoming insolvent. How could these two things be true?

That night, I glanced through the photocopy of Edis' opening statement – and wondered if there was any more breaking news for Monday morning. I was looking forward to the buzz of covering the case, but the early morning starts had left my body – long used to the freelance writer's nocturnal rhythms – exhausted. Monday would be my last day in court.

That last day, as Edis stood up to finish his opening address, the sound in the annex failed. The BBC's main regular producer, Gaetan Portal, banged the speakers and checked the cables – to no avail. Great. A technical malfunction was going to ruin my last hurrah. Then I noticed other journalists discreetly leaving the room. I followed, and the trickle of reporters became a flood. Most headed to the lifts, but I knew they moved at the pace of an arthritic snail, so I began the first of one of my many races up the stairs to Court 12.

I was among the first dozen or so hacks to arrive. With no seats anywhere, I crouched and began to tweet out Edis' account of Rebekah Brooks' reaction to the arrest of Clive Goodman in August 2006 – a letter in her name to the PCC saying her journalists 'work within the law.' He then spoke about the early *Guardian* reports in 2009 by Nick Davies, which made the rogue reporter line held by the company 'untenable.' He covered the *New York Times* investigation of 2010 and the Sienna Miller lawsuit which led to the 'emails that closed the *News of the World.*' While seeking to keep News Corp's bid for BSkyB alive, News International had, in January 2011, handed over three emails showing evidence of phone hacking to the

Metropolitan Police, prompting its new inquiry, Operation Weeting. Edis then went through the *Guardian* scoop on 4 July 2011 about the targeting of Milly Dowler and the impact on Brooks.

The human drama was vivid in the room. While Brooks and Coulson sat side by side, now outed as lovers, their nemesis, Nick Davies, made notes only feet way in the press seats. (Davies had told me that Coulson had hissed 'traitor' at him during the Tommy Sheridan perjury trial).

Distracted, I'd failed to notice my Twitter interactions were buzzing again, and some were quite angry. One tweet seemed to stir a few journalists.

> Edis on Dowler voicemail 'deletions' and 'false hope' moment alleged in Guardian. No evidence that Mulcaire deleted voicemails

Neil Wallis, former deputy editor of the *News of the World*, was making great play of this, saying the *Guardian* had falsified the story about deleting voicemails. Foolishly, I responded, sticking to the phrasing used by Edis there was 'no evidence Mulcaire deleted voicemails.' Wallis didn't like this, and told me I was showing bias. It was an important lesson I'd learn several times – the hard way – about judgmental comments on my tweets: don't interact. As a court reporter you can't risk joining the outer world of comment and speculation. If I had my own opinions of the evidence, I couldn't afford the luxury of expressing them. Yet.

> 'I am ring fenced properly… if we don't launch the Sun on Sunday this weekend…' BREAKING: 8th July 2011 SUN ON SUNDAY already planned

As the prosecution ran briskly through the email deletion/reten-
tion policies at News International, I also (inadvertently) got my
last breaking from his opening. Edis was reading an email Brooks
wrote four days after the Milly Dowler scandal broke, and I was
halfway through a tweet when I realised it was breaking news.

For anyone who had followed the scandal, the fact that News
International was already planning the *Sun on Sunday* before the
*News of the World* had closed confirmed a long held suspicion. The
court later heard that in April 2011 senior News International
executives had decided the redtop's brand was 'too toxic.' This revelation rather sank the argument that it was Nick Davies who put
hundreds of journalists out of a job.

Edis ran through the closing case on Counts 6 and 7, and
some call data between Hanna and Charlie Brooks on the day
of his wife's arrest. Then he started playing the black and white
CCTV footage from the car park below the Brooks' flat at Chelsea
Harbour in London, where Charlie had hidden a bag containing
his pornography and a laptop computer.

In the press annex, which I'd returned to, we could see the
footage much more clearly. And sometimes laugh. And speculate.
From day one the consensus was that the case against Rebekah
Brooks on phone hacking was 'circumstantial' or 'inferential.'
There was no smoking email, no 'top left' tasking of Mulcaire (the
private investigator recorded who commissioned him on the top
left-hand corner of his notes) and no call data from her editorship
of the *News of the World*. The general opinion was that Brooks
was in greater danger from Count 5, the conspiracy to commit
misconduct in public office charge over her approval of payments
for a *Sun* journalist's 'number one military source.'

Andy Coulson's case looked a whole lot worse. I'd say that most
journalists thought, at the time, that although Brooks would be
acquitted on phone hacking, Coulson would be convicted. Some
people assumed he was being the loyal NCO, jumping on a live
grenade to save his former commanding officer and sweetheart.

But all this was conjecture. At any rate, we didn't know what the jurors were thinking. Talking to them was a complete no-no. James Doleman told me how he found himself on the same bus as a juror during the Tommy Sheridan perjury trial in Glasgow. (For fear of contempt of court, he promptly got off).

In a departure from the norm and perhaps as a sign of his concern, Timothy Langdale, Coulson's counsel, made his opening remarks to the jury immediately after Edis, rather than wait until the prosecution had completed its case. I tweeted Langdale's remarks even more furiously because I wanted to prove there was no bias in my reporting. Coulson's defence was simple: he couldn't have been expected to read in detail the 'blizzard of emails' that went across his desk as deputy editor, then editor, of *News of the World*.

Emails, emails: the *News of the World* had been killed by emails. Three emails had ignited Operation Weeting in January 2011. Coulson's defence team had been fighting all year against the use of emails associated with Clive Goodman, on the grounds that the police searches for them had failed to comply with the Regulation of Investigatory Powers Act 2000 – the same law Coulson was being charged with breaking. The ironies were already piling high when, after Langdale finished his opening, Justice Saunders made a surprising ruling:

> BREAKING: I've been told we can live tweet from day to day now, depending on evidence. #hackingtrial

This may have been great news for transparency and open justice, but what was I going to do? I never thought any judge would allow live blogging of such a complex, contempt-fraught trial. And he left me in an invidious position. I'd gained almost 10,000 new followers on the basis I was live tweeting the trial. Many were looking forward to my continued coverage. There was only one hitch – I couldn't afford to do it. As I went home and managed to squeeze the last of my credit card to buy food, I discovered some kind anonymous soul had donated £10 to me using my public email address found on my blog (yes it's possible).

As I lay in bed that night, I realised I'd have to explain to my followers why I was halting my coverage. But that £10 donation sowed the germ of an idea. Perhaps someone might offer to pay me to stay at the trial? Highly unlikely, but I had to explain my absence, and perhaps hint at a way to prevent it. Unable to sleep, I got up again at 2am, and went back to an old blog I'd used to launch my book two years previously, to write a rather self-pitying explanation:

> *As a freelancer I have no retainer to cover my time there. I get paid per piece, and with a likely offer of one piece per week being published for the remaining months of the trial, £200 per week will not cover my living expenses in London. Actually, given the cost of living here, they barely cover a day…. Prior to the trial, without having to be in court all day, I've managed to cross-fund the time through other work and dip into my savings. But now I'm broke (mortgage defaulting broke to be honest) and so will have to seek other work in the months ahead.*
>
> *This is not a pity plea or pitch. There are others who survive on much less than I do. But it is worth noting for those who celebrate the 'everything for free' era of Google….*
>
> *Some kind soul sent me some money through PayPal through my peter@peterjukes.com account just so I would continue live reporting. I haven't figured out how to return that, so I might just email back and offer to do a Q&A for that person, or attend a session of their choice. Some other tweeters have kindly offered to set up a crowd funding account. I'm neither a saint nor a martyr, and given the importance of this trial for 'British justice' as the presiding judge put it, I will not ignore further requests. If there's a popular demand for more*

*coverage, I will respond and carve out as much as time as possible to return to the court...'*

By the time I woke up the next morning, the response was phenomenal. The Twitter link had been retweeted nearly 100 times, with dozens of sympathetic comments. The blog itself had been re-blogged elsewhere and had nearly 1,000 views. Meanwhile several commentators, taking up my PayPal hint, suggested I crowd-fund my coverage. Former tabloid hack turned comedian and documentary maker, Richard Peppiatt, was the most vocal.

I wasn't entirely unfamiliar with crowd-funding. My book on Murdoch had been pre-sold on this basis by *Unbound,* and I'd looked at this model with Marcos D'Cruze, co-writer of my musical *Mrs Gucci,* who had crowd funded some recordings. I logged on to Indiegogo and within 10 minutes had assembled a crowd-funding site.

The next stroke of luck was the video. Video pitches sell projects more effectively than text. I had the advantage of the newly-minted CNN interview on YouTube. Thanks to the experience of crowdfunding my book, it didn't take me long to think of 'pledges' – signed copies, extra briefings, launch parties, which could generate more money. I hated the idea of constantly pitching for support, so set a deadline of six days. With no pride left to swallow, I hit the publish button, tweeted out the links and ignored the internet for the next few hours. When I checked the site again, I'd raised half the money. Or rather, others had.

One of the most inspiring things about crowd-funding is not the money, but the interaction with people interested in your work, and several complete strangers had become advocates, tweeting and retweeting links to the fundraising. Gabrielle Laine Peters, Jon Lippitt and Claire Pollard – three people I'd never even heard of let alone met – would become key figures supporting my work throughout the trial. As well as raising money, I had crowd-sourced three talented people.

Within an hour my campaign was half funded. I added a rider to my blog:

> *UPDATE; putting pride aside for public demand, I created a crowd funding page at IndieGogo in order to cover the trial till at least Christmas. An amazing response in the first hour or so*

The BBC website covered the crowd-funding. Even TabloidTroll praised it as a possible new model for journalism. Within six hours I had hit the target and, within 24 hours, had overshot it by 50 percent. I was exhausted, humbled, and most importantly – since some of the money came through immediately – able to pay my mortgage. There was only one downside: I'd have to get up the next morning, go back to the uncomfortable chairs in Court 19 and risk jeopardising the trial with a single ill-judged tweet.

◆ ◆ ◆

Typically, my first day back was the first (and only) day Justice Saunders banned live-tweeting.

That non-livetweeted session concerned two men who had met Brooks on holiday in Dubai in April 2002, the weekend the Missing Milly story was published in the *News of the World*, with Milly Dowler's voicemail messages as part of the early editions. One witness, William Hennessey, remembered Brooks had disappeared to talk to her office about a 'missing Surrey schoolgirl.' He also had a nice line in self-deprecating replies. When told by Laidlaw that his client, Brooks, could not remember the meetings in Dubai, Hennessey simply said: 'Why would she?' The second witness, Dean Keyworth, a friend of Andy Coulson's, could only remember talking to Kemp about leaving *EastEnde*rs and his fondness for Hermes toiletries. In his cross-examination of Keyworth, Langdale secured a quick character reference for his client, Coulson. But what was Laidlaw going to do? These two witnesses were important for Brooks' case. He had to discredit the story that Brooks was concerned by Milly Dowler that weekend in April 2002. How would he do that?

Laidlaw then launched one of the most cunning defence tactics I've ever seen: a device he would deploy at regular intervals in the months ahead, a formidable weapon which would leave witnesses quivering, the jury compliant, and the rest of the court submissive and cowed. He deployed repetition and tedium. He went through the details of their various lunches and drinks by the poolside in swish Dubai hotels, blow by blow, again and again. It was a Cartesian approach, to question events repeatedly until they became so boring you wished they would disappear, and the whole courtroom dissolved in a mist of doubt. During a two-hour long cross examination of a police officer later in the trial, Goodman's QC David Spens could be heard muttering to another barrister 'How much longer is this going to take?' Laidlaw himself recognised the ordeal and apologised to the jury: 'Sorry that was a bit hard going. '

Finally he got to the point with Keyworth: 'Mrs Brooks really struggles to remember the details,' he said. Sensing what was happening, Edis got to his feet. 'If my learned friend would ask the witness a question…' Trying not to look annoyed, Laidlaw cut straight to his Hamlet-like 'to be or not to be' question: 'Do you actually remember meeting her? '

'Yes,' Keyworth said, cheerfully, seemingly unaffected by the existential hole the rest of us had fallen into: 'Very vividly. It was great publicity for the hotel.'

Quick as a flash, Saunders stirred from the boredom and joked: 'I'm not sure he was expecting this sort of publicity. '

# SEX, LIES AND VOICEMAILS

*Jonathan Laidlaw QC: I am not, in any sense, being critical…*

Throughout the trial the publicity problem remained. Virtually every day before the jury entered the court in the first few months the defence teams would complain about a magazine piece, newspaper article or tweet. Generally the judge would shrug off these complaints and remind Laidlaw that the jury had been directed to ignore comment. But Laidlaw wouldn't relent. His second, Clare Sibson, insisted Justice Saunders deal with a *Metro* newspaper headline and an *Evening Standard* piece that erroneously suggested former England football manager Sven-Goran Eriksson experienced six years of continuous hacking – an allegation potentially injurious to Brooks' case.

Justice Saunders deftly solved the problem. When the jury filed back in, he warned them: 'Some reports in papers may be misleading. There is a sub editor looking for an eye-catching headline. But eye-catching headlines don't catch the tenor of the case of the whole… An example of that is Sven-Goran Eriksson. The suggestion that the *News of the World* was hacking his phone for six years or so is not an established fact, or necessarily part of the prosecution case. 'The warning, designed to please the defence, also had a perverse corollary – it was an implicit criticism of the industry shaped by Brooks and Coulson in their heyday. 'Listen to what the advocates are saying here, and particularly what witnesses are saying,' reiterated Justice Saunders: 'Don't rely on newspaper reports.'

He needn't have worried. The headlines were beginning to fade, and most of my followers on my timeline complained mainstream media outlets were burying reports of the trial. After the salvoes of Edis' opening, which generated media coverage of shock and awe proportions, the trial now shifted to door to door fighting. And what a slog that would be.

> Re: #hackingtrial Some of my recent tweets might seem dry and repetitive compared to prosecution opening: but this is reading in evidence

Reading in evidence – when a lawyer reads a statement or a report to the court – is a laborious process which has not been represented in any fictional trial I've ever seen, for good reason. It could almost be done by computers. Take the timelines. Though only visible to counsel and the jury, these large graphical fold-up papers showed the hacking of selected targets and their connections in colour coded lines. As the trial wore on and the defence lawyers added so many of their own bundles to the Crown's A3 timeline, they almost threatened to topple over onto jurors.

Each prosecution timeline represented thousands of hours of detective work, as Mulcaire's notes of targets and access numbers were married to the available call data from thousands of phone records (only a small fraction of the whole that survived). Targets' phone numbers had to be proved by billing information from the phone companies; there were often dozens of people around a celebrity, politician or member of the public the news desk was surveilling. Hacking is really a network tracing activity. People don't leave messages on their own voicemail. If you want to know what a celebrity or politician is saying, hack their family and friends.

People of interest were then tallied to potential stories in the *News of the World*, culled from the newspaper's archives. Voicemail tapes or transcripts were cross-referenced. One-off payments to Mulcaire, or his retainer fees had to be tracked down through the invoices of News International's payment systems. And for each of these elements, witness statements had to be taken, redrafted, signed and sworn to bring the evidence 'up to proof. '

Reading in this kind of evidence was never going to set the press benches alight. As Edis' junior Mark Bryant-Heron went through another call data list or payment schedule with his stentorian voice, some unfortunate police officer had to stand in the witness box confirming every assertion with a repetitive 'yes, 'or 'that is correct.'

Hours were spent following these audit trails, and an amazing amount of factual information about hacking would be laid down. I was never quite bored enough to stop tweeting, because I knew every date and name was part of a massive three dimensional jigsaw which – when put together – showed how briefly being caught in the searchlight of *News of the World* could lead to someone's love life, health problems, business plans and personal angst exposed to a lucrative publicity machine.

Despite *Private* Eye's complaint about the number of press tickets, by this point there was no court official on the door of the annex to check them. Having never been entirely full, the annex thinned out. The number of journalists dwindled to about a dozen stalwarts, who could somehow survive the complex details of voicemail settings of the mobile service providers or the niceties of cash contributor payments at the *News of the World*.

To anyone who wants to know how real detective work happens, this section of the trial was instructive. One simple example: every victim in the multiple timelines had to give a statement that they did not know Glenn Mulcaire and had not given him permission to access their voicemail. Tedious and pedantic questions they might be, but potential gaping loopholes in the realities of an adversarial court system, where one police oversight would be picked up and re-examined again and again, as an example of either incompetence, presumption of guilt or abuse of power. And soon they would be. But there was another aspect to these timelines which could easily be missed.

◆ ◆ ◆

During November, timelines for more than 20 victims of phone hacking were read in to the evidence. Excluding the royal targets relevant to Clive Goodman (Helen Asprey, aide to the Duke and Duchess of Cambridge; Paddy Harverson, Communications Secretary for the Royal Family; Jamie Lowther-Pinkerton, Private Secretary to Princes William and Harry: and Mark Dyer, Royal Equerry to the Prince of Wales and the Royal Princes) – what do the following personalities (all of whom had timelines) have in common?

Sven-Goran Eriksson and Faria Alam
Andy Gilchrist
David Blunkett and Kimberly Quinn
Delia Smith
Wayne Rooney, Patricia Tierney and Laura Rooney
Tessa Jowell and David Mills
Lord Prescott
Mark Oaten
Sir Paul McCartney and Heather Mills
Gordon Taylor
Nigel Farage and Liga Howells
Calum Best and Laura Hogan
Jude Law, Sienna Miller and Jade Schmidt
Lord Archer and Edwina Freeman
Charles Clarke and Hannah Pawlby
Kerry Katona

With the exception of Delia Smith, all the other political, sports, music, film or television personalities were suspected of (or close to someone suspected of) some kind of illicit liaison or marital dysfunction.

At first I thought this subtext of sex, lies and voicemails was deliberately chosen by the prosecution to highlight the hypocrisy of the two former editors of *News of the World* who were having an on/off affair for when these individuals were targeted.

Two successive Home Secretaries, David Blunkett and Charles Clarke, figured prominently. Blunkett had his relationship with a married woman exposed even though he was a 'friend' of the *News of the World* and News International executives. Clarke was targeted over a bogus rumour he was having an affair with his special adviser even though he had willingly given interviews to the paper and was a friend of a *News of the World* executive. In the timeline for the former fire brigade union leader, Andy Gilchrist, Brooks' *Sun* had branded him a 'love rat' and 'lowlife fornicator' for an affair which had ended the previous decade.

Police and prosecutors had chosen these individuals from among the *News of the World's* victims, not to highlight any hypocrisy on the part of Brooks and Coulson, but because they had chapter and verse in terms of evidence: a tasking by Mulcaire, call data to show hacks and related stories in the newspaper. Sometimes Mulcaire had made recordings of the voicemails too.

Nonetheless the *News of the World* was indisputably the market leader in kiss and tells. Under the editorship of Brooks and then Coulson, it became even more interested in private lives. This was nowhere more apparent than in the encounter between Andy Coulson and David Blunkett at his constituency home in Sheffield in August 2004, when Coulson confronted the Home Secretary about his relationship with Kimberly Quinn, publisher of *The Spectator*.

On 7 November, the jury were played Blunkett's recording of the meeting. It was inaudible in the annex, though Coulson's barrister, Langdale, replayed the tape during his defence the following year. Here's some of what I tweeted the second time round:

*'There's no desire to cause you damage. It precedes my editor-ship,' says Coulson to Blunkett as the Home Secretary talks about the principle of privacy and how he defended the Tories in the 80s on this issue. Blunkett emphasises to the News of the World editor how his friendship with Kimberly Quinn isn't a secret. Coulson replies: 'You've been much more than friends' and then adds how he is 'extremely confident of his information:' they had a three year affair, spent nights together at Blunkett's holiday cottage.*

*Blunkett seems incredulous: 'What's it based on?' Coulson seems confident: 'extremely reliable sources.' Blunkett scoffs: 'Everyone says that... it's not evidence.' But then Coulson suggests he has something more than gossip: 'Forgive me for being crude about this, but I'm not going to lay out photos of you and this lady in a bedroom.'*

*Blunkett puts up a valiant defence: 'My private life is my own... I've been divorced for 14 years.... what do you expect me to say '. Coulson explains the problem: the allegation that he's having an affair with a 'married woman '. 'You're asking me to say I've had an affair with a married woman?' asks Blunkett. 'Yes and nothing more,' Coulson replies.*

After the Prime Minister, Blunkett was probably the most powerful government minister, in charge of policing, prisons and counter terrorism. Yet here was a young redtop journalist telling the divorced politician that his affair with a married woman wasn't quite 'a resigning matter.' Meanwhile, that same young tabloid editor was having an extramarital affair with his fellow editor.

Brooks was in contact with Coulson the night before that meeting, and also the following night as the *News of the World* published the story of the Blunkett affair with an as-yet-unnamed woman. The next day Brooks' *Sun* named her. As Coulson predicted, the Blunkett affair then became a tabloid feeding frenzy. Though News International were not the first to reveal Quinn's pregnancy, its management already knew about it, because Mulcaire had hacked voicemails left for her by a pregnancy clinic.

> **BREAKING:** NI Lawyer had copy of birth certificate of Kimberly Quinn's child in his safe

Later admissions revealed there were 300 messages on micro-cassettes in that safe. A year later, in 2005, Blunkett would resign over allegations he helped fast-track a visa application for Quinn's nanny. Later that year, the court heard, he was targeted by Mulcaire again over an alleged liaison with Sally Anderson – a woman he had met in Annabel's night club. Anderson had already been in contact with journalists from the *Daily Mail* – though Blunkett didn't know that, and his plaintive taped voicemail messages to Anderson were played to the court. After a story about them was published, the politician told Anderson the press were 'absolutely vile' – 'real bastards' and 'hyenas' – and hoped they would 'rot in hell.' On one recording of a Blunkett message to Anderson, Mulcaire could be heard saying: 'Just say I love you and that's £25 grand.' Mulcaire, though, was not the only one to record the voicemails:

> **BREAKING:** Max Clifford recorded the voice mail messages left by Blunkett on Sally Anderson's voicemail and showed to Sunday People

◆ ◆ ◆

Max Clifford would remain an important figure throughout the trial. The ringmaster of tabloid sleaze came to prominence during the John Major government in the nineties, claiming the scalps of several prominent Tory MPs and ministers. Clifford figured frequently in evidence, but because he was being tried at Southwark Crown Court for indecent assault (he was found guilty) his name could not be reported at the time.

In Court 12 of the Old Bailey, the jury heard Brooks and Coulson had a difficult relationship with Clifford, and for several years refused to use his services. However, the evidence suggested that the breakdown wasn't over scruple, but money. Clifford had sold the story of David Beckham's relationship with Rebecca Loos to News International as an exclusive in 2004, but elements of the story had appeared in rival newspapers. When, after the original police investigation into hacking in 2006, Clifford found out that he had been hacked by Mulcaire, he engaged the lawyer Charlotte Harris, who was intent on forcing the private detective to name names in the civil courts. In 2010, Brooks ended Clifford's lawsuit by making a 'commercial decision' to pay him £1 million for future stories.

If the ethos of the redtop press was in the dock at the Old Bailey, one of its most famous figures appeared in legal argument. Piers Morgan, then a CNN host, started following me soon after the hacking trial began. He said he couldn't retweet my crowd-funding campaign because so many of his friends were in the dock. Morgan had been Coulson's predecessor as editor of the *Sun*'s Bizarre showbusiness column, and edited the *News of the World* before Brooks.

Unknown to me at the time, he was also potentially a witness. While editing the *Daily Mirror* Morgan had attended a birthday party for his friend Coulson, at which Brooks, then editing the *Sun,* was also present. Another guest, Ambi Sitham, a lawyer who attended the party as the girlfriend of the publicist Neil Reading, was a prosecution witness. She would claim that Brooks and Morgan, editors of Britain's two best-selling daily papers, openly joked about phone hacking at the party in a Balham steakhouse. That testimony would come later. At this point all we knew was that Morgan was wanted by the defence to counter Sitham's evidence. But the argument about Morgan provided a useful insight into the intricate legal rules about calling witnesses.

For prosecution evidence, witness statements which are not contested by the defence may be read to the court. However if the defence challenge their evidence, witnesses must appear in person. The Crown is not allowed to ask any questions beyond the 'evidence in chief' of the original witness statement. However during cross-examination the defence can go beyond the existing prosecution statements, and adduce new 'evidence in rebuttal.' This difference between evidence in chief and evidence in rebuttal was central to Laidlaw's demand that the prosecution rather than the defence should call Morgan. That way, the prosecution couldn't wander beyond his witness statement to other matters. As always, Brooks' team were obsessed with publicity. As Justice Saunders summarised it, Laidlaw was hesitant to call Morgan in Brooks' defence because he 'engenders contrasting polarised reactions in people.' 'Some people's reactions are very favourable to him and others are very hostile,' Justice Saunders wrote: 'The defence are concerned that if some of the jury have a hostile reaction to him that will reflect on Rebekah Brooks and will colour their view of her. '

Meanwhile, the prosecution refused to call Morgan because he 'may not be a reliable witness,' partly because of his evidence to the Leveson Inquiry, where he denied knowing about hacking.

Justice Saunders ruled against ordering the prosecution to call him. In a complicated ruling, he quoted a report of a 1994 Court of Appeal Case by the then Lord Chief Justice Taylor: 'The Crown were under no duty to call witnesses to give evidence in respect of witness statements which had never formed part of the prosecution case.' Justice Saunders added in clearer English: 'For the trial judge to have pressed the Crown to call the witnesses would in effect have required them to act as both prosecution and defence. '

◆ ◆ ◆

While Laidlaw was fighting for Brooks, it was the turn of Coulson's lawyer, Langdale, to score his first real victory against the prosecution in front of the jury. It came, somewhat unexpectedly, in the shape of Calum Best, son of the late footballer George Best.

Calum Best had carved out a career on shows such as Celebrity Love Island and appeared in Mulcaire's notebooks in March 2005. Looking debonair in a suit but lost in the witness box, Best confirmed details of his service provider, an old mobile number from many years ago, and his texts to a glamour model, Lorna Hogan.

Langdale's cross examination of Best was indicative of the defence's strategy when it came to several phone hacking timelines: the paradox of celebrities who sought favourable publicity but reviled the negative. 'You wouldn't have appeared on Celebrity Love Island if the press hadn't been interested in your personal life, and personal relationships, 'Langdale said to Best, following up with a final rhetorical question that seemed to answer itself: 'Some media intrusion you have actively encouraged yourself? '

'Correct, 'Best replied, cheerfully agreeing it could lead to well-paid TV appearances. 'And therefore earning money,' continued Langdale 'running into thousands rather than hundreds. 'The implication was clear. If celebrities complained about the papers making money out of their stories, they were still beneficiaries of the eco-system when it suited them.'

Langdale's second line of attack would also become a staple during the months ahead: most of the *News of the World* stories hadn't come from phone hacking – they had come from sources. He listed an array of these around Calum Best; Phil Hughes, his father's agent; Regulat, who organised personal appearances, who was a friend of Ross Kemp; Adey Phelan who ran a hairdressers in Soho called Blow and allegedly received money from a *News of the World*'s showbiz reporter, Rav Singh. Best said he'd known Singh since around 2004, but couldn't remember crashing parties with him. Out of the blue Langdale asked if Singh alerted Best to tabloid stories prior to publication. Best replied: 'I can't remember that.' This seemed like an innocent aside at the time, but would become a crucial line of defence later. Langdale was laying down a marker.

To confirm his first point about celebrity collusion, Langdale went through a series of tabloid stories about Best. The cumulative effect of the headlines was like watching a bloody wildlife documentary of sharks in a feeding frenzy around a victim:

2 May 2004, *Calum: How Dad Drove Me to Drugs*
20 February 2005, *11 Minutes of Shame*
27 February 2005, *Calum Confesses*

In November 2005 there was a splash about George Best five days before he died and on 11 and 18 December articles by his son in the *News of the World* about his death. On 27 March 2006, the paper headlined a story of Best having sex with the glamour model Laura Hogan before his father's memorial service in Manchester: *Lust Like Dad*. On 16 April 2006, the *News of the World* printed: *I'm Having Calum Best's Baby* about Hogan's pregnancy. On 21 May 2006, another article appeared: *Best's First Grandchild*.

The last three stories were sourced through the *News of the World's* northern reporter, Chris Tate. Giving evidence after Best on 13 November 2013, Lorna Hogan, the model, confirmed that Tate paid her between £3,000 and £10,000 for exclusive gossip sourced from celebrities she met at nightclubs. Hogan insisted she was not paid for a scan of her baby with Best, who had texted her: 'How could you be so low as to sell pic of unborn child?' Hogan later contracted Max Clifford.

◆ ◆ ◆

Another drama quietly played itself out during the morning of Best's evidence, 13 November. Within minutes of Best leaving the witness box, another defence team had found an email about him in its bundle of News International data. A month later, Langdale called the officer in charge of the email evidence in the Calum Best timeline, Detective Sergeant John Massey, and gave him a roasting. 'How come you missed that?' asked Langdale in his most disappointed voice. Massey was placatory: 'I can only apologise it seems to have been missed.' Langdale wanted to hammer home the point: 'How could you have missed it? It was obviously relevant.' Massey apologised again: 'The fact remains quite palpably it was missed, I apologise.' That wasn't enough for Langdale: 'Nobody drew the defence's attention to the fact there was evidence related to Calum Best, due that very day,' he complained. 'It was only as Calum Best was leaving the stand that the defence were given a password to that disk from the prosecution. It was only because [not named for legal reasons] team provided that email to me I could put that email to Calum Best. '

By then, however, it was quite clear why Langdale was hitting the police so hard about this particular timeline. It culminated in an email Coulson sent a colleague on 20 May 2006, about worries that Best was being tipped off about Hogan's deal with the paper, in which Coulson commanded: 'Do his phone.' Though Langdale made much about the 'last moment' nature of the recently recovered Chris Tate email, the strategy had actually been set out many months before. In the pre-trial submissions six months earlier in April, Clare Montgomery QC had indicated their defence for this apparently damning email: 'Do his phone' was not an instruction to hack the footballer's son but was a request for the billing information on Rav Singh who was in regular contact with Best, and who could have tipped him off about Hogan.

A few weeks later, on 4 February 2014, DC John Massey would retract his apology for missing the newly discovered email: it wasn't on the database of News International emails being searching. 'I didn't have anything else to hand,' said Massey, 'and wasn't in a position to argue, so I conceded that if I missed it...' Justice Saunders intervened to reassure the detective: 'Don't worry, we're not accusing you of perjury or anything.' However, that wouldn't stop Langdale using the oversight as an integral part of his attack on the police and a 'systemic failure in the disclosure system.' Once the prosecution phase of the trial was over, Langdale would use this as grounds to dismiss the whole case against his client.

◆ ◆ ◆

After a few weeks I thought I was getting into the swing of the trial. Though exhausted most evenings, and slightly shell-shocked by early morning rises, the evidence continued (in my mind) to break news and provide irrefutable evidence of what really happened at Britain's best-selling newspaper. I won't repeat all the 'breaking' elements here: they're all publicly available. But pride always comes before a fall.

> BREAKING: Goodman emailed Coulson about P Harry's health with 'scanned from Asprey' (Royal Aide) NOTW article on medical problems next day

It was a regular day. On 13 November the jury were being taken through the hacking timeline of the royal aide Helen Asprey. An email from Goodman to Coulson on Prince Harry's medical problems was briefly shown on the screen and read out but the annex screens were down.

I heard the word 'scanned.' Others, with sharper hearing and vision, saw the real word 'scammed.' The next morning, during the usual litany of defence complaints about press coverage, Langdale's junior, Alison Pople, stood up and started talking about a 'prejudicial tweet.' I was half paying attention, and then she mentioned 'Mr Jukes' and the 'scanned health inf' email. It was like a lightning bolt. Everyone in the annex seemed to turn and look at me with horror and pity. As Justice Saunders said he would refer the tweet to the court's expert on media matters, my heart raced and I desperately went back through my timeline to delete the tweet.

Had I undermined the trial of the century by failing to add 'To Coulson '? Would I be thrown out of the court for the lack of a preposition? Or be indicted for contempt?

Other reporters laughed. It was a minor mistake. The *Independent* had mistakenly reported that 15 royal directories had been found at Coulson's house, rather than Goodman's, but I didn't have the cover of a masthead and felt sick. It was a stark reminder that even in the most tedious or humdrum days one couldn't relax. For days afterwards, Nick Davies would josh me – 'in trouble again, Jukes' – or tell security: 'Don't let this guy in.' It was like a hazing ritual. To be mentioned in court was simultaneously a badge of humiliation and honour.

# DEMOLITION JOB

*Jonathan Laidlaw QC: You've had this since last week, Mr Edis!*

*Mr Justice Saunders: Alright, thank you: it's only Monday.*

As the trial headed further into November and December, we were taken deep inside the machinery of the *News of the World*.

'Follow the money' as the saying goes, though in this case the money was hard to follow. Private investigator and phone hacker extraordinaire Glenn Mulcaire's annual fee averaged £100,000 for six years – less than the paper's astrologer, but still one of the top five retainers on the paper. Anything over £50,000 was beyond the authority of the editors, and should have been referred up to the managing director of the holding company, News Group Newspapers. Yet because the private detective was paid weekly, his payments were within the threshold of a desk editors' authority.

Though often dry as dust, the evidence about Contributor Payment Requests, cash payments and 'desk head limits' changed my mind about what happened at Wapping. Prior to the trial, I'd assumed that the volume of phone hacking at *News of the World*, and the amounts of money involved, must have meant that everyone in News International was aware of it. But Mulcaire's payments were constantly modified to keep them under weekly thresholds. As Edis put it, someone was 'cooking the books.' The question was: who?

I've since been told by News International executives that editor's budgets were protected from management interference. That these payments should have been so craftily concealed suggests to me that Mulcaire's worth may well have been hidden from News Corp – and Rupert Murdoch. This would explain why, with the one exception of the Missing Milly story, articles inspired by hacked voicemails were often concealed by 'friends say' or another purported source.

On 20 November, Court 12 heard from Andy Gadd, another private investigator or 'trace agent' employed by *News of the World* and (though this was never mentioned in court) an early collaborator with Glenn Mulcaire. Gadd said he legitimately traced individuals using a variety of public sources. One startling fact emerged, though: for a three-day week the *News of the World* paid him £70,000 a year.

Not all the evidence in the hacking trial portrayed the Sunday tabloid as a den of intrigue. Many of those who abhorred the cover-up of the scandal mourned the demise of a great national paper. And in the testimony of Harry Scott, the engaging night editor of *News of the World*, the court got an impression of the excitement and camaraderie of the Saturday evening as the paper was 'put on stone': the hive of activity between the front, middle and back benches, a slightly nostalgic trip into a vanishing industrial process. To those who worked at the paper, like the former showbusiness reporter Tom Latchem, who challenged Brooks at a fractious 'town hall' meeting during the paper's closure in 2011, it was the reminder of a lost world.

Though the hacking trial lasted only eight months (compared to the 168 years of the *News of the World*) it's worth picturing the front, middle and back benches of its press.

◆ ◆ ◆

Pride of place were the journalists upstairs, sitting in comfy green upholstered chairs, even if they were shoved under the public gallery to make way for solicitors. Tristan Kirk from Central News, who had a desk with a power socket, looked the part of a court reporter: intense, tall and bearded, with an air of authority that, allied with his knowledge of court procedure, meant he would often challenge reporting restrictions on behalf of the press. Behind him Nick Davies from the *Guardian* would attend most days, dressed in jeans and leather jacket. His colleague Lisa O'Carroll wrote incessantly, and I soon learned not to ask too many questions. With her Irish lilt, she'd protest: 'I'm filing, Peter!'

Fiona Hamilton from *The Times* was another regular with a gold ticket. She only missed a few days when she had to attend other high profile trials. Her reports were comprehensive, though I felt *The Times* buried them a little. Vanessa Allen from the *Daily Mail* used to sit with us ne'er-do-wells in the annex until she was upgraded to the main court. She was always helpful, as was Jane Croft from the *Financial Times,* who would come down to join us if she had to leave for another court case. Lisa O'Carroll, the BBC's Robin Brant and James Old from *Sky News* were my main rivals on live-tweeting. Since they were also working on news reports, they couldn't match the volume of my output, but they caught courtroom colour and reactions in the public gallery or dock that I missed in the annex. They'd often pop down to check out what the naughty school-kids were up to.

In the annex, with no jury to contempt or judge to annoy, we checked quotations and evidence and discussed the different prosecution and defence tactics. The BBC's Gaetan Portal sat by the annex door where he constantly negotiated with the Crown Prosecution Service for the release of emails, photos, CCTV and phone data and organised daily reports. The Beeb has a small airless studio in the Old Bailey basement, and depending on who was giving evidence, we'd be joined by the royal correspondent Peter Hunt, or Tom Symonds, a home affairs reporter. Producers from ITN or Channel 4 would sit in, doing alternate 'wet man' duty with TV crews on the rainy streets outside.

Behind the broadcasters sat the diligent journalists from the agencies who seemed to note down everything, and were always reliable to cross check any quote. At first quiet (probably because they were working so hard) were the agency reporters. Michael Holden from Reuters seemed enigmatic, almost delphic in his knowledge, while Jeremy Hodges from Bloomberg revealed to me he had been trained as a chef by Gordon Ramsey, and that journalism was easy compared to that. A roving band of correspondents from NBC, CNN, France and Barcelona would turn up occasionally, but the foreign press was regularly represented by Jill Lawless for *Associated Press* and Jenny Gross for the *Wall Street Journal*. Gross wrote an early piece about my crowd-funding coverage, but there were several debates as to whether her paper should receive CPS releases of evidence and legal arguments from the court since the *Wall Street Journal* (a News Corp company) had not signed up to a non-disclosure agreement. I was briefly told that handing over any material to it could land you in prison. It was an exaggeration about the rules, but yet another potential minefield. Many of the other journalists who passed through would say they didn't feel they needed to be in court every day, because they could read my tweets. I should have billed them.

Over the eight months, even love lives would be shaped by the trial. Within two months of it beginning, Lizzy Millar, a reporter for the London Media agency, got engaged. When planning a date for the wedding, she and her fiancé estimated the case would be over by spring. In the end, they wed in early June when the jury were considering their verdicts. 'I had to actually make a conscious decision not to think about it,' she said. 'And when we went on honeymoon, I said to my husband: 'Please take my iPhone, take my laptop, and I'll try not to listen to the TV or the radio because if there is a verdict I'll be all over it like a rash'.'

Attendance in the annex would go up and down depending on who gave evidence. But no matter how misbehaved we wanted to be, we were constrained by the police presence in the back of the room. Scotland Yard detectives came in force through the prosecution phase, some having made, or about to make, an appearance in the witness box. Some Elveden detectives turned up if there was evidence connected with their investigations, and there was a police officer from Scotland throughout Coulson's time in the witness box.

An increased number of detectives was usually an early warning sign something significant was going to take place. For the first few months they were quite wary of the press, and remained stony faced and unresponsive. Perhaps – given they had arrested over 100 journalists – they distrusted journalists in general. But as the days wore on, and they saw we were really interested in the minutiae of the evidence, they would open up. By the end of the trial I'm told they found our discussions so useful they would often hang around in the annex picking up our conversation, and then head upstairs to the main court to remind the prosecution of a piece of relevant evidence. And in a few days they were going to ask me to be a witness.

◆ ◆ ◆

Real trials are nothing like TV dramas. The staples of the genre – the sudden ambushing with a new witness, the devastating discovery of forensic evidence or a knockout blow by counsel – are extremely rare. Not once did I see any hint of the explosive cross examination where witnesses lost their temper and exploded, like Jack Nicholson in *A Few Good Men*: 'You want the truth? You can't handle the truth!' On the whole it was gruelling, fact-driven stuff, though cross examination would soon show that destruction of a witness's credibility still plays a key part in a criminal trial.

At first there was no hint of what was to come. Monday 25 November was a dull morning with another Weeting detective confirming some News International emails from Brooks, which we (unlike the jury) couldn't see. By now the prosecution case was being badly disrupted. There were endless debates when the jury were not present about how to present the 'top left' schedules. The disruption appeared to be a key part of the defence strategy; surprise sabotage attacks on the prosecution's supply lines.

The next live witness would be the first devastating full frontal attack. Few in the annex knew who Eimear Cook was until she stepped into the witness box. She was the former wife of the golfer Colin Montgomerie, from whom she filed for divorce in 2003. Because of Montgomerie's fame and wealth, the break-up was conducted in a blaze of publicity. In 2002 Mulcaire targeted her, noting down her Vodafone mobile number, default PIN, bank details, address and numbers for her sister in Alabama, her mother, and her mother's friend, who looked after her when she was ill. In 2004, Mulcaire wrote down the headquarters of Montgomerie's agent.

Cook described the press coverage of her as a 'hatchet job' which ignored the real nature of the marital breakdown. Stories claimed she was having 'numerous multiple affairs.' 'It was extremely wholly unexpected and extremely upsetting,' Cook told the jury: 'To have all these lies published about me… There were reporters outside the house all day. I was followed to the shops.'

Because she had been extremely badly treated, a friend, Jo Manoukian, organised a 'well-meaning effort' to make her 'feel better about the media' by meeting Rebekah Brooks, then editor of the *Sun* and a friend of her husband, Rafi Manoukian. Cook said: 'They introduced me to Rebekah Wade, as she was then. They invited me to lunch in their house in Pond Street. Four of us.' She told the court she thought the lunch was probably in September 2004.

She told the court she thought the lunch was probably in September 2004 and recalled that Brooks had come all the way from Wapping to Knightsbridge, and was late, but was soon talking about 'public figures… in a gossipy fun way.' Brooks included herself in gossipy indiscretions. Cook remembered Brooks 'laughing' about her own appearance in the papers after a 'domestic row' with Ross Kemp. Crucially, she said Brooks also spoke about phone hacking. Cook told the court: 'She said that it was so easy to do and she couldn't believe all those famous people who have all these advisors and they don't know they need to personalise their PIN codes to make their voicemails secure…She told me it was ludicrous people weren't aware of the simple way people could protect their voicemail.'

The conversation turned to Sir Paul McCartney and Heather Mills who were frequently appearing in the papers with well-publicised bust ups. According to a story in the *News of the World*, headlined Feud of the Rings, Mills and McCartney argued so badly that the former Beatle threw their engagement ring out of the window of a Miami hotel. Cook maintained that as Brooks spoke about the ring throwing session she had the impression she was talking about voicemail messages.

When Laidlaw rose to his feet, he told Cook to sit down (she had been standing throughout her evidence in chief). He added rather ominously: 'You might be there some time.' In the annex, those who had been twiddling on iPads or taking phone calls, went quiet.

Laidlaw asked Cook to reflect on her statement 'I've never talked to the press.' Cook replied quite firmly: 'Not about my marriage.' Laidlaw went back to read her original statement line by line, with an air of extreme scepticism, reciting her words: 'I've never courted the press, or sought media attention, and always strived to have a private life…I've never given my address, numbers, or private details to any journalist or member of the press.' For all the disapproval in his voice it was difficult to see what Laidlaw's 'gotcha' moment would be. Golfer's wife talks to journalist? Hardly likely to bring the prosecution case tumbling down.

The minutes ticked by, and you could sense Laidlaw was circling his prey as he went through Cook's statement about the *Daily Mail*, *Mirror* and the *Sun* asking for interviews. He cited a *Hello!* magazine article from 2003, 'The wife of top golfer talks frankly about past marital difficulties,' suggesting she was doing 'precisely the opposite to her witness statement.' Cook said that was during a period they had got back together but when she 'filed for divorce from Colin I thought I was no longer in the public eye and deserved my privacy.'

Laidlaw was getting closer: he told Cook of another *Hello!* article in September 2004, beyond the date of filing for divorce. Cook replied it was just a fashion shoot, which she did as a favour for a friend: 'I didn't talk about the marriage,' she said: 'I don't think giving a glossy photo shoot is the same as giving permission to access my private life.' Laidlaw reminded Cook 'you are on oath' – as if she were lying. What was the import of his portentous, almost menacing tone?

If Brooks' barrister was suggesting that Cook was guilty of double standards by only criticising press coverage when it didn't suit her, then even then this line of attack backfired. Going over a January 2005 *Daily Mail* article by Richard Kay, Monty Still Won't Talk To Me, Cook said it was 'extremely embellished' from a 'couple of comments' she made at a party to another Mail reporter, Helen Minsky. Of Kay, who claimed to have talked to her, Cook said: 'I've never met him.' A second *Mail* article from February 2006 implying she'd talked to the paper again was 'completely untrue.'

Laidlaw was unperturbed. Slowly, almost casually, he turned to the crucial lunch meeting with the Manoukians and his client, Brooks. Again he reminded Cook that she was 'on oath.' This tried the patience of Justice Saunders who intervened to reprimand him: 'That's just comment.'

Then Laidlaw sprang his trap. He produced an entry in one of Brooks' desk diaries which set the lunch in September 2005, rather than September 2004. Cook didn't seem too bothered by this. It was 'definitely before my divorce' and the decree absolute wasn't until 2006. Laidlaw said the reference to Kate Moss losing her Chanel contract confirmed the date: 20 September 2005. Cook shrugged.

Laidlaw jumped on her: she'd 'told lies' and made 'serious allegations' in her police statement in March 2012. (Oddly enough the written version actually specified 2005 for the lunch meeting with Brooks). Laidlaw quickly went to Cook's account of a 'frank and open' discussion with Brooks about her assault on Ross Kemp. He sounded incredulous at Cook's claim that the journalist was 'laughing while regaling me with the story' about Rupert Murdoch's reaction to her night in the cells. To Laidlaw, this seemed to be final proof the whole conversation was confected. Cook stuck to her line: 'Yes she was light hearted,' and said she could see the incident 'in her mind's eye.'

And at that moment, I had my own déjà vu. But the questioning was moving on before I could even process this eerie feeling. Laidlaw was now at his most scornful, openly accusing Cook of lying on oath: 'Did this happen?' Cook sounded cornered, torn between anger and distress: 'Why would I make this up?'

Then Laidlaw snapped tight the jaws of his trap. It was 'quite impossible' that Brooks confided in Cook about the night in the police cells: 'She wasn't subject to this event till November 2005,' he pointed out, derisively: 'six weeks later.' 'Not only did this not happen…. it could not have happened. It's a lie,' he said.

Cook was shaken badly now. 'I did not make it up,' she said: 'I have no grievance against Mrs Brooks.' But Laidlaw wouldn't let up: he now went to motive, saying Cook had a 'vendetta' against his client. 'Absolutely not,' protested Cook: 'I was asked by the police to be here.' The barrister said she'd 'made these things up' because she wanted aggravated damages for phone hacking, and that the whole conversation about phone hacking and McCartney Mills was 'a lie.'

As Laidlaw sat down, I realised I'd just witnessed a brilliant takedown of an important witness by a top barrister. It's their job to test the evidence. It's their job to defend their client to the utmost within the rules. This was all in the rules, and if I were a defendant in a criminal trial I'd want someone like Laidlaw as my counsel.

Edis tried to rescue his witness in re-examination. He took Cook through the McCartney Mills story in the *News of the World* in June 2002 (under Brooks' editorship): Cook told the chief prosecutor she'd never heard the story before, 'only from what Miss Wade told me.' Edis even tried to imply that Brooks could have been talking of a different incident with Kemp before November 2005. Cook said: 'She didn't say she'd been arrested.' But it was desperate last ditch stuff.

Whatever Cook had said about phone hacking was undermined by her inaccuracy over timing. How had the police overlooked this obvious anomaly regarding the dates? How could they have not seen that it would neutralise Cook's initial witness statement? Of course, this was just one of hundreds of witness statements and there were millions of emails, payment records and billing details to go through. But that's their job. And it's the defence's job to stop someone being imprisoned on erroneous facts.

Laidlaw would make great play of this evidential oversight, both during Brooks' defence witnesses and in his closing speech. The very next day he was all over the Weeting detective, DC Andrea Fletcher, who created the Eimear Cook timeline. He reminded her of her duty 'to be at all times of an open mind' and to follow the evidence wherever it led. He got Fletcher to agree that 'any police officer who allows any agenda to take over… would have lost their way' and that it 'wouldn't represent good policing to take a witnesses account without testing it.' 'Have you approached that task with an open mind?' Laidlaw asked the detective. She replied: 'Yes I have.'

Laidlaw then proceeded to blast the McCartney Mills timeline of phone hacking, and to ask Fletcher how much checking she had done on the Feud of the Rings story. With no call data from 2002 the detective couldn't prove a hack had taken place. And Laidlaw was much more interested in another source for the story. The Metropolitan Police had evidence that the story came from Annette Witheridge, a freelance journalist in the US, who had been told about the ring throwing by an employee at the hotel's beauty salon.

Again, another point for the defence. Though Edis had said in his opening that phone hacking was rarely if ever the sole exclusive source of the story, Laidlaw was effectively suggesting the Weeting investigation had closed off any alternatives. Witheridge would appear again as a witness to fact in Brooks' defence in the New Year. If the police and prosecution didn't see this coming, I noticed several journalists were interested in my timeline during this particular bit of evidence: including my old friend TabloidTroll, who retweeted Laidlaw's comments assiduously.

As Cook left the witness box, I had mixed emotions. Laidlaw had hectored her to destruction. But if truth be told when other defendants got facts or dates wrong, that was explained as an honest mistake or faulty memory rather than malign intent. Laidlaw was eager to emphasise Cook's bad faith on Brooks' account of the incident with Kemp.

But this part of Cook's account resonated with my direct experience. I had encountered Brooks at the Hay-on-Wye book festival in 2006. We started talking and dancing at a late-night party. Though I was a stranger, her first line to me was: 'Everyone hates me' (in those days the festival was sponsored by the *Guardian*). We sat for the next few hours, drinking and talking in a corner. Just as in Eimear Cook's evidence Brooks was funny and indiscreet, and was soon laughing at herself, telling me of the brief night in police cells the previous year – in the same tone and terms as she had in Cook's testimony.

As the court wound up, one of the police officers from the back of the annex who had overheard my story took me to the side and told me I should make a statement about the Hay-on-Wye encounter. I think he was half joking, and told him he should buy a copy of *The Fall of the House of Murdoch*, where I gave an account of the meeting. He smiled, and went on his way.

◆ ◆ ◆

Though the lurking fear of being summoned as a witness or locked up for contempt began to fade I was now having problems getting locked out of my Twitter account. I was posting tweets so often the micro-blogging platform's algorithms automatically assumed I was spamming and sent me to 'Twitter prison' regularly, which meant all my court reporting got locked away in drafts for 15 minutes or so.

I tried to contact Twitter support to no avail, and eventually had to crowd-source my customer servicing. After dozens of complaints, Twitter UK changed the settings on my account. I also sourced a new Logitech keyboard, to replace my battered one, on which I'd done two million keystrokes. The latter statistic came from database whiz Jon Lippitt, who was by now regularly compiling my tweets on my blog. Another tweet follower, Claire Pollard, who worked on 3-D printing, summarised my tweets in a twice a day 'Storify' movie. They refused any payment.

Much has been written about the problem of free online content and how it has sucked revenues away from print journalism. Yet here was the other more benign side of free: the free association of ideas and individuals: the volunteered expertise of strangers who somehow thought my reporting served a public interest or a personal passion. Jon Lippitt had turned my thousands of tweets into spreadsheets that could be searched by date, location, witness and charge. This was amounting to something else – an open-source information that could be used by anyone. As it was, I know my tweets have become a resource to other journalists, academics, and lawyers. Add to that the daily spelling corrections, comments, links and encouragement by the thousands of followers, the power of the crowd – or rather the kindness of the strangers within it – was probably the only thing that kept me going through the harder phases of the trial, as the stress of live-tweeting wore me down and the inevitable winter man 'flu turned live-tweeting into an endurance test. I needed them, since the trial was about to enter a long dark tunnel.

# MISTRIAL OF THE CENTURY

*Mr Justice Saunders: Even Radio 5
thinks this trial is boring now.*

In reality, a trial is a contest of narratives. The defence and prosecution are like competing playwrights working on the same story. Cases are won and lost by who has the most compelling narrative. In most trials, the prosecution have all the advantages. They have the police on hand to cast the villains, forensic services to provide a backdrop of evidence. All but a tiny fraction of defendants rely on legal aid provided by the state, and what countervailing evidence, witnesses or expert testimony they can garner.

What made the hacking trial exceptional was not just the high profile of the defendants – media executives who had befriended powerful people in showbusiness, sport, policing, politics, and in Brooks' case, three prime ministers. It wasn't even the calibre of witnesses that ranged from archdeacons and a former Archbishop of Canterbury to Hollywood stars. The gathering of legal talent was unprecedented. The defence teams led by the QCs Timothy Langdale, Jonathan Laidlaw, Jonathan Caplan, Trevor Burke and William Clegg, and Neil Saunders (described to me as 'the best paid junior in the country' and coincidentally married to Alison Saunders, the Director of Public Prosecutions) had stellar reputations. The hacking trial was a gathering of the best criminal barristers of a generation. But what made it unique was not just the array of talent, but the way they were paid.

Most criminal barristers do legal aid work. While commercial law is paid for commercially, and civil litigation bills can run to millions, ordinarily both sides of a criminal trial are publicly funded. To have one privately paid for criminal defence is exceptional. To have six is unheard of, especially for a case that would demand their presence month after month. It represented a major payday for lawyers, and an inversion of the usual power relationship between prosecution and defence.

Since News Corp has buried the specific details of the costs of the trial in the hundreds of millions it has spent cleaning up phone hacking, settling civil actions and maintaining its Management and Standards Committee, the cost to Rupert Murdoch's company can only be estimated – and probably underestimated. But as a rule of thumb, a top QC can command up to £800 an hour on the commercial market, and the billable hours would stretch to at least 10 a day. Juniors earn £400 an hour. So one defence team of two people is about £12,000 a day, or £60,000 a week. Because News Corp funded most of the defence teams (all but Edmondson and Goodman in the original indictment) its bill for barristers at the trial alone would be around £10 million.

By contrast, a publicly-funded QC earns from £500 to £800 per day, with a junior receiving as little as £150. With four regulars on the team, this meant that the Crown's entire hacking trial team earned less a day than one of the six privately-funded defence teams received an hour. Even adding the cost of running the Old Bailey court estimated at £50,000 a week – the public purse was outspent six to one by a corporation. Whatever the final figures, the impact on the trial was clear. I don't think Justice Saunders had this in mind when he said 'not only the defendants are on trial, British justice is on trial,' but it was true that the Crown was outgunned.

As a result, the barrage of legal argument from the defence was serious and sustained. By December there were so many formal objections from the defence teams that it was impossible to keep track of them, and you could sense the judge and prosecution were struggling. There was still the ongoing background noise about prejudicial coverage. Laidlaw for Brooks often complained about the BBC, and was joined by David Spens QC, counsel for Clive Goodman, about a mix up over charges on the BBC website.

♦ ♦ ♦

Because my Twitter feed had to go silent during legal argument, I doubt many outside the legal profession understand how substantive these debates are. In December five issues dominated the court in a way which was much more dramatic than anything heard before the jury: a tranche of new email evidence; the potential calling of the hacking supergrass Dan Evans as a prosecution witness; battles over how to format the 'top left' schedules of Mulcaire tasking; the guilty pleas of a public official from another trial; and the ongoing absence of Ian Edmondson, the eighth defendant, who would eventually be deemed 'unfit' to stand trial.

Here's a brief example of how these formal submissions worked in the case of Mark Hanna, News International's head of security, who was alleged to have been involved in the Charlie's bags plot. A forthcoming witness called by the prosecution would allege that on the night the *News of the World's* closed Hanna spoke about burning stuff in his garden. Hanna's QC, William Clegg, tried to argue the witness was inadmissible as he was not relevant to the dates of his client's indictment. He lost that argument. The evidence had been ruled admissible under a 'bad character' application – in other words it was not germane to the 'facts' of the case, but to the proclivities of a defendant.

Bad character applications are a new phenomenon. Until the Criminal Justice Act of 2003 a defendant could not be tried on their past behaviour, only on the charge before the court, though there were circumstances in which the accused could lose the 'shield' of their presumed good character. That Act formalised ways in which the prosecution could adduce evidence of previous 'bad character.' This has since become a routine tactic of the Crown – applying to use evidence of a defendant's past behaviour to encourage them to plead guilty, or to undermine their defence. Because the evidence about Hanna 'burning stuff' also concerned his client, Rebekah Brooks, (Hanna allegedly said it after praising Brooks as a boss), Laidlaw was now arguing that Hannas should be severed from the trial.

This submission required all the formalities: skeleton arguments to be written up for the judge, then argued over between defence and prosecution, with Justice Saunders taking down notes, and then – having considered the issue for some time – issuing a written ruling. All this sounds very polite and formal – and most of it was. But tempers frayed over the days of attrition. The tone between Brooks' counsel and the judge was by now somewhat frosty, though it was better than Laidlaw's relations with the prosecutor, Edis. Though the two QCs shared chambers, Edis could be heard calling Laidlaw 'Johnny' in a brief aside, to which the silk reputedly replied: 'Oh fuck off.'

Because there were so many interlocking conspiracy charges, which required guilt from more than one party, there was also a degree of natural co-operation between the different defence teams. By helping another of the accused on a conspiracy charge, a defendant had a good chance of breaking down the conspiracy element, and therefore exculpating themselves. It should be no surprise then that the various defence silks appeared to be divvying up their attacks on the prosecution between them. Laidlaw's speciality was prejudicial coverage and abuse of process by the police. Langdale's big beef was disclosure –and the sudden discovery of a new tranche of emails gave him more ammunition.

Email evidence was vital to the prosecution case. Indeed, without the 'three emails that closed *News of the World*' the case would not have reached the courts, let alone made it into the public domain. These were retrieved from the files of Harbottle & Lewis, an employment law firm who had trawled the News International's email server for information after Goodman's allegations about hacking in 2007. These incriminating remnants were subject to long legal argument over the summer as Clare Montgomery, Coulson's barrister at the time, tried to have the retrieved emails thrown out under the same act as an 'improper search' of a public broadcaster. Ironically, Montgomery had homed in on the metadata in the headers of the emails as part of her argument, and this had inadvertently given a police computer expert another line of inquiry.

By mid-November, using the metadata in an email index from 2010, the police had discovered a public folder called Lowndes dating from the time of the Harbottle and Lewis search. Though the original Goodman/Coulson emails weren't in this reconstructed folder, nearly 1,800 new emails were discovered. Edis told the court how he'd spent 11 hours reading through 2,142 pages of the complete archive, and many were duplicates or irrelevant. (He added, in passing, that the metadata in the files showed that some 1,000 emails were missing from the relevant period; probably due to email deletion.) However he'd thinned down the new cache to 81 pages. Some of this was 'highly material' to the case.

Given Justice Saunders had imposed a guillotine on new evidence at the end of October, the defence had a real chance to counter. Langdale would lead the charge, but first Laidlaw went over the top. He wasn't going to make a written submission because an initial search had only come back with 30 hits for Rebekah (only one related to a hacking victim, the footballer Marcel Desailly). But Laidlaw, for Brooks, still objected to the 'management of the case and the lateness of the material.' He thundered: 'This is the point when the court should say 'enough'!'

For Coulson, Langdale rose to speak of his 'mounting concern' and demanded witness statements from Mr Lowndes who had created the folder in 2007, and the police officer who'd reconstructed it. 'Until I receive in statement form where this all this comes from,' Langdale complained: 'I'm not in a position to say whether I accept or reject this material.' However, Langdale was in a position to make a wider point about his 'pessimism' regarding the 'proper preparation' of the hacking trial. He rued: 'Each time we seem to see the light at the end of the tunnel, immediately the roof falls in. A picture emerges that your lordship gives time, the prosecution produce more evidence.' He insisted that the schedule of the trial would now have to be delayed, telling the judge: 'We can't allow the defendant we represent to be disadvantaged.'

Even David Spens QC, Goodman's counsel, objected to 'another blizzard' of emails going before the jury. He'd read the 81 new pages, which he said provided little new knowledge but would add to the length of the trial. At this rate the trial threatened to go well beyond Easter already. 'Enough is enough,' Spens said. Jonathan Caplan QC, Kuttner's barrister, also made one of his rare but effective interventions in this battle. Caplan shared the concerns of others but reserved his judgement and promised a formal written submission. Justice Saunders, who was now dealing with his own blizzard of emails, asked Caplan to make it short, remarking: 'The art of summary seems to have disappeared with copy and paste.'

While new battles raged, old conflicts wore on. The weekly skirmishes over the 'Top Lefts' – how to represent the journalists who tasked Mulcaire over six years – were now becoming particularly bitter. The prosecution wanted to link Mulcaire's targets to their appearance in *News of the World* stories. But Coulson's defence team argued that there was no definitive proof the stories were the direct result of phone hacking and the individuals were of general news value, and could give jurors the false impression that Coulson must have known about phone hacking.

With an eye to fairness, Justice Saunders suggested removing the news stories from the schedules. Edis objected. Then Brooks' counsel objected to the objection. Sounding at the end of his tether, the judge asked the counsel to settle the matter among themselves and added that this way of settling the top-left schedules was becoming a 'fiasco.'

The calling of witnesses was the other major area of dispute, and from week to week legal wrangling made it almost impossible to know who was going to testify. Paul Nicholas, former deputy to Kuttner as managing editor of *News of the World,* was originally going to be called by the prosecution, but the Crown changed tack after Harry Scott and editorial assistant Bev Stokes covered the same ground. Langdale wanted Nicholas to appear to discuss day-to-day running of the paper and the contributor payments system. (Nicholas never gave evidence). But for every submission they lost, the defence lawyers would always gain somewhere else. The judge acceded to their demand that Susan Pannuccio, former chief operating officer for News International and now higher up in News Corp, give evidence.

Around this time Justice Saunders joked to the various counsel: 'That's 12-All by my reckoning.' His scrupulous attempts to be even handed in his rulings no doubt helped his elevation to the bench. His legal rulings would be thoroughly scrutinised in the event of an appeal. But by being fair on an uneven field, the defence onslaught was gaining ground.

Another pending witness was causing more concern to Coulson's team. By late summer it was apparent that Dan Evans, a former *News of the World* reporter who was helping the police, had become a prosecution witness. Previous attempts to exclude his evidence had failed, but Langdale wasn't giving up. Thirty-eight pages of Evans' various witness statements had already raised howls of protest. Two new lever arch files had now been served and Langdale made his obligatory complaint about 'late service and delivery' of relevant paperwork. By now, Coulson's lawyer was demanding a hearing without the jury before Christmas to formally present an 'abuse of process' argument against Evans appearing. If that failed, he wanted to schedule the appearance of the actors Jude Law and Sienna Miller to coincide with Evans. That in itself was a logistical nightmare because of their filming commitments.

With all these shifting variables and contested evidence, the prosecution's timetabling was in disarray. To ensure that the jury weren't left with nothing to do, Edis offered to bypass the morass that bogged everyone down in the phone hacking evidence and move on to the two Elveden charges against Brooks – allegations of payments to public officials and conspiracy to commit misconduct in public office. Laidlaw wasn't having that, though. Because the prosecution case was 'so chaotic' he hadn't even begun to look at this part of the case. It felt like 'tails I win – heads you lose' for the Crown. Its narrative was being fractured by the opposition, who then complained the fragmentary nature of the prosecution case was holding things up.

And there were always personal issues to deal with. Jurors needed time off for scheduled medical appointments, funerals, or other day-to-day matters. Stuart Kuttner, who had suffered a heart attack and a brain stem stroke since the hacking scandal broke, was rarely in the dock. Clive Goodman suffered from heart problems. Unreportable, because of future trials, were arguments relating to other pleas over convictions for misconduct in public office. At the end of one particularly gruelling argument, even Andrew Edis QC seemed to be losing the will to live. He joked, wearily: 'Life is too short, even if the trial is too long.'

◆ ◆ ◆

Apart from illness, one personal matter would preoccupy the trial throughout and emerged again in these long December debates in the absence of the jury: the unsent Brooks love letter to Coulson.

After losing his attempt to have none of the letter aired, Laidlaw wanted now to show the letter in its entirety to the jury. Only a couple of paragraphs had so far been cited in Edis' opening, and those were about how the lovers would deal with their work relationship after the end of the affair in 2004 (this turned out to be a temporary break). Rumours about some of the more graphic language in Brooks' letter had circulated from the beginning of the trial, but Edis had described it as passionate, intelligent, heartfelt and articulate. The only reason I could see that Laidlaw wanted the whole thing adduced was to evince the jury's sympathy and support.

However, the fact that the jury were going to see the whole letter not only piqued the prurience of the press, it also touched on an important principle. If justice was to be done, it had to be seen to be done and the public deserved to see all the evidence as much as the jury. Adam Wolanski, counsel for the *Guardian* and other newspapers, made his formal submission for the press. He argued that the letter was an important piece of evidence in the hacking trial, and elements of it had been reported extensively during the opening six weeks earlier; the press acted as a public watchdog, and the principle of open justice was paramount if the judicial process was to be trusted and transparent.

This was not the first time Justice Saunders had to rule on the love letter – nor would it be the last. The same issues were rehearsed again the following summer when the jury retired. It's clear from the judge's ruling in December 2013 that he found the competing issues at stake some of the most difficult of the whole trial to resolve.

Justice Saunders summarised the submission by counsel representing Brooks. Laidlaw said his client wanted the jury to see the letter, with a tiny number of linguistic redactions so that the jury could understand 'its true meaning.' He didn't want the full text of the letter released to the press, not because of Brooks' Article 8 or privacy rights (once again, Laidlaw bemoaned these are 'long gone'), but because the content of this 'intimate and unsent letter does not contribute to any debate of general or public interest.' The *News of the World* editor's office might not have agreed with him on that.

It was Langdale, however, who opposed the press application to release the letter, not on behalf of his client Andy Coulson, but Coulson's three children. It was their Article 8 rights which were enjoined, and they would suffer in a further wave of publicity about their father. In one of the endless ironies of this trial, Langdale cited the case of ETK versus News Group Newspapers (a News International subsidiary) in 2011 when the Court of Appeal ruled that an actor's affair couldn't be exposed to the public because of his children being bullied. As *Private Eye* later asked: 'Which was the devilish newspaper which was proposing to expose the extra-marital shenanigans in the public interest… The *News of the World*?'

In his ruling, Justice Saunders came down against releasing the letter in its entirety. He agreed the affair had 'received a great deal of publicity.' He went on: 'There will be some, particularly those who consider that their own family life and their children's family life were affected by stories in the *News of the World* or the *Sun*, who take the view that it would only be just for the same to happen to the Coulsons… That is no justification either legally or morally for the children to suffer.' While the judge appreciated the right of the press to report everything the jury heard in court, he had received a letter from Coulson's wife saying further information could still threaten 'the security of their family unit.' The press's demand to see the full terms of the letter was 'outweighed by the likely effect on the children.'

# I'LL BE THE JUDGE OF THAT

*Anthony Edis QC: Life is too short, and this trial is too long.*

During one of these dark days of legal argument, talking to a defence barrister outside court during a break, I asked him about the chaotic progress of the trial. He pointed out that the longer it went on, the more likely it would be subject to appeal. Previously, any trial that exceeded three months could be deemed too long for a jury, he said, and we were heading for Christmas with no sign of the end of the prosecution case. Slightly surprised, I pointed out that it seemed to be the defence teams who were delaying things. He smiled enigmatically and stubbed out his cigarette.

'Fog everywhere,' Charles Dickens wrote in his vivid opening to *Bleak House*, depicting the streets between Old Bailey and Chancery Lane in primeval terms as a muddy, misty metaphor for the obfuscations of the law. What the defence lawyer on his fag break was telling me was that protracted legal arguments are a form of filibuster: a way of undermining a trial through procedural delay.

Brooks' QC, John Kelsey-Fry, was more responsible than anyone for this advantage at the pre-trial hearings under Mr Justice Fulford. Initially the CPS had wanted to try Brooks separately for the charges she faced; an Operation Weeting trial for allegations of phone hacking; an Operation Elveden trial for allegations of payments to public officials; and an Operation Sacha trial over accusations of perverting the course of justice and concealing evidence from the police. But Kelsey-Fry argued successfully that his client was such a prominent public figure that it would be impossible to try her separately for the different counts. The publicity around one verdict would escape any news blackout. Therefore, to prevent a jury being prejudiced, Brooks would have to be tried on all the counts at the same time.

At a stroke, Kelsey-Fry had turned the phone hacking trial into an unruly and unmanageable enterprise. During one hearing in July 2012, in the larger Court 1 of the Old Bailey, the entire three benches were filled with wigs and the 13 suspects spilled out of the dock. By February 2013 some of the Sacha defendants had been severed, leaving nine suspects to answer on phone hacking; but the prosecution was still burdened, in their minds, by the addition to the main case of the conspiracy to pervert the course of justice charges against Cheryl Carter, Rebekah Brooks, Charlie Brooks and Mark Hanna.

At a dismissal hearing in March 2013, several defendants, led by Coulson's barrister Clare Montgomery, claimed there was no case to answer as the relevant part of the law on phone hacking was imprecise. Montgomery argued that listening to phone messages that had already been heard could not be 'interception' in 'course of transmission.' Fulford disagreed but this point was taken all the way up to the Supreme Court, where it finally failed in June 2013.

Around the same time Kelsey-Fry was trying to get individual hacking counts thrown out. Before they had all been combined into a single conspiracy to intercept, Count 1, there had been many individual hacking charges. (For instance Milly Dowler was Count 2: David Blunkett Count 6, Charles Clarke Count 8, and Calum Best Count 14).

Since he had already been convicted in 2007 for phone hacking, Mulcaire himself couldn't plead guilty to 'conspiracy' to intercept voicemails, since it would involve double jeopardy. But once he did plead guilty to some single substantive counts, this cleared the way for the prosecution to reduce the phone hacking charges into one conspiracy charge for the remaining defendants. Though an overarching conspiracy charge had the benefit of simplifying the trial and legal submissions, it also reduced the penalties available to the court, as a single conspiracy charge carried the same maximum custodial sentence as each substantive charge.

In May 2013, when he took over from Fulford, Justice Saunders made a rare mistake. He told the defendants that, given the prolonged build up to the trial, any time they spent on an electronic tag would count towards a 'qualifying curfew' and a reduction of the final sentence. The three *News of the World* news editors, Miskiw, Thurlbeck and Weatherup, pleaded guilty to conspiracy to hack phones. The qualifying curfew plus the third off for pleading guilty could mean they would spend no time in prison if the trial was long enough. It was months before it was discovered that Saunders had misinterpreted the law on this matter, and a portion of that time would be struck off their final sentence. But it was too late to help the prosecution, who had lost several potential witnesses who might have incriminated other defendants. As their final mitigation would make apparent, at least two of the former desk editors were willing to name their bosses as conspirators in open court.

It didn't all go the defence's way, though. Since Coulson's case was heavily tied to Brooks' (Fulford had already alluded to the affair cryptically by describing their conversations as 'beyond what was ordinarily necessary for colleagues'), Edis argued that the same problem of publicity applied to the charges against Goodman and Coulson over alleged payments to police officers for the royal phone directories and those charges remained joined to the main trial. No one thought much about this until the summer when Goodman's counsel revealed the 'rogue reporter' was going to go fully rogue against his former bosses.

◆ ◆ ◆

Deep in December 2013, those case management problems returned to haunt Edis and his team. The continued absence of the remaining desk editor in the trial, Ian Edmondson, was holding up proceedings. After seeking expert medical advice from a prosecution-appointed doctor, Edis agreed to sever him from the case. On one of the rare days (it seemed) the jury was in, Justice Saunders told them that they were dismissed from considering charges against Edmondson who would face another trial at a later date. His would not be the last illness to delay and nearly derail the trial.

Not only did the trial lose a defendant, it was soon to lose one of the seven counts. DC Tilbury and DI David Kennett, two Operation Elveden detectives tasked to examine alleged payments to public officials, were cross-examined in detail by Laidlaw over Count 4. The evidence for that was a £4,000 cash payment to a Sandhurst employee for a photograph of Prince William in a bikini. The heir to the throne had dressed as a Bond girl for a themed 007 party he'd attended with Kate Middleton, and in June 2006 a *Sun* journalist sent an email to his Brooks requesting a Thomas Cook payment, which she authorised within 10 minutes.

With his brilliant ability to break down emails into fragments of imprecise grammar, Laidlaw suggested the alleged payment could cover not only two potential officers serving at Sandhurst but also a 'third man,' a middleman, who may or may not have been a public official. Of the two military suspects, one had died in action, and the other was overseas (the military refused to 'post him into jeopardy' by returning him to the UK).

A subsequent witness, Sandhurst official Major Julia Parke-Robinson, who appeared on Wednesday 11 December, agreed that the photo could have been taken by one of the many guests at the Bond party. In 2006, before the widespread use of camera phones and explosion of social media, the services didn't really place major restrictions on photography. Count 4 was now riven with doubt and complication. After Christmas, Laidlaw would submit a motion to dismiss this charge on the basis there was insufficient evidence. Justice Saunders agreed. Though the prosecution could have gone on to appeal his decision, it would have delayed the trial for another three weeks, to the point it would run into danger of losing jury members. Once again, the complexity and length of the trial was working in the defence's favour.

◆ ◆ ◆

Two months into the trial, with the prosecution losing ground and often looking in disarray, Nick Davies reiterated to me his initial belief from the early days of the trial, that Brooks was safe but that Coulson was still in trouble. Gaetan Portal, who had been following the *News of the World* story for years, was also coming to the same conclusion. One morning he came in saying he'd had a brainwave in the middle of the previous night and announced to the annex: 'She's going to get off everything.' Other journalists and visitors to the public gallery had noted that at least one of the jurors was smiling regularly at Brooks.

More disaster loomed for the prosecution with the promised appearance of Ambi Sitham by video link from Los Angeles. She was the witness who was going to tell a hacking anecdote about Brooks from Coulson's birthday party. But Brooks' lawyers were up in arms when they discovered Sitham had written a blog for the Huffington Post in 2012 in which she explained how she had met former MP Dr Evan Harris and actor Hugh Grant from the *Hacked Off* campaign after she had decided to give a statement to the Leveson Inquiry. Nick Davies was also at this meeting and Laidlaw made great play on another 'vendetta' against his client.

As Sitham swore her oath from a room in Los Angeles on 11 December accompanied by an FBI officer who made sure she wasn't being intimidated or coached, we all sat back to watch another Crown witness fall apart under intensive cross examination.

The Crown went through Sitham's statement. She told the court that in January 2003 at Coulson's birthday party at the steakhouse in Balham she found herself sitting next to Brooks, editor of the *Sun,* and in front of Piers Morgan, editor of the *Daily*

*Mirror*, on a narrow table of 18 to 20 guests. The dinner was 'a very relaxed, intimate gathering' but Sitham drank only a glass and a half of wine all evening because she was so nervous. 'These people had all climbed the ladder together,' she told the court. 'At the time they were both editors of quite big national tabloid newspapers.'

'They were both very busy trying to finish off the last details of their front covers for their newspapers,' Sitham recalled, alleging that Morgan joshed Brooks: 'I know what your splash is because I've been listening to your messages.' According to Sitham, Brooks quipped back: 'Been hacking into my phone again have you, Piers?' Morgan had the last word: 'Well, you've been looking at my emails. But I've left a false trail, I've led you up the garden path.'

Sitham, who was working on privacy cases against newspapers (including a *Mirror* exposé of supermodel Naomi Campbell's visit to a rehab clinic) told the jury she found Brooks 'very lovely and very welcoming and very nice' and offered her contact details so they could talk about future cases and 'try and settle a bit more amicably.' But she said that as she handed over her phone number to Brooks: 'Piers turned to me and said 'Careful – she'll tap your phone'.' Brooks 'saw my expression' and reassured her: 'Don't worry, let me give you my number instead.'

As Claire Sibson, Laidlaw's second, started her cross examination by going through the date of the Balham birthday party, it looked like we were about to witness another timing error which would discredit Sitham. Sibson said the party could not have in been in 2003. Sitham shrugged. It was just before her relationship with Reading ended. She would go back and check dates. Sibson challenged Sitham over the moment Brooks asked for her number, suggesting that the *Sun* editor would have never reacted that way. But Sitham didn't budge, insisting: 'I was concerned. She saw that.'

Brook's junior counsel then went through a series of emails between *Hacked Off*'s director Evan Harris and Sitham in the lead up to her making a statement to the Leveson Inquiry (which was not used). Sibson focused on a passage about timing Sitham's evidence to the Leveson Inquiry to gain 'media impact.' Sibson asked: 'Is this whole exercise not just about publicising yourself?' 'That was never the objective of doing this,' Sitham replied. 'This whole process has given me an ulcer and lost friendships.'

If this was a hatchet job, the former lawyer seemed to have come out of it with barely a scratch. Compared to Laidlaw's slow and ruthless destruction of Cook, Sibson seemed to lack the aggression, or perhaps just the ammunition, to destroy Sitham.

Edis – who seemed more alert to the danger to another Crown witness – was quick to his feet for the re-examination. Since the Brooks teams had introduced the Harris/Sitham emails into evidence, he drew attention to a passage Sitham had written to Harris about her fears of going public: 'I do dread the wave of vitriol that I am pretty sure will come my way.' She added that she decided to go ahead to cast light 'into the workings of the media industry and the incestuous nest of vipers that exists within that industry who are so powerful that people are intimidated from coming forward and speaking the truth.'

It was a powerful statement of the 'dog doesn't bite dog' code of loyalty in the newspaper business. Sitham explained how she had lost friends by going public. Since she had agreed to give evidence, Neil Reading, who had remained a best friend after the end of their relationship, had severed contact.

If Sitham's final appearance was a relief to the prosecution, the whole court was provided some light relief courtesy of Sir Michael Peat, Private Secretary to Prince Charles for 10 years from 2002. Peat had been targeted by Mulcaire in 2003 after suggestions of an affair. Called to the witness box by Mark Bryant-Heron on 12 December, the courtier was shown the tasking note and asked: 'In 2003, were you then engaged in an affair?' (Bryant-Heron was expecting a denial.) There was a dramatic pause as Peat reddened, and asked imperiously: 'Could you please explain the relevance of that question?' Justice Saunders quickly told the jury to leave.

With the jury gone, Peat complained that he had been nagged incessantly to provide a statement by detectives and gave the impression he thought his appearance in court an irritating waste of his time. Justice Saunders tried to placate him. He told Peat: 'Your evidence is relevant to this case. However much you were nagged by the police, we would be grateful if you would spend a few minutes of your time to answer questions.' But Peat wasn't having it. 'As long as I feel it is relevant,' he replied.

It was one of the rare moments Justice Saunders showed the steel beneath the charm, a flash of the ceremonial sword on the wall, usually obscured by his silk robes. 'It is not your decision if it is relevant or not,' the judge said: 'It is not your decision. It is my decision – because I am the judge in this court.' He told the court usher: 'Let's have the jury back in….'

As the jurors returned, Justice Saunders explained the reason for the hiatus: 'We have done our utmost not to require people to answer questions about their personal life. Sir Michael does not want to answer the question. We will carry on without the question being asked.' He indicated the Crown barrister should continue. Bryant-Heron said: 'I have no further questions. Thank you my lord,' and sat straight back down.

◆ ◆ ◆

Though the privately-funded defence teams might have had access to resources which could match or exceed that of the prosecution and police combined, the onus to deal with new evidence still fell heavily on the silks in court. With the police discovery of the 'Lowndes' email cache, even the indefatigable Laidlaw, reputed to be earning around £8,000 a day, was close to exhaustion. As he told Justice Saunders, his team were struggling with 'overload': 'The challenge is simply beyond everybody, even if you stay up every working hour,' Laidlaw complained, but with a nice line in self-awareness. 'I know it's a refrain, but it is not a difficulty which is falling away. So if you see me coming to court late, or being tired, or being tetchy, you know why.'

Always on hand to defuse the situation, the judge smiled: 'I hadn't noticed you being tetchy.' Laidlaw shook his head wearily: 'I am tetchy.' Mark Bryant-Heron affirmed: 'He is, my lord.'

None of the emails in question would be particularly germane to the case against Brooks. When Justice Saunders finally ruled on allowing these further emails into evidence his reasoning was primarily addressed to Langdale. Coulson's barrister had said they would 'overload the defence and overload the jury with information' and 'extend the length of the trial.' The judge pointed out that the emails had only been found on existing electronic data bases because of questions instigated by Coulson's defence team. He also said he was satisfied the prosecution had 'exercised reasonable expedition' but were now hampered because there was 'less co-operation from News International than there had been in the past.' Justice Saunders took a middle course, allowing about a third of the 81 new emails into evidence.

The judge's ruling gave the media some red meat shortly before the Christmas break: a reference to a royal disclosure withheld from the original hacking trial. But before the press could get sight of these, we had to go through almost the entire police interviews given by Cheryl Carter and Stuart Kuttner – at the insistence of their QCs. Though interesting to see how detectives question suspects (they're much politer than on the TV) it was excruciatingly dull. And the jury were subjected to days of police officers and barristers re-enacting a formal interview in even more formal voices. Justice Saunders was irritated by the lack of editing, especially when one of the jurors fell asleep.

The judge asked wearily: 'And the interviews are as short as we can get them?' Jonathan Caplan, for Stuart Kuttner, replied: 'I wouldn't say they were short, but they are as short as we can get them.' The judge noted that Kuttner's team was staffed with senior barristers, observing: 'That's the trouble with having two leading counsel. It's been so long since either of them had to edit interviews that they can't remember how to do it.'

Edis finally got to the royal hacking into evidence on 19 December. As redacted versions of Goodman's transcription of the voicemail message were read out in court the annex rapidly filled. Though the hacking of the young royals themselves had been revealed a while back the release of voicemail transcripts to the jury was new.

Prince William was quoted as saying to Middleton in 2006: 'Hi, baby. Um, sorry, I've just got back in off my night navigation exercise,' was just one such example. 'I've been running around the woods of Aldershot chasing shadows and getting horribly lost, and I walked into some other regiment's ambush, which was slightly embarrassing because I nearly got shot.' Goodman's Blackadder column in the *News of the World* in January 2006 was based on this transcribed message, and even used the 'babykins' phrase Prince William left on her voicemail. In another message left for Prince Harry, Prince William put on a falsetto and pretended be his brother's girlfriend at the time, Chelsy Davy: 'I really miss you,' he joked. 'Hopefully I'll see you very soon, you big hairy fat ginger.'

All this was a gift to the journalists who had suffered two months of often dull legal wrangling. For a change, reporters called their news desks with a strong story.

◆ ◆ ◆

Before Christmas Justice Saunders also issued his ruling on Dan Evans. Without knowing quite what the former reporter was going to say, all the journalists knew his testimony was important, if only because of the amount of effort going into stopping him. The battle to stop Evans arriving in court had been a long and bloody one, even if it seemed to take place out of the main theatre of war. Andy Coulson was present through all these hearings about

Evans, as he was through most of the legal argument in the trial. He took notes and listened intently. Indeed, he looked more attentive and focused than most of the journalists and lawyers present; an impressive feat given how many days were devoted to arcane disputes. You could see why he made a good newspaper editor and an even more impressive director of communications for David Cameron and the Conservative Party. His attention to detail was unflagging, and his ability to be present during the constant knocks and blows was stoic, if borderline masochistic.

As we would hear in the New Year, Dan Evans claimed that in 2005 Coulson had recruited him to the *News of the World* from the *Sunday Mirror* because of his phone hacking skills. Though he stopped using phone hacking as a source of stories after Goodman and Mulcaire's arrest in 2006, he did revert again to hacking phones in 2009. Using his own mobile, he had dialled the unique voicemail number of the designer Kelly Hoppen – and was quickly tracked and arrested. He signed an affidavit for the civil claims court saying he had hacked Hoppen by mistake because of the 'sticky keys' on his mobile phone. Suspended from work on full pay, Evans had remained on News International's payroll until the closure of *News of the World* in 2011.

For Coulson, Langdale's defence against Evans was quite technical. He cited Section 78 from the 1984 Police and Criminal Evidence Act, which allows a judge to refuse any evidence which would have 'an adverse effect on the fairness of the proceedings.' Langdale claimed that in trying to secure his co-operation the Crown Prosecution Service had misled Evans and had simultaneously breached its own guidelines. Also, by letting the former *News of the World* journalist believe he would get immunity from prosecution in exchange for being a witness for the Crown they had effectively forced him to confess: a breach of another section of PACE (76) which renders confessions under duress or inducement 'unreliable.' To further his argument, Langdale needed to examine large amounts of paperwork from Evans' legal team and the CPS, and live witnesses were sworn in to examine the process by which Evans sought immunity in return for becoming a prosecution witness.

In the old days, such co-operation was dealt with through a letter to the judge who could take it as mitigation. The process was formalised in the Serious Organised Crime and Police Act 2005 (SOCPA) to prevent abuses. Evans had been advised by a QC and his law firm, Peters & Peters, to seek a deal guaranteeing full immunity from prosecution in return for being a prosecution witness. His lawyers had first approached the CPS at the end of April 2012. But before any agreement could be discussed Evans needed to do a 'cleansing and scoping interview' with a dedicated SOCPA team so that the Crown could know what he was saying.

Alison Levitt QC, principal legal adviser to the Director of Public Prosecutions, took the final decision on the deal, advised by Gregor McGill, a senior employee of the Crown Prosecution Service, who arrived at the witness box of Court 12 to give evidence. McGill said it was common knowledge that full immunity from prosecution was granted only in exceptional cases, involving organised crime and threats to life. The information about phone hacking from Evans' interviews went all the way up to the Deputy Assistant Commissioner of the Metropolitan Police, Sue Akers, in charge of Weeting. As they analysed Evans' confession, the detectives gave leading journalists at the *News of the World* codenames based on flowers: Dan Evans was 'Snowdrop,' Andy Coulson 'Tulip,' and another senior *News of the World* executive 'Geranium.' Akers agreed Evans' testimony was worth a reduction of sentence by a third, but not full immunity. In January 2013 Evans refused the deal, then changed solicitors, changed his mind, and finally agreed to become a prosecution witness in the summer.

Justice Saunders did not agree with Langdale that his evidence had been procured from him 'unfairly.' Rather than use Evans' confession as 'a bad character application,' he ruled that Evans should be included as a co-conspirator in the Count 1 phone hacking charge.

Having lost Edmondson, the trial now had a new defendant. It was a gift to the prosecution and a blow to Andy Coulson. Evans was scheduled to appear in the New Year, soon after the Christmas break. The appearances of Jude Law and Sienna Miller had been scheduled to coincide with his evidence – Hollywood stardom and long-rumoured supergrass in one week. Finally the trial was about to live up to its billing.

# HOSTILE WITNESS

*Mr Justice Saunders: This will live in my nightmares, this particular bundle.*

Christmas was not going to be much of a break. With my funding due to run out in the New Year and rumours rife that the trial would go well into the summer, I devised a new crowd-funding campaign, asking for substantially more than before. I didn't think this would be easy, but given the slog of the court days, I wasn't sure I would be gutted if it turned out to be impossible.

The truth was the 'Trial of the Century' was feeling like an anti-climax. In a way, it was supposed to be; Justice Saunders didn't want a media circus. I had lost a few Twitter followers, presumably through sheer tedium. I decided to send a questionnaire asking my funders whether they liked the level of detail I was providing (all but one said they did), and whether there was any other service I could offer.

Given the time limit for funding, I needed to re-launch when there were maximum eyes on my feed. But when would that be? The appearance of Jude Law, Dan Evans and Sienna Miller in January, followed by the defence cases, starting with Rebekah Brooks, would be ideal. Cast as my own mini news agency, I was having to think about marketing. There were upsides to this independence, though. My blog was getting thousands of hits per week now, mainly when Jon Lippitt arranged my daily tweets in neat time lines. But my occasional posts of photographic evidence released from the press, or articles on side issues (without commentary) were also getting a lot of traffic. It was fantastic to communicate directly with an audience without having to go through all the checks, delays and attendant shenanigans of commercial media bureaucracies. But on the other hand, as somebody warned me, it did leave me 'terribly exposed.'

No writer can deny wanting to influence other people. What do fiction writers do, if not invade your dreams? I enjoy my anonymity, though. Even this seemed in danger thanks to my tweeting. Before Christmas I had travelled by train to Oxford one lunchtime to do an interview with the author Phillip Pullman for *Aeon* magazine. Twenty minutes into the journey a young guy in a suit started glancing at me. At first, I wondered whether I had put on enough de-odorant. But when he looked at me again he was holding an iPhone showing my Twitter page. 'That's you,' he said: 'You're famous!' 'In my own lunchtime,' I replied. He turned out to be a lawyer. A lot were following me at that time. And journalists; I had mixed feelings about that, given that most couldn't or wouldn't fund me. But there were more worrying interactions with others in the trade. There was regular background noise from some inveterate opponents, complaining that my 'BREAKING' tweets only favoured the prosecution and showed bias. It was annoying because we were still on the prosecution case, but it made me all the more determined to cover the defence cases just as diligently.

Some of this background noise was more ominous. During evidence about Mulcaire's various whiteboards, recovered from his office during his 2006 arrest, Detective Sergeant Jim Guest of Operation Weeting read out some of the writing on the complicated flow diagrams. Though Guest's Rotherham accent was loud and clear, the sound wasn't great in the annex and we couldn't actually see the boards because they were out of camera shot. I transcribed as much as I could. Normally, when I got a name wrong or queried a date or fact, someone on Twitter would come back with a data search and correct me in real time. I always retweeted their corrections or rewrote the tweet. But during DS Jim Guest's evidence I suddenly got an email marked: 'Urgent, Mice not Maz.'

The correspondent, who called himself Conrad Brown, pointed out that my version of one white board: 'SOE, Maz, money, ideology, compromise, ego' was incorrect, and drew my attention to the Wikipedia entry explaining the M.I.C.E. acronym. He also pointed out that the *Guardian* had tweeted 'Mice' (with no doubt the advantage of actually being able to see the white board) and continued with this vaguely worrying rider: 'It is my understanding that Maz (Mazher Mahmood) has never been suspected in the police enquiries as having any connection to phone hacking and that he would not be happy for his name to be wrongly linked in this way by your recent tweet. Can you please re-check what was written on the whiteboard and delete or correct the offending tweet as a matter of some urgency before it is retweeted.'

I was more than willing to do so and corrected the email immediately with a capitalised CORRECTION. But I was still a little concerned about the line 'he would not be happy.' I didn't want to antagonise the man famed as the Fake Sheikh and responsible for some of the most famous journalistic tabloid stings against would-be drug buyers or match-fixing cricketers. The guy writing the email had an unremarkable name, Conrad Brown, and untraceable email. I asked: 'Are you representing Mr Mahmood in any capacity?' He replied thanking me for the correction and praising my Twitter coverage, adding: 'I'm a long-time colleague of Maz's. I hope you can understand his concern at his name being mentioned in connection with this debacle. I'm pretty sure he accepts it as an honest mistake.'

Pretty sure? But not certain? I later discovered that a Conrad Brown was a long-time associate of Mahmood's, specialising in surveillance. Memo to self: in the near future don't buy any Class A drugs or fix any Test matches.

◆ ◆ ◆

With the prosecution case against Coulson on Count 1 stalled because of the delay around Dan Evans, Justice Saunders tried to keep the show on the road, and told the defence teams for Cheryl Carter, Mark Hanna and Charlie Brooks to get ready. This made for a welcome change of tone – their barristers Trevor Burke QC, William Clegg QC and Neil Saunders all had lighter, more affable styles and regularly provided comedic moments. But though Edis had spoken in his opening about 'memorable moments' from CCTV footage, it was fairly commonly held opinion that the prosecution team didn't really want to be dealing with the charges of perverting the course of justice. As time went by, we would see why.

Though it might not have been the prosecution's favourite material, much of the evidence around Carter, Hanna and Charlie Brooks was revealing in its own right, for the wider light it shed on News International.

With the appearance on Monday 6 January of Nick Mays, News International's archivist, my timeline got a little fillip of followers – mainly fellow archivists who were probably unused to seeing a member of their profession participating in a high profile criminal trial. Meticulous and precise, Mays complained to Trevor Burke, Carter's QC, that 'people use the word 'archive' loosely' without realising it was a legal requirement for companies to safeguard important corporate or historical records. Burke, who was one of the few barristers not deploying a cut-glass English accent, used his blokeishness to great effect, pointing out that his client – like most people – wouldn't know the difference between archive and storage for personal memorabilia. 'I'm a professional archivist,' Mays replied punctiliously. 'I would expect the same of lawyers.'

Mays' precision soon made him the butt of barristers' jokes. Edis later remarked: 'Whether archivists are the life and soul of the party is not known,' before emphasising Mays' meticulousness. In his closing speech for Cheryl, Burke riffed further on the 'life and soul of the party' line. Only Justice Saunders stepped up to defend archivists in his summing up. He said of Mays: 'Just because he is an archivist, it is suggested he is rather boring,' adding: 'He may not have as exciting a life as top QCs. [But] Neither Mr Edis nor Mr Burke will be giving the speech at the archivist dinner this year.'

(This didn't stop the judge having his own joke at the expense of another former News International archivist who appeared the next day, Eamon Dyas. After a whole day's discussion of archiving policies and practices, Dyas finished his testimony in the witness box and asked if he could take his statements with him. Justice Saunders responded quick as a flash: 'If you would like to keep them for historical purposes, yes.' He was probably the only quick witted person in the court that day….)

Another News International staffer, Jane Viner, Chief Operation Officer, explored the 'deep carpetland' of the executive floors during the tumult of 2011. Viner was Hanna's line manager as Head of Security for News International, as he dealt with protests following the Milly Dowler story and threats to senior executives. She explained what happened during Brooks' resignation and then arrest in July 2011: how the chief executive was escorted out of the building by noon on July 8 as she became a person of interest to the police. Viner was present later that day when the police sealed off Brooks' office but somehow neglected the storage cabinets in the pods around Brooks' two personal assistants, where many documents were stored. Viner supervised the packing up of these items later, when they eventually found their way back to Brooks.

The endless filing lists of what did or did not make it from News International, back through Brooks, then through her solicitor to the police was such a complicated, mind-numbing affair, documented in various lists (one inventory was 131 pages long) that even the judge lost the will to live at some point, saying 'This will live in my nightmares, this particular bundle.'

Apart from the typical corporate procedures, the real revelation was just what a family business News International was. Mark Hanna's nephew was employed by the company, as was Cheryl Carter's son, Nick. The husband of Deborah Keegan, Brooks other PA, was employed as one of her occasional drivers (he was one of several witnesses who tweeted me to thank me for impartial coverage); Clive Goodman's sister Fran worked as a *News of the World* sub editor; Charlie Brooks had various contracts with his wife's employer, as well as several electronic devices tagged as belonging to News International. 'You were quite a trusted associate of News Corp,' Edis pointed out during cross-examination of Charlie. 'It's quite a family orientated company,' Charlie replied. Of course, News Corp itself, though a global media business, is still controlled by the Murdoch family trust, so this emphasis on family is hardly inconsistent. It could also explain some of the clannish loyalty.

One aspect of this loyalty almost went awry for one of the witnesses. Deborah Keegan gave a rather neutral witness statement about her involvement in filing materials for archives and storage for her former boss. But during cross examination by Laidlaw (who began a little unctuously with 'You're one of Mrs Brooks' PAs: I'm one of her lawyers') on 8 January 2014, Keegan seemed to veer from her original testimony, saying she'd actually helped file the seven boxes now missing from archives. Laidlaw also went through the contents of Brooks' filing cabinets in exhausting detail – another of his effective uses of repetition to emphasise his client's busy life and campaigning work on Sarah's Law, Military Awards, youth charities, comprehensive school background and volunteering project. He also made great deal about Brooks' use of notebooks – or lack thereof. One interchange reveals the (effective) powers of suggestion that can be hidden in an apparent question.

> ***Jonathan Laidlaw QC:*** *(to Keegan) Now, the use of notebooks and what you saw during your time with Mrs Brooks. When I say she did not use either of these sorts of notebooks during the period when you helped her, I mean habitual use, routine everyday use, I'm not suggesting she might not on occasions have picked up something like this, written something*

*briefly in it, taken one away with her when she was looking*
*for something to write on. But what I mean is the habitual use*
*of notebooks. So I can illustrate, there are some people who use*
*one of these things like a diary or journal, note things down,*
*the events of the day, what they are thinking…*

*Mr Justice Saunders: Think we feel a question coming on,*
*do we?*

By the time Laidlaw had finished with Keegan – which was quite
some time - Edis, looking furious, seemed to have noticed some
change in the executive assistant's testimony. He quickly established that Keegan had met with her good friend and fellow PA,
Cheryl Carter, six times since her initial statement in November
2011. Permission had been granted by News International's chief
lawyer Kathleen Harris, and had only taken place in the presence
of a *Sun* journalist, Sally Brook. Keegan also confirmed she and
Carter had since exchanged various text messages.

The jury had to leave as Edis told the judge he now wanted
to turn Keegan into a hostile witness so he could re-examine her
with rebuttal evidence. The implication was clear – Keegan had
changed her story to suit Carter and Brooks. Defence counsel
objected, and the judge said he'd need to take submissions and
make a ruling before he decided. It was over a week before Keegan
was invited back to finish her testimony. It must have been a gruelling period for her. While a witness or suspect is giving evidence
they cannot speak to their legal teams or anyone else about the
substance of their case.

Before Justice Saunders would allow Keegan to be recast as a
hostile witness, he questioned her himself over the packing of the
seven missing archive boxes. As it was, Keegan backed down from
saying she was actually present when the seven boxes were packed,
and Justice Saunders ruled this would be sufficient instead of sub-
jecting her to a full prosecution grilling.

The prosecution also had a setback with an expert witness, Dave Cutts, a mobile phone network consultant for the Met. On Tuesday 14 January he was called to talk about some cell site data which showed the movements of various participants in the Count 7 charges. By confusing telephone masts and durations, Cutts had placed Hanna and another security operative in the vicinity of the Brooks' Oxfordshire residence, Jubilee Barn, for over half an hour on the morning of Brooks' arrest. With a brilliant forensic set of data of his own, William Clegg QC (a prosecutor said Clegg commonly reduced drug dealers into quivering wrecks) established that Cutts had got key bits of data wrong from the masts around Chipping Norton. At best the data would only support a 10 minute visit, thereby undermining the prosecution's inference that Hanna could have gone to the Barn to strip the place of electronic devices or other incriminating material. In the final battering of the expert witness, Justice Saunders had to step in the ring and declare a knockout.

*Dave Cutts: Both were measured in the vicinity of Jubilee Barn.*

*William Clegg QC: Why does the statement say the opposite?*

*Dave Cutts: It would appear to be a mistake.*

*William Clegg QC: Another mistake?*

*[A long beat]*

*Mr Justice Saunders: (exasperated) Just say yes.*

*Dave Cutts: [A short pause] Yes.*

On 15 January the cross-examination of the cleaner at Chelsea Harbour, Fernando Nascimento, provided one of the most bizarre moments of the trial, and emphasised the clash of worlds between the upper-class tones of the barristers and cosmopolitan range of witnesses they interact with daily at the Old Bailey. Nascimento had discovered Charlie's bags behind the wheelie bin the morning after they were hidden there, and handed them to his supervisor, who had called in his manager, who had in turn called the police.

Despite Neil Saunders' booming voice and dominant personality, Nascimento, speaking through a Portuguese interpreter, stood his ground, and even injected a bit of humour into the lesbian pornography in the recovered bag. Saunders kept on trying to suggest the cleaner had tampered with material inside the bags. Saunders boomed: 'You took it out, I suggest if you had you wouldn't have forgotten, because inside was a magazine whose title was 'Lesbian Lovers'.' Nascimento laughed when the interpreter translated this: 'I didn't see anything. … I didn't see anything like that. I don't understand English, so the only thing I noticed was the computers.' Alluding to the pornography, Charlie Brooks' barrister barked: 'There wasn't much writing on it!' Nascimento laughed again. Slowly his interpreter translated his words: 'If I had seen it, maybe I would have taken it.'

With the thick mist of obfuscation upon all this evidence about Charlie's bags – bad cell site data, fingerprints on double-bagged bin liners, pizza deliveries, bottles of wine, and missing devices which may have been mislaid or never existed, it's no wonder the jury came to the decision they did on Count 7. Even to this day, I have no idea what happened. And suspicions that the porn was planted or the pizza delivery a cover or that something nefarious was going on involving so many security operatives obviously didn't meet the burden of proof for a criminal charge of perverting the course of justice. On the other hand, a successful cover-up would never admit to any other conclusion.

◆ ◆ ◆

This sensation of co-ordination, that the six corporately-funded defence team were working together, became even more acute when

Neil Saunders, Charlie Brooks' barrister, on 23 January started a day of cross-examination of police witnesses on Operation Kilo, a Scotland Yard inquiry into leaks from Operation Weeting. Superintendent Mark Mitchell, chief investigating officer, had been called because the inquiry was relevant to 'what Charlie Brooks knew' on July 17 2011 when he, on his own admission, hid his bags from the police. Brooks later claimed part of the reason was because he was worried about police leaks.

It emerged that soon after his much-trailed arrest in July 2011, Coulson's lawyers had written to the police and named *Guardian* journalist Amelia Hill as a recipient of leaks from Weeting. In response the Metropolitan Police set up a covert anti-corruption inquiry, Operation Kilo, which traced texts between Hill and an interview strategy adviser, Detective Constable Peter Cripps, from the Weeting team, leaking details of arrests and possible charges. Both were interviewed by detectives, and a charging file was sent to the Crown Prosecution Service. 'There was no evidence of financial inducement,' Superintendent Mitchell told the court, 'and that was why the CPS decided not to prosecute.'

So much so unremarkable you might think, especially in a trial which was concerned with paying public officials – particularly police officers – for tittle tattle about mayors having affairs, or celebrities caught napping in their cars after wild nights out. But this strand of the defence (along with reported blue chip hacking allegations about lawyers and corporations) would become a theme in the coming months. Not only Rebekah and Charlie Brooks, but also Coulson and Goodman would use these suspicions of a police leak to the press to justify their actions.

It was another example of the classic hacking trial irony – the press complaining about the press. The anomaly was even more glaring when emails revealed that News International had its own source inside Operation Weeting. (On the eve of her resignation the next week, Will Lewis emailed Brooks to 'call [name redacted for legal reasons' to find out more). For all their complaints about police leaks to the *Guardian,* News International executives seemed more than happy when they received police leaks themselves.

But even more intriguing than this institutional internecine warfare between journalists was the way the evidence on Operation Kilo seemed to have been well flagged up in advance. On the day Superintendent Mitchell gave evidence my tweets were retweeted within seconds by two *Sun* columnists: the former Conservative MP Louise Mensch, who had sat on the parliamentary committee that grilled Brooks over phone hacking, and the blogger Guido Fawkes. Guido had retweeted my reporting on previous occasions, particularly the affair, albeit not briskly. Mensch was a new follower. Why were they both all over this story so quickly?

That sense of an air campaign – the media offensive which worked in concert with the ground warfare of the court – would intensify in the months ahead. But who was fighting whom in the sky? An email would soon emerge from the height of the hacking scandal in 2011, with Brooks complaining to James Harding, editor of *The Times,* that the Milly Dowler story was 'a proper Guardian, BBC Old Labour, hit.'

If there was internecine warfare between the tabloid press and the *Guardian*, it rages on. During the trial I was invited to the Press Club Awards lunch where my hacking trial blog was nominated one of the best three news sites. A free lunch beckoned and I was sat next to a veteran *Mirror* journalist who had reported many Old Bailey cases. He was a gent, full of fascinating stories. But when we got to the subject of the phone hacking trial, he said to me, confidentially: 'You know who is to blame for all this?' I shook my head, waiting for a bit of insider information I might have missed. He said: 'The *Guardian!*'

A trial about the biggest newspaper in Britain, involving executives of a global media conglomerate, was bound to cause problems of contempt. But it was also destined to reveal the way that the media interact with the court process. Apart from six defence teams funded by News Corp, there were also at least three dedicated note takers from the company, as well as regular attendance from journalists from the *Sun, The Times* and *Wall Street Journal.* Multiple sources of information could be going back to other columnists and employees without there being any co-ordinated collusion. Perhaps a joint interest in seeing the company survive and former associates vindicated explains the synchronicity of those events. But as Dan Evans was due in the witness box, the convergence of interest became ever more apparent.

◆ ◆ ◆

Before that happened, however, I had a drink with the Murdoch biographer and New York columnist, Michael Wolff. He was in London to write an article on the trial for the British edition of *GQ* magazine, and we met after a dull day in court at a nearby wine bar. I'd interviewed Michael down the phone for a couple of features on the phone hacking scandal, and quoted him extensively in my book. He could write brilliantly at times, but on Twitter could shape shift, and only six months or so before he had accused me of having a dead style and the controlling heart of a press regulator. But he was a good sport and I was still keen to meet him. In person he was less acerbic, and much more gossipy and self-deprecating. He too, like everyone else in contact with News Corp HQ in New York, relayed Rupert Murdoch's conviction that Brooks would escape all the charges. We chatted for a couple of hours about the courtroom gossip, and relatively onerous contempt laws in the UK. His ultimate response to that was 'Shit. I'm not going to be able to write anything.'

Six weeks later the April edition of *GQ* hit the streets, with Wolff's piece teased on the front cover *Hacking Exclusive: Michael Wolff at the Trial of the Century.* There was a furore. Reading it again now, half the essay was novelistic scene setting. And Wolff's points about the prosecution's 'laborious sometimes stumbling efforts to connect the scattered dots' and how it could seem 'muted' compared to the

'booming voice' of the defence was accurate. But because he had
so few facts to report, Wolff couldn't help making (in legal terms)
controversial comments, calling Brooks' case a 'magician's defence'
and asking: 'How can you convict a man called Charlie?'

In Court 12, Laidlaw, for Brooks, was first to object, and
read out a passage in which his client was described as 'clever,
sharp, winning, seductive, cunning – well prepared to do what
is required.' 'This is, on the face of it, contempt,' he continued.
'It's objectionable, the comment, the tone, the language used – it's
utterly, utterly inappropriate.' Given his comments on the prosecution case, Wolff managed to achieve rare unanimity between
Laidlaw and Edis. The article was referred to the Attorney General
for contempt of court. Though many think the current contempt
of court laws in the UK are heavy-handed, it did gall reporters in
the annex that Wolff felt he could waltz into court for a few days
and write a long commentary, while we stuck to the reporting
restrictions. He also erroneously suggested Nick Davies dropped by
late most mornings when he was a punctual and regular attendee –
and sniped that people had 'made a living' out of the hacking trial.
Perhaps more revealing were Wolff's closing lines suggesting that
Murdoch was planning some form of redress against his enemies.

Outside the courtroom, my rising profile was causing some
unwanted attention. By now detailed evidence had been cited
in court about how Mulcaire had hacked senior editors at News
International. Brooks and Coulson were hacked regularly by the
private investigator. Brooks told the court that she was shocked
to be told by a Scotland Yard detective in 2006 that Mulcaire had
obtained her PIN; she'd changed her PIN years ago – but declined
to be a prosecution witness. Both Andy Coulson and Neil Wallis
were regularly hacked, as well as the *News of the World* showbusiness reporter Rav Singh. So too were two *Mail on Sunday* journalists to get a spoiler of their exclusive on John Prescott.

I decided to write a blog on journalist victims of phone hacking,
making a fairly innocuous distinction between hacking for industrial

sabotage and for gleaning personal information. At this point
Dennis Rice, one of the *Mail on Sunday* reporters whose phone had
been hacked, was debating the court's revelations with *Hacked Off*'s
Evan Harris. Foolishly, I joined the discussion, and suggested that
having your stories pinched through a rival's hacking was different
from having your own personal life exposed in the papers.

Rice took exception to this and told me that his family had
been targeted. I replied I was very sorry to hear that and updated
my blog, writing: 'Twitter is not the ideal place to have a nuanced
argument, and Rice has since revealed his family was targeted.
This is a privacy violation of the first order.' This failed to placate
Rice, who accused me of 'stalking' him on *Linked In* (he'd come up
in a search I'd done when writing up his timeline from the trial).
He added that he was a potential witness, and I was 'harassing'
him so he was thinking of reporting me to the Attorney General.

Again, I should have remembered not to interact with people
during the trial – and promised to myself to leave Rice well alone.
He blocked his timeline anyway. Two weeks later Rice unblocked
his Twitter feed and was back online saying that 'fellow hacks' had
encouraged him to correct a blogger's 'factual errors' and saying he
had a settlement from News International worth more than that
awarded to the MP George Galloway. Civil settlements are usually
confidential and Rice had warned me off engaging with him as a
potential trial witness, but I did update the blog with newspaper
links. This clearly wasn't enough and Rice somehow read my blog
as demeaning journalists as second-class citizens. 'It's now 24 hrs
since I showed @peterjukes that his smear blog about my family
was factually incorrect,' he tweeted, 'yet he still refuses to alter it. So
I'm now going to blog about @peterjukes & his family.' There were
some mutterings about me being too afraid to meet him face to face.

I was more concerned about the tone of his subsequent
comments. 'His blatant refusal to remove these falsehoods invites
me to look as an investigative journalist what else is going on
here,' Rice tweeted about my 'malicious' 'smear blog,' saying I

was 'wetting your pants when a real journalist turns his gaze on you. I'm coming.' I was not sure what Rice meant when he said he was 'coming,' though I knew he had taunted someone else on Twitter after checking their business details at Companies House. Through the months ahead I anxiously anticipated some kind of blog about my financial background or my family. Rice locked down his feed again.

Another account, TabloidTroll (which Rice vigorously insists he has nothing to do with) mentioned me regularly, my crowd-funding and even suggested I should give some of the proceeds to my ex-wife. It wasn't pleasant, but a tiny example of a much larger debate at the heart of British journalism, a battle which would amplify considerably when Dan Evans – the *News of the World* hack who had repented about the 'Dark Arts' – finally arrived at Court 12.

# THE OFFICE CAT

*Andrew Edis QC: Shall we do something exciting with dividers whilst we've got this file open?*

*Justice Saunders: Yes, it'll calm us all down.*

Few witnesses brought into such sharp relief both the legal and personal meanings of 'contempt' than the much awaited and delayed appearance in the witness box of Daniel Evans on 27 January 2014.

For a start, the reporting restrictions imposed around his appearance were voluminous: they covered more than 20 names from News International and Mirror Group Newspapers. We already had a dozen or so restricted names because of two imminent trials and these additional names were too numerous to memorise easily. During the week Evans gave evidence reporters in the annex constantly asked each other if a name mentioned in evidence had to be redacted, and whether the code 'executive' or 'editor' was too explicit.

The perils of tweeting were never greater. For my part, I managed to avoid these 20 names and actually went overboard, deleting a tweet innocently naming a *News of the World* journalist as part of an email exchange. (Noises off from the usual suspects told a colleague tabloid journalists were furious with me for tweeting his name out).

Yet it was the other meaning of contempt that had a more profound impact. For legitimate evidential reasons, Coulson's counsel had insisted that Evans' appearance should be book-ended by the two most famous witnesses: Jude Law and Sienna Miller. The legal argument for this was solid. Evans' witness statement revolved around his claim to have hacked the phone of their friend Daniel Craig in September 2005. Evans claimed he played a tape of a voicemail message from Craig's phone to Coulson and other senior journalists at the *News of the World* to land the story that Miller (who was in a relationship with Jude Law) was having a fling with Craig. According to Evans, Miller told Craig in the message that she was with Law in the Groucho private members' club in Soho, adding: 'I love you.' Since Law was the subject of many tabloid stories at the time as a result of this particular triangle, he wasn't just a starry witness – but essential to the facts.

Soberly-dressed and trim, Law stepped into the witness box on 27 January 2014. Langdale's cross examination of him about events 'that took place in 2005' which may have 'some bearing on another witnesses' evidence' was mainly a reprise of his favourite theme: there were sources other than phone hacking for *News of the World* stories. Langdale took the jury to the *News of the World*'s *Sienna Cheats on Jude* article, and another titled *Layer Fake* (Miller and Craig had starred in the film *Layer Cake*): 'I'm not going to ask you to read it,' Langdale told the actor. Law replied: 'I'd rather not.'

Then, in one of the most dramatic moments in the trial, Langdale asked the actor if he was aware that a close member of his family was in contact with the *News of the World* about his anger with Craig over Miller. Stoically, Law said he didn't know at the time, but that the family member had explained things in 2011 and they were reconciled. However, Law paled when Langdale told him that the relative had been paid for the stories. Law said quietly: 'I've never been aware of that.' Langdale then wrote down the name of the family member on a piece of paper and handed it to Law for him to confirm, which he did. Langdale also wrote down the names of a close friend and a publicist who had been talking to the Sunday tabloid and handed it to him. The actor said he had also been made aware of these sources 'very recently.' He sounded subdued.

Though both the judge and the prosecution tried to limit the damage, a trial about gross privacy intrusions was bound to compound the original harm. Several defendants, too, would lose their rights to privacy as a result of testing evidence, with Rebekah and Charlie Brooks subjected to intense scrutiny of their private lives. But sometimes the defence attitude to victims of phone hacking seemed casual, almost brutal. When earlier making random points about the formatting of Mulcaire's notebooks, Laidlaw for Brooks alighted on the actor Hugh Grant and the police officers Jacqui Hames and Dave Cook, which seemed gratuitous given their experiences. But if the lawyers in court seemed less than caring about Law's personal relationships, the newspapers followed up the next day with more egregious examples of the problem. The *Star* used some of the evidence produced in court to run a new front-page story about a 10-year-old affair between Daniel Craig and the fashion model Kate Moss. Meanwhile, even *The Times* fell into the celebrity trap. Rather than reporting on the explosive evidence of Dan Evans (who gave evidence that afternoon), its front-page story was about how Jude Law was betrayed by a member of his own family

Perhaps my editorial sense is faulty; I'm not employed by a major news group, after all, but I considered the first live witness to admit phone hacking to be front-page material.

◆ ◆ ◆

Of all the witnesses who appeared at the trial, none was as blasé and blunt as Dan Evans. After months of speculation about what he would say and who he would implicate, Evans spelled out baldly the daily life of a phone hacker – and how it was an integral part of the newsgathering operation at Andy Coulson's *News of the World*. 'Even the office cat knew' about hacking, he said blithely. Caught hacking again in 2009, trying to find out a connection between Kelly Hoppen and director Guy Ritchie, Evans remarked: 'Curiosity killed this particular cat.'

Evans went through his phone hacking rampage in tabloid newspapers. He had first worked at the *Sunday Mirror*, where he was taught how to hack. He said: 'I was taken aside by a very senior exec and told I was tasked for something secret... and shown how to hack a voicemail.' He was given a list of famous people and told 'this is your job, you have to hack and crack the numbers. 'Over a period of time I did this quite successfully... too successfully... forsaking all the stuff I enjoyed doing... I wanted to get out.'

He was such a strong story-getter that the *News of the World* made several attempts to headhunt him. During one of those attempts, James Weatherup, *News of the World* news editor, introduced Evans to another executive at Boot's Bar in Wapping, where he was offered work with Mazher Mahmood, the Fake Sheikh. Evans was keen to get into undercover investigations. 'Things had slipped too much into phone hacking at the *Sunday Mirror*,' Evans told the court. 'My interest was piqued by James' approach.... but I didn't want to arrive there as his pet phone hacker.'

Evans said that by the time of a second approach by the *News of the World* in 2004 'my head had been turned, definitely' and he met one of the paper's executives, whom he described as 'a bombastic character.' The executive allegedly asked Evans: 'We know you can screw phones, but what else can you do?'

Then, crucially, Evans met Andy Coulson and another executive at One Aldwych hotel, London, for breakfast on 1 October 2005. Evans said that at this 'nearest formal thing to an interview' he alluded to hacking and told Coulson 'I can get you big exclusive stories cheaply.' According to Evans, Coulson replied: 'You've got something which can shift units from supermarket shelves.' Evans continued: 'Every week there was a humdinger of a story in

*Sunday Mirror....* achieved through this method. Andy knew the context.' When the 25-minute interview was over, the *News of the World* called Evans five minutes later and offered him a job on a salary of £53,000. His contract was biked around that afternoon.

Key to his recruitment, Evans told the court, was his master list of celebrity phone numbers. He said the journalist who recruited him took him into a glass office on his first day at work and gave him 'a contacts list to get cracking on....' Evans handed over the email to Operation Weeting when he agreed to testify. This list of phone hacking targets and numbers ran to more than 10 pages and included the DJ Zoe Ball, John Birt, the former director general of the BBC, and the singer and TV presenter Cilla Black. Another list of names and numbers, annotated by Evans, was 26 pages long.

Given that Mulcaire pleaded guilty, and could not be compelled to give evidence, Evans' testimony was electric: the closest the court got to hearing the daily life of a phone hacker. Evans told the jury that at the *News of the World* he'd hack phones 'most days.' 'So I want to find out about you,' Evans told Edis: 'We'd get billing data. Who you called first thing, last thing. Significant others. Can we hack their voicemail? Oh, there they are... let's go along with a photographer. That's kind of how tabloid journalism worked in those days – that was life.' He said management referred to phone hacking during conferences as 'special checks,' and unlike the *Mirror* group, News International wanted everything on email.

During his four years at the *News of the World* Evans admitted doing thousands of hacks to more than 100 mobile phones, but his most important testimony was about a single hack – of Daniel Craig's phone.

Evans claimed he was depressed at not doing proper investigative journalism and getting 'bullied' and 'monstered' over getting a front-page scoop. One day in September 2005, the journalist who recruited him told him: 'As far as I'm concerned your USP is the phones. And I suggest you get on with some more.' Evans then hacked all the numbers he could until he got to Craig, the new James Bond, and heard a message: 'Hi it's me. Can't speak. I'm with Jude at Groucho's. I love you.' The name 'Jude' would have probably been enough to give Evans a clue, but he said he also checked Sienna Miller's number from a list in his Palm Pilot. When he brought a Dictaphone recording of the message into work the following Monday, Evans claimed in court, he played it to the journalist who recruited him, who got 'very excited,' started writing copy and 'started an operation on it,' with the help of the showbiz columnist Rav Singh. Evans then played it to Coulson, the editor, who got 'very animated' and told the assembled journalists: 'I told you so!' Evans said another newspaper executive shook his hand and congratulated him, saying: 'You're a company man now.'

Evans said Coulson told him to make a copy of the tape and make it look like it was delivered anonymously. Evans copied the tape, put the new tape in a Jiffy bag (careful all the while to use a handkerchief to avoid fingerprints) and had it delivered to the front desk. He said Rav Singh picked up the Jiffy bag and said: 'Look what I've found.'

I'm not a court expert, forensic psychologist or expert interrogator, but after years in drama I have a strong sense of what is fiction and what is hard to make up. We'll get to the classic Brooks/Carter MI5/MFI joke later, but the scenario Evans described did not change significantly between his witness statement and appearance at the Old Bailey. It also had the merit of being vivid and believable. Another journalist in the annex, who knew some of the personalities involved, said he could imagine them saying all these things. That's not a sufficient test, and as Langdale rose to cross-examine Evans there was a common feeling that the lawyer had something big on the journalist. When he asked to delay his cross-examination until the next morning, that expectation increased.

◆ ◆ ◆

When it finally began the following morning, 29 January, Langdale's three-day cross-examination of Evans was a master class in trying to discredit a witness, through a variety of tactics. The first obvious weak spot was the deal with the CPS to become a prosecution witness. Just as he had done in legal argument during the jury's absence, Langdale tried to imply Evans was frightened and effectively forced to co-operate by the authorities. He agreed he was frightened when he got arrested again in 2011 during the height of the phone hacking scandal, remarking: 'Caught between the Prime Minister and the tabloids, caught between high paid lawyers.'

Throughout Langdale maintained a tone of world-weary disappointment, his cynicism sometimes sounding more like contempt, seemingly aimed at provoking a reaction from Evans. 'To be fair, I didn't really understand the ramifications of all this,' Evans said about his scoping police interview. Langdale said ominously: 'I'll discuss later.' Evans chipped in: 'Can't wait.'

Then Langdale went to the statement Evans made in the civil case brought by Kelly Hoppen in in 2009. 'Yes I lied,' the journalist said of his laughable excuse that 'sticky keys' on his phone made him call Hoppen's voicemail. But he reiterated his claim he was told by News International lawyers to concoct the alibi. 'I was part of a conspiracy,' he said. Langdale wasn't going to be distracted: 'You decided to deny the truth…' he persisted. 'I'm ashamed to say I did,' Evans replied. With a feline mix of languor and menace, Langdale said: 'We'll see how ashamed you are.'

Then the septuagenarian lawyer performed one of his favourite tricks. He would touch on a subject, casually obtain an admission, and move on – only to return in force later. The target he was circling was the precise date Evans claimed he played the Sienna Miller message to Andy Coulson. Given the timing of the story's publication, Evans conceded this must have been on Tuesday 27 September 2005. Langdale quickly changed the subject, and went on to Evans' police statement that the use of the 'dark arts' left him 'drinking too much, using drugs, conflicted inside, and generally unhappy.' Evans admitted using cocaine every couple of weeks, as a form of self-medication. He told the jury: 'Having an enormous secret and delving illegally into the lives of people who didn't deserve it made me unhappy.'

The way the veteran QC circled his prey before finally pouncing in for attack made some of us in the annex try to come up with a good code name for Langdale. James Doleman had already christened Edis 'The Cobra' for his ability to mesmerize and then strike. 'The Cat' Langdale seemed to be the best animal soubriquet for Coulson's sharp but sly counsel. He played with his opponent as if he were batting around a tremulous mouse.

♦ ♦ ♦

The legal battering was clearly working. The next morning, 30 January, Evans changed his testimony. In his police statement he claimed to have hacked Kelly Hoppen's voicemail in 2005, and heard a tearful message from Sienna Miller (her step daughter at the time) about her romantic difficulties. Evans now revised that testimony, saying the message may have been Miller's sister, Savannah. 'This document jogged my memory…. after many, many years and thousands of hacks,' he said: 'Sorry if I misspoke my evidence.' It looked like the prosecution's star witness was cracking.

Langdale went through Evans' *News of the World* articles, sounding shocked that the journalist in the witness box was admitting to fabricating quotes. Now it was Evans' turn to sound world-weary. He told the court casually: 'This is a tabloid newspaper… not every quote is nailed as the truth. When it says 'a source says' it's just made up.' As for Langdale's forensic attempt to prove the articles of the time all came from legitimate sources, Evans explained: 'I would editorialise a bit about sisters closing ranks around the love rat. Four of five paras of editorialised tabloid fluff.' Trying hard to prove the Miller Craig story didn't come from phone hacking, Langdale went on to quote related articles from the *Daily Mirror* and the *Daily Star*. This move Evans easily parried with a laugh: 'The *Daily Star* is a notoriously dodgy paper,' he told the court, 'a nest of inaccuracies.'

Yet something in Langdale's voice suggested he was still toying with the witness. He went back to the 'I love you' voicemail from Miller to Craig. How did Evans identify her? Evans repeated his explanation that he'd identified the actress partly from context 'I'm in Groucho's with Jude' and a number he had in his Palm Pilot. Now Langdale pounced. The number in Evans Palm Pilot (disclosed to the defence months before) was a new one – a number she hadn't received till months after the hacking.

Evans looked startled, stymied. Justice Saunders intervened: 'Just take a deep breath and concentrate for a bit.' Langdale backed off a little. Moments before the lunch break, the lawyer ratcheted open the jaws of his trap, revealing to Evans he had fallen for a fatal error. 'I'm going to suggest,' said Langdale, sounding triumphant, 'that nothing of any significance was happening at all in relation to this voicemail message you say was played on the morning of the 27th.' Evans blinked. Langdale growled. 'What do you say to that?' Evans was all tabloid bravado: 'I say bring it on!' But once again Justice Saunders had the last word: 'Shall we bring it on at five past two?'

It looked like another Eimear Cook situation, another date the prosecution had casually entered which – with the benefit of Brooks and Coulson's desk diaries – would turn out to be impossible, and threaten to undermine an entire testimony. Back after lunch, Langdale pushed home his advantage. He went back to Evans playing the tape to Coulson on a 'twilighty' late afternoon – before telling him this was impossible. The *News of the World* editor was not in the office that day. (It would later emerge that he was at the Labour Party conference). But Evans was steadier than Eimear Cook: 'Perhaps it was the following day, later in the day,' he said. 'It doesn't alter the fact, playing the tape... and remarks made... happened. Certainly salient elements are clear in my mind.'

Still Langdale harried. If he wasn't sure about the day, how could Evans be sure Coulson and another senior executive were present? He harried so much the judge had to intervene: 'Stop… this is becoming comment.' Evans stuck to his guns. 'My memory isn't clear of exactly when it happened, but happen it did,' he said, 'in the early part of the week.' If Evans' original testimony was out, it was only out by a day or so.

Evans was barely hanging on now. But Langdale was not done with him. Having attacked Evans' credibility, and now the accuracy of his account of the Miller voicemail, Langdale had a third point, which he proceeded to press home during a long day: Evans had not hacked Craig's phone. There was no call data evidence to support the notion. There were other sources for the romantic bust up: confidential human sources (we saw why the Jude Law pre-amble was so vital to Langdale's case) – and indeed other news articles. Langdale cited a *Mail on Sunday* piece about Jude Law and Sienna Miller at her sister's wedding. Coulson's QC insisted Evans must have read this that weekend, which drew the memorable response: 'Not necessarily, mate,' he said, turning an offence into a defence: 'I would have been drunk after a night going out.'

For all the bullish joking, Evans was tiring and losing his temper, describing a follow up question as 'meaningless.' It was hard to know whether Langdale was growling or purring when he ended that day's cross-examination with the line: 'That's the appropriate place to pause.'

◆ ◆ ◆

I'd never met Dan Evans before we nodded to each other outside Court 12, though I know someone who worked with him and counted him as a friend. In person, you could still sense the wild, fun-seeking tabloid journalist who liked being in the centre of events, addicted to adrenaline and a memorable phrase. No doubt, given the clannish nature of newspaper journalists (and though I've enjoyed working with them, I've never met quite such a tribal profession) Evans will be seen as a traitor. Other former senior tabloid editors mentioned in evidence were quick to disparage him on Twitter for his drinking habits (despite the contempt threat).

I know many reporters in commercial and public service TV and radio and I've never heard any of them ever express the kind of groupthink repeatedly uttered by print journalists. A reporter who became a good friend during the trial told me the first rule of the press is, 'you never betray your own.' Admirable sentiments in one sense, especially if you're in a tight corner, and the amount of co-operation among the press in the Old Bailey was heartening. Nevertheless, taken to the limit, 'Never betray your own' could mean covering up crimes for a colleague.

◆ ◆ ◆

The next morning, 31 January, Langdale resumed for his third day of cross-examination. Though neither the jury nor the public knew it yet, the lawyers and journalists attending knew that Sienna Miller was due to speak by video link in the afternoon, so the cross examination would be limited. Langdale's overall plan for the week was becoming clear. Evans didn't get the crucial Miller voicemail message by hacking: the story came from another source. He'd suggested part of that with Jude Law. Now he would box Evans in with Sienna Miller, and claim victory.

In the hours before the actress made her appearance though, Langdale had to disprove the source was phone hacking, and therefore was in the odd position of getting Evans to deny his acknowledged criminality. He tried to prove an article written by Evans about Eva Green being the new Bond girl was not obtained through hacking Craig's voicemail. Evans was getting punchy now. Things became even more fractious over the filing of a new piece of paper

**Timothy Langdale QC:** *Did you manage to put it in the file?*

**Dan Evans:** *Do you want me to?*

**Timothy Langdale QC:** *I said did you manage to, the answer is 'no'.*

**Mr Justice Saunders:** *OK, OK, just put it in the file*

**Dan Evans:** *Where do you want me to put it? I thought you said put in the back of the file.*

**Timothy Langdale QC:** *[exasperated] Just put it wherever you want to.*

**Mr Justice Saunders:** *OK, OK. Let's just get on with the case.*

Despite the judge asking him if it was avoidable, Langdale went through some internal *News of the World* emails that contained some very personal details of Sienna Miller's health and state of mind during the bust up with Jude Law. Langdale's point was that these details came from a source close to Miller, rather than hacking. But he was labouring the point by now – and using some untested and unproven allegations about Miller to bang it home.

Another potential tricky moment for Evans was an expenses claim to News International for a 'meal with Daniel Craig contact' which Langdale produced with a flourish as another 'gotcha.' But Evans had the perfect explanation for that: 'I was having a meal with my girlfriend.' When Langdale sounded shocked about this 'fiddling of expenses' the former journalist brought the lawyer up to date about that part of Fleet Street: 'This was a tabloid way of life, part of our culture at the paper.'

Langdale shouldn't have been so surprised: he later suggested that Clive Goodman was pocketing some of the money he claimed for sources. But this was yet another example of the clash of different values between Fleet Street and the Inns of Court. The lawyers present were focused on truth and evidence. In many of the newspaper stories adduced, truth and evidence were secondary matters.

As the morning wound down, and Langdale went back to the other crucial event for his client – the recruitment at One Aldwych – Evans began to rally, knowing he was nearing the end without any further major slip-ups or changes in testimony. He reiterated his version of the morning meeting, and went into more damning detail. He said he even told Coulson how various *Sunday Mirror* front pages were sourced from phone interception. In a phrase which would echo throughout the trial (rather like the office cat), Evans said he told the *News of the World* editor how phone hacking was 'a good way of getting big stories cheaply.'

◆ ◆ ◆

That afternoon, Sienna Miller gave evidence by video link from New Orleans, taking her oath in the presence of an FBI officer. We were all waiting for Langdale's big killer question that would explain the whole week: a devastating piece of evidence from a movie star which would damage the prosecution's star witness, Dan Evans. Knowing what could be coming, Edis, for the prosecution, questioned Miller on the context of the voicemail message that was at the centre of Coulson's defence

'My membership was always a little bit of a hazy issue, but I was there a lot of the time,' Miller told Edis of her attendance at the Groucho Club. But she confirmed it was 'likely' she called Daniel Craig. 'I was in constant communication with him. It's likely I would have called him. And likely I was there,' she said. As for the part of the message that animated the newsroom at the *News of the World*, Miller had an innocent explanation: 'Since we'd become close friends, I always left a message 'I love you.' I often did with family and friends. That makes it most likely.'

Not much room for doubt there. What did Langdale have in his locker? As the veteran barrister stood up to cross examine the actress, he sounded much less menacing, and more kittenish, especially since there were (once again) problems with the sound. First Miller confirmed some details about her sister's wedding, and contacts with her former stepmother. Langdale then asked her to open a prepared bundle. Was this the time bomb? Miller tore open the sealed envelope to discover a picture of herself in a *News of the World* article in mid February 2005, in the company of the newspaper's showbiz correspondent, Rav Singh.

Miller denied she had spoken to Singh at length, or that the article was based on her own words. She 'just posed with him at a party... it's common for journalists to ask for a picture,' she said. The rest of the article was 'misconstrued and invented.' She said she would have never have told Singh she loved Law so much she wanted to marry him. At most she would have said: 'Stop! He's one of the nicest, kindest people I know and you're misrepresenting him.' Langdale persisted in his attempt to find another source for the story of the affair. But Miller wasn't budging from her testimony, telling Court 12: 'That sounds like a message I would have left.' Langdale followed up with: 'Was that message an expression of friendship, 'I love you?" But by this point the lawyer and actress were talking over each other. There was a pause. Langdale apologised and seemed lost. Miller followed up: 'Sorry, you just told me you loved me, and then I interrupted you.' The court erupted in one of the biggest laughs of the trial. Langdale had his own riposte: 'Miss Miller, are you by any chance an actress? That was very well timed, if I may say so.'

By now, the sting had gone from Langdale's cross-examination. Once again seemingly failing to understand a tabloid newsroom, Langdale sounded incredulous that the whole affair story could have been inspired by a misreading of an innocuous term of endearment. Miller was adamant that her relationship with Craig was a 'brief encounter' and how upsetting it was for this to be 'released

to the world media and be vilified for.' She said the timing of the
message and the story was 'very significant' and absolutely disagreed it was too slender to form the basis of a major tabloid story.
'If a journalist got hold of that piece of information... it could be
the basis of a story,' she told the jury: "I love you' could be exciting
to a journalist who didn't understand our relationship.'

Game, set and match to Miller.

Edis' re-examination of Miller was brisk and relieved. He went
back to an email which provided extra background information
on Miller in 2005, from someone who knew her mother casually.
Miller itemised the allegations: 'I don't remember losing half a
stone in weight, or being flat chested, I've always bitten my nails,'
she said. Edis sounded mortified, and immediately apologised: 'I
didn't mean to make you answer a question to say all that.' Justice
Saunders reiterated his apologies before Miller signed off, telling
her: 'I am very sorry that what has been said in court and reported
in the press has caused you upset but it has been necessary.'

That weekend, the coverage continued. Not only had newspapers like the *Daily Star* repeated the privacy invasion without
revealing the context of the trial (which involved illegal privacy
intrusion) other papers seemed to be ignoring the substance of
what had happened. Just as *The Times* had led on Jude Law's
family member, the *Sun* had bracketed the week of Dan Evans'
appearance with two front pages about another Hugh Grant
love-child and Sally Bercow kissing someone: anything about the
trial was buried deep within the paper. For this observation I was
reprimanded by the *Sun*'s showbusiness editor, Dan Wooton, and
upbraided by the *Mirror*'s showbusiness editor Tom Bryant for
'commentary.'

Around this time too, there were reports from the usually
reliable True Crime blog that other journalists were thinking of
coming forward as witnesses after Evans' testimony. Late one
night, I carelessly retweeted it. The next morning I heard another
of the 'There's been a tweet, My Lord' interventions from the

defence. I turned to look at James Doleman, who blanched. A
few days previously he'd had to delete a tweet that had transposed
two of the defendants. Now Justice Saunders was talking about
how long it took Twitter to respond to 'take down' notices from
the court. I tried to reassure Doleman: they couldn't be talking
about him because the tweet had already been deleted, then Justice
Saunders asked: 'Is Mr Jukes in court?'

I ran up the eight flights of stairs to Court 12. By the time I'd
got there the court had moved on to other business, but Justice
Saunders saw me enter and nodded to me to speak. Still breathless,
I said 'My lord. You mentioned a tweet. Can you... Can you let
me know which one it is and I'll delete it.' Justice Saunders said:
'You'd better speak to Mr McCulloch.' As I went outside with the
court amicus, I heard the courtroom laugh. I was later told Justice
Saunders grinned about my sudden appearance from the bowels of
the Old Bailey and said: 'I didn't know I had such power.'

In the waiting area outside the court, McCulloch explained to
me it wasn't a tweet of mine, but the True Crime tweet from the
previous night I'd retweeted. I was immediately relieved, but also
a bit aggrieved I'd been mentioned as the source. 'Why me?' I
asked. McCulloch smiled: 'Everyone follows you, Peter.' Back in
the annex, I was ritually ribbed for nearly derailing the trial, again.

But we'd survived this far. With Dan Evans over, and a little bit
of mopping up to do with prosecution bits and pieces, we were now
due to get to the highlight of any trial – the defence case. It was here
the high stakes and drama really exist, when the defence are allowed
to rebut the inferences of the evidence so far, and then the prosecution can cross examine. In many trials, defendants avoid the witness
box for fear of letting something slip in the crossfire of questions.
But in the hacking trial, all the defendants planned to give evidence,
opening the prospect of some amazing set pieces.

By now, I'd nearly finished my crowd-funding, and overshot
the target again. But right away, my feed went dark for a week as
defence counsel fought a rear-guard action to halt the trial.

# INTERLUDE: THE TRIAL
# THAT MIGHT HAVE BEEN

*Andrew Edis QC: As your lordship pleases.*

*Justice Saunders: I've always thought that was
a nice phrase, 'as your lordship pleases.'*

*Andrew Edis QC: It was intended to be graceful.*

'The traditional half time break as lawyers argue the toss,' was how a journalist described it to me. After the prosecution rested its case on 5 February after 13 weeks of evidence, the defence teams argued the trial should be halted on the grounds that there was no case to answer. Normally these debates take a day or so. But nothing was normal at the phone hacking trial and, given the number of defendants and privately-paid counsel, a week was set aside. Though dull and technical-sounding, this half-time debate – like all legal argument conducted in the absence of the jury – amounted to an assessment of the whole case.

Unlike courtroom dramas, where prosecutors tell the jury what crimes the suspects have committed and emphasise means, motive and conspiracy, real-life prosecutions can only adduce evidence gathered by the police. Everything must be disclosed to the defence well in advance, even if unhelpful. Rather than join the dots of evidence, only a bare narrative of the facts may be set out; though the jury may be asked to draw inferences. The defence's job is to challenge and disrupt that inferential narrative: challenging exhibits, expert testimony and the credibility and memory of witnesses. So the half-time submissions gave both an insight into the inferences the prosecution were asking the jury to make – and the defence's counter arguments.

Four defendants – Rebekah Brooks, Cheryl Carter, Charlie Brooks and Mark Hanna – made a 'no case to answer' submission. (Coulson's barrister Timothy Langdale had another strategy, going for a procedural dismissal because of a 'systematic failure' in police and prosecution disclosure 'creating an unfair bias against his client.' Justice Saunders dismissed this application in a separate ruling, pointing to the millions of emails and problems of co-operation with News International.)

Before he addressed them, Justice Saunders stressed that his job was to check the evidence objectively; important subjective decisions on the reliability of witnesses were for the jury.

In an age where *CSI* and other dramas about science and forensics have reduced our notion of guilt and innocence to scientific proof, it's worth remembering this more human element of a court trial. Most crimes aren't just about acts and events which can be filmed, tested in a laboratory, or captured in electronic data and spreadsheets; they are about intent, the state of mind of the defendant. With the exception of 'strict liability' offences (like contempt of court) where intent is irrelevant, most crimes depend on both a guilty act (an *actus reus*) and a guilty state of mind (a *mens rea*). You took someone else's iPhone from a pub table and walked away. Did you think it was yours? Did the owner give you permission to borrow it? Were you planning to return it? All those elements, beyond the mere fact of removing the iPhone, are crucial to determining whether you committed theft. Hard objective evidence tends to produce guilty pleas – or very short trials. In determining the subjective state of mind of the accused, the courts pass the matter to a jury of our peers.

Justice Saunders explored what weight the jury might put on the evidence.

◆ ◆ ◆

The judge rejected the application for Rebekah Brooks. Given the absence of any direct communication with Mulcaire, or an incriminating email about hacking, or many confirmed hacks during her editorship of the *News of the World*, Justice Saunders described the targeting of Milly Dowler – which did so much to shape public attitudes towards the paper and for which there was much evidence – as 'the high point' of Count 1 against Brooks.

Milly Dowler disappeared on 21 March 2002, and her disappearance appeared in editions of the newspaper over the next three weekends when Brooks was editing the paper. The following weekend, 14 April 2002, Brooks was away in Dubai, but the judge said that because of her campaign for Sarah's Law: 'The jury could properly infer that Rebekah Brooks would have been interested in this story which was ongoing when she went on holiday.'

The admissions or 'agreed facts' had established that Neville Thurlbeck had put Mulcaire on the Dowler story by 10 April. Sometime between 10 and 12 April, Mulcaire hacked Milly's phone and picked up a message, intended for someone else, left by Monday's Recruitment Agency about an interview with a firm in Telford. Up to nine reporters, photographers and desk editors were put on the story. In the end Milly wasn't found, and on 14 April the paper splashed on actor Michael Greco's claims about the BBC soap *EastEnders*. 'Despite the large following of *EastEnders*,' Justice Saunders wrote, 'the jury might infer that the return of a missing 13-year-old to her family through the efforts of the *News of the World* despite a large police operation might have taken priority.'

As well as call data showing Brooks was in regular contact with her office, and her deputy Andy Coulson, the jury had evidence from Keyworth and Hennessey that Brooks was constantly on the phone, with Hennessey saying she talked of a 'missing Surrey schoolgirl.' So the jury 'could infer that she was told of the search going on in Telford and the reason for it.' The jury could also conclude, because her managing editor, Stuart Kuttner, had spoken to Surrey Police about it the day before she returned from holiday, that she might have been told about that.

Moving to the time of her arrest, nine years later, Justice Saunders also said the jury might decide Brooks had not given 'truthful accounts' in a letter to Surrey Police on 5 July 2011, when she said she'd only been aware of the *News of the World*'s hacking of Milly Dowler when it was reported by the *Guardian*. 'Prior to that date she had been requesting that her 2002 diaries were found and also emailing her previous husband Ross Kemp wanting a discussion about phone hacking,' the judge argued. 'The jury could infer that those enquiries related to Milly Dowler,' and therefore she knew about the hacking in 2002.

Justice Saunders then went on to look at the other twelve occasions where there was evidence from Mulcaire's notes that he was hacking during Rebekah Brooks' editorship. The defence had already admitted the hacking of Andy Gilchrist – 'a person who was of great interest to the editor of the *News of the World* which was running a strong and personal campaign against the leader of the fire brigade union's strike action.' Beyond that, there was the story about Sir Paul McCartney and the ring in the *News of the World* on 2 June 2002 which, according to Eimear Cook, Brooks had implied came from a phone hack. 'Her [Cook's] credibility has undoubtedly been dented as part of her account has been proved to be inaccurate,' Justice Saunders said, 'but Mr Laidlaw accepts that it does constitute some evidence.' Though there was already Annette Witheridge's evidence that the Feud of the Rings story came from a tip-off. 'The fact of a human source does not exclude the possibility that there was also a phone hack.' If the evidence against Brooks had relied solely on Cook, the submission of 'no case to answer' might have succeeded, Justice Saunders said. But it didn't rely solely on that.

◆ ◆ ◆

For Cheryl Carter, Trevor Burke QC simply argued that she never archived her boss's notebooks, and by removing them of her own accord wasn't conspiring with Brooks. Though Carter did travel to Oxfordshire the day after she retrieved the seven boxes from archives, it was to see Brooks' mother. Though they were in the same vicinity of Jubilee Barn, she never met her boss.

Justice Saunders disagreed: 'The jury might conclude that it was strange that she volunteered to Nick Mays that she had applied a misleading description to items she was archiving and strange that she said in another email to Mays, News International's archivist and a man she scarcely knew, that she had spent the weekend reading her old columns.' The description on the archiving form for the seven boxes was 'All notebooks Rebekah Brooks (nee Wade) 1995 – 2007.' Though Keegan had argued that Brooks didn't use notebooks, 'it will be a matter for the jury to decide which evidence they prefer and what their view is of Deborah Keegan.' That the two PAs worked closely together for Brooks and 'carried out her instructions and took over jobs, mainly personal ones, to ensure that she was free to devote herself to her job' could be counted towards a consideration of conspiracy.

Justice Saunders drew attention to the wider context around Carter's actions. The boxes were removed 'on the day after it was announced that the *News of the World* was closing and the day after the *Guardian* had leaked the fact that Andrew Coulson was to be arrested.' He added: 'It also may be of significance that it is close to the time when Mrs Brooks was instigating enquiries about where she was at the time the Milly Dowler story was published.' The jury were entitled to infer Brooks was the beneficiary of hiding property that the police might like to see: 'The jury could properly infer that not only were the boxes removed for Rebekah Brooks' benefit but she must have known about it.'

Ruling that Carter still had a case to answer on Count 6, Justice Saunders said the jury could conclude: 'Either Cheryl Carter was acting out of a sense of loyalty and altruism that she got the seven boxes out of the way without any knowledge on the part of Mrs Brooks, or she was acting jointly with Rebekah Brooks.'

◆ ◆ ◆

The submission of no case to answer for Charlie Brooks and Mark Hanna was simpler still. As Neil Saunders argued, the only item Charlie Brooks was trying to conceal was his soft porn collection, because he was concerned the police might leak its existence to the press. On Hanna's behalf, William Clegg QC conceded that the head of News International security took Charlie's bags away and hid them – but there was no intention of removing anything that the police could be interested in, because it was personal, embarrassing property belonging to Charlie. Since he wasn't trying to hide anything germane to the police investigation, there could be no conspiracy to pervert the course of justice.

Again, Justice Saunders dismissed the idea these arguments were absolute and that no other interpretation was possible. Since Brooks was travelling to a pre-arranged interview with police at Lewisham police station on 17 July 2011, the jury could infer her husband suspected she might be arrested and their properties searched. That was confirmed by the prior presence of solicitors at both Thames Quay and at Jubilee Barn in Oxfordshire that day. The judge pointed out that the jury could properly infer from the items recovered from behind the wheelie bins at Thames Quay that 'someone brought items from Jubilee Barn to London on that day.' The fact that Charlie Brooks removed a computer and a Jiffy bag from his London flat, which was collected by Hanna, could also be read by the jury as an attempt to hide material from the police.

The return of two bin bags to Thames Quay later that evening was also something for the jury to consider. Hanna had texted a second security operative 'have a plan' and a guard, Daryl Jorsling, had returned later that evening with property sealed up in bin bags, put them behind the wheelie bins and delivered a pizza to Charlie's friend, Chris Palmer. The judge said: 'The jury could infer that the reason for the purchase of the pizza was to provide a justification for entry to the flats and provide cover for the real purpose which was to take the bin bags there.'

Justice Saunders then turned to Clegg's contention that there was an 'innocent explanation' for all this. So why, when arrested the following year, did Charlie make a 'no comment' interview to the police? 'The jury would be entitled to infer,' wrote Justice Saunders 'that he realized that any explanation he could give would not stand up to scrutiny so he didn't want to give it.' He continued: 'Mr Brooks is an intelligent man. He must have realised that what he had done was incredibly stupid and, as a result of his stupidity, not only he but his wife was facing a charge of conspiracy to pervert the course of justice. If there was an innocent explanation, why not give it in a prepared statement, if he didn't want to answer questions?'

More graphically, Justice Saunders also drew attention to a key moment in the CCTV evidence: shots of Brooks in the underground car park, the day after her arrest, looking on when Charlie realised the bags stored behind the wheelie bins were missing.

'When they got out of the car, Charlie Brooks and the chauffeur went over to the bins for the purpose of recovering the bin bags,' he wrote, recapturing the scene caught on the underground car park's cameras. 'She waited until they returned empty handed.... The jury could infer that Charlie Brooks would not have gone over to retrieve the bin bags while she was there unless Rebekah Brooks knew what was going on.' Brooks also refused to answer questions when arrested in 2012 over the allegations of perverting the course of justice. 'Why shouldn't she tell the police she knew nothing about it or give an innocent reason why property was moved from Oxfordshire if there was one?' he asked. 'The jury would be entitled to infer that whatever the reason for the movement of material on this day Rebekah Brooks knew about it. Accordingly she has a case to answer on Count 7.'

◆ ◆ ◆

And so there, with a snapshot of the judge's weighing of the evidence after the Crown rested its case, you have an indication of various routes the trial might have taken had the jury made different inferences. As the defence opened its case, we'll now see what actually happened.

# HOLDING COURT

*Jonathan Laidlaw QC: Mr Edis talks about elephants in the room. Let me identify a second – because it's possible to have two in the same room.*

*Justice Saunders: Only if it's big enough.*

In February 2014, cameramen and photographers massed outside the Old Bailey. Suddenly the annex was busy again, with glamorous TV news anchors and foreign reporters swelling the ranks of bloggers and court reporters. Rebekah Brooks, former head of News International and uncrowned queen of Fleet Street was unequivocally a crowd puller. Along with Milly Dowler, she was the iconic image of the hacking scandal. Little of this had to do with evidence, and much to do with her personality, and the optics of the media she'd done so much to shape. So much hinged on her appearance in the witness box, you can understand why (even after two years waiting) she needed extra preparation.

But before Brooks even entered the witness box, there were two interesting pieces of information that, after weeks of legal wrangling, could finally be entered into evidence. The first was the 'Plan B' email Brooks sent to James Murdoch, which planned to 'slam' the outgoing editor of the *News of the World,* Colin Myler, and a senior News Corp executive, for the failures of governance and cover-up at the defunct Sunday tabloid. The judge ruled that it was relevant. (Sources close to News International at the time informed me that this slamming had indeed taken place in some newspapers the day after the email was sent.)

A second email was more explosive. This was the now famous email from Brooks to James Murdoch relaying an hour-long conversation she had had with Tony Blair after the announcement of the closure of the *News of the World*. According to her account, the Labour politician had suggested she set up a 'Hutton-style' report, chaired by a major figure like Lord Macdonald, the former Director of Public Prosecutions, which would clear her. Blair also offered to act as an unofficial adviser to James and Rupert Murdoch.

Initially Laidlaw had objected to any of the email being adduced, because of 'the unfair impact' it would have, though he conceded that James Murdoch's response to Brooks – 'What are you doing on email?' – was relevant and admissible. For Edis and the prosecution, the document was relevant because it showed Brooks' state of mind as she tried to manage the unfolding crisis. Laidlaw protested that any mention of Tony Blair would cause enormous media comment and adverse publicity that 'will divert the jury from the issues that they have to consider and may well be prejudicial to her case.'

Justice Saunders ruled some of the email should be released, but left it up to Laidlaw and Edis to decide which parts. To everyone's surprise, Brooks' defence team suddenly ditched all their objections, and the day before she was due to arrive in the witness box, said the whole email should be released – creating exactly the kind of publicity predicted. The next morning, after Blair's office released a statement saying he was just trying to help a friend, Laidlaw was back on his feet complaining about prejudicial comment from a senior politician. Justice Saunders said Blair's office should be contacted immediately to prevent any more comments on an ongoing trial. There was a pause. With perfect comic timing, Brooks piped up from the dock: 'I have his number.'

So the Brooks defence team were ultimately responsible for the release of the whole Blair email. But why? Perhaps they tired of the legal argument, or decided the publicity could be better for their client. However, it should also be remembered that, having previously been a good friend of Rupert Murdoch's, and a godfather to one of his daughters, the former Labour Prime Minister had reportedly spectacularly fallen out with the media mogul because of his friendship with his wife, Wendi Deng. In the months leading up to Brooks' evidence, various emails suggesting Deng was infatuated with Blair were leaked from Deng's old News Corp email account. There's little chance Laidlaw would have any professional interest in conducting a media vendetta against Blair, but ultimately he was under instruction from his client.

◆ ◆ ◆

As she entered the witness box on 20 February, Brooks had the best overture she could hope for. Justice Saunders asked the jury to appoint a pro-tem foreman so they could dismiss the Count 4 charge of conspiracy to commit misconduct in public office. As new evidence emerged that the photo of Prince William in his bikini might have been taken lawfully, the prosecution wanted to change the charge to include only Brooks, a *Sun* journalist, and a member of the services who provided the photo to the paper. But Justice Saunders wouldn't allow the removal of a fourth person, the alleged taker of the photograph. Edis was all set to appeal this decision on the basis there was misconduct of office between the *Sun* and the seller of the photograph, regardless of where the photo came from, because the member of the services had a duty of care towards the prince. The problem, however, was the length of time it would take to lodge an appeal against Justice Saunders' ruling.

As the judge explained: 'It is of course a matter for the prosecution whether they seek to appeal my ruling on Count 4. I am extremely concerned as to the effect that it would have on the course of the trial if I were to expedite the hearing in the Court of Appeal. Assuming that the appeal were to be heard in a week, sending the jury away for another week would undoubtedly be unsettling for them. We have told them they will retire in the middle of May and we do have a duty to try and ensure that that happens.'

Again, the complexity and length of the trial was benefitting the defence. In this instance, Edis dropped his suggestion of an appeal.

As I tweeted the dismissal of Count 4, I noticed unusual activity again in my Twitter feed. Louise Mensch, the former Conservative MP, was clearly watching closely, and retweeting my reports about the dismissed charge avidly within seconds of me reporting them. I can't say she was forewarned, but only legal advisers or friends of Brooks would have known what was coming. I'd become used to sections of the media using my coverage when it suited, but disparaging me when it didn't. But on this occasion Mensch went a bit further, and began to suggest the whole prosecution was as flimsy as Count 4. Contempt works both ways – you can't make comments about the prosecution any more than you can about a defendant or a witness. Unless you're reporting something a barrister has said in court, proclaiming a prosecution is a waste of time is also prejudicial. I tried to warn Mensch gently with the standard Twitter hashtag for legal issues #carefulnow. She replied instantly 'No, you be careful!' My mistake. I should have remembered my motto. Don't interact too much on Twitter during the trial.

◆ ◆ ◆

The notion of a trial as a contest of narratives was confirmed as soon as Laidlaw opened his defence case for Brooks. In place of the often chaotic prosecution bundles, he gave the jury stacks of beautifully presented laminated files. Handing them out, Laidlaw apologised for the chaos of Edis' case. 'As the order was lost, as we jumped around from topic to topic, it must have been difficult,' he said, waving at prosecution files and timelines: 'They aren't of much great help at all…. Indeed they're in something of a mess.' Much of the mess was of course down to the tactics of the six-privately funded defence teams. But as Nick Davies later pointed out in a piece for the *Guardian*, the Crown were hampered by a lack of resources for photocopying and arranging bundles. (When, in the teeth of defence objections, Edis received approval for jurors to have an electronic version of the evidence to look at in retirement, funds were so short he offered to pay for it himself.)

In contrast, Laidlaw had prepared what Davies called 'a Rolls-Royce' defence. Given the outcome, Brooks' three week appearance at the hacking trial will probably be studied by lawyers and advisers for years to come as an epic narrative. At the time, to many in the annex, the point of this great narrative seemed pretty obvious, often skirting over key elements, and with an emotive overtone which verged on the manipulative. (One former Murdoch employee quipped it was about as unscripted as Jeremy Clarkson's *Top Gear*). The jury might have seen it differently. A friend of mine, who became my regular spy in the public gallery around this time, began to see the chemistry between several of the jurors and Brooks. She smiled at several of the female jurors on the front row and they smiled back.

Indeed, except for a few odd days when she looked worn out or stressed, Brooks was nearly always engaged with everyone: judge, jury, lawyers, and journalists. She made jokes, she shed tears, she looked harassed at times, but she never lost attention. (An eight-month trial preceded by two years of preparation is a kind of prison sentence in itself). Brooks has wealth and powerful friends, but in Court 12 she was in the dock alone. It's a lonely place, where you cannot seek legal advice, hide from the cameras or rely on PR advisers. Brooks' strengths and weaknesses were on display in the three weeks she gave evidence. If it was a carefully scripted performance (as Andrew Edis QC later implied) it was the performance of her life.

During his two-week examination of Brooks, Laidlaw made constant reference to the former chief executive of News International as a likeable if flawed human being: young female features writer in the macho world of Fleet Street; then a campaigning editor who took on the establishment of the police and military; above all, a daughter; and now, a mother. Whether any of these emphases was influenced by the fact the jury was composed of nine women and three men, we may never know. Given the millions of pounds spent of her defence and PR advisers (Bell Pottinger were reportedly paid £1 million for the first year alone) it seems likely that her team would have considered the makeup and apparent characters of the jurors.

Though Laidlaw was the narrator, the star of the show was indubitably Brooks. Laidlaw's legal narrative was as insistent, sometimes incessant as a 19th century moralist. But it merely provided a backdrop against which his colourful and empathetic client would stand out. For it was Brooks – her character, humour, likeability, foibles, anti-establishment campaigning – that was the central theme. Her defence was essentially the story of how she battled against misogyny, corrupt patriarchal institutions like the prison, army and Parliament, was ultimately hounded by baying mobs and paparazzi, and persecuted by the police. As a work of fiction, it would be like *Vanity Fair*, rewritten to make Becky Sharpe an innocent victim.

Rooted in personal biography, Brooks' defence had to begin at the beginning, and so the first days were like an episode of *This is Your Life*. Brooks explained how she was born in 1968, the only child of a father who was 'basically a gardener,' her mother a PA in an engineering firm. Her grandmother wrote poetry for a local newspaper, giving her granddaughter the idea of becoming a journalist. Her parents divorced when she was in her twenties. Then she started working, part time, at Eddie Shah's *Warrington Post*. When the *Post* closed she followed other journalists who went to work at News International, and after a three-month probationary period, got a staff job at the *News of the World* in 1989.

Asked by Laidlaw how common it was to be a woman in Fleet Street, Brooks explained that the *News of the World* was unusual because it had a female editor, Wendy Henry. Brooks worked for the magazine department, referred to as a 'Pink Parlour' by the male news hacks because of its focus on human interest and celebrity. She became a features writer and then an executive. One day she found the news desk had compiled a list of her stories headed Twat 1, Twat 2, Twat 3. 'I was unusually young, and a woman,' Brooks said. 'There was a bit of old school misogyny added in to competition.' In 1995, she was promoted to deputy editor – at the age of 27. 'Because of my age and lack of experience,' she told the jury 'I was given the job of acting deputy editor.' Her skill was in 'buy ups' of celebrity stories. Brooks said: 'The *News of the World* had a very strong relationship with Max Clifford. I dealt with him a lot.' Her 'buy-ups' included Paul and Cheryl Gascoigne on domestic violence, and Divine Brown, the prostitute who had an encounter with Hugh Grant in Los Angeles. Though interested in celebrity, Brooks was also interested in 'campaigning journalism.'

As an example of her early campaigning style, jurors were shown a feature by her about the release on licence of prisoners serving life sentences. As the jury read the article, Brooks said: 'The prison service felt it was right for the rehabilitation of people [imprisoned] for murder to go out into the community and work. Some members of the public didn't think that was right. I was trying to use the *News of the World* for a debate.' Justice Saunders, looking a little sceptical, pointed out the headline was: *Killer's Day Out*. 'Doesn't look like much of a debate,' he observed wryly. Quick-wittedly, Brooks replied: 'It provokes a debate.'

In 1998, Brooks was promoted to deputy editor of the *Sun*, because management wanted to make the paper less 'blokey.' By then, she had helped found 'Women in Journalism' (dubbed by some colleagues the 'Whingers'). 'It was just the redtops that had female editors,' she told the court: 'The broadsheets hadn't come even close.' During her time at the *Sun*, she worked alongside Andy Coulson, the showbiz editor, and in the frenzy of the dotcom boom they set up an online celebrity site for News International, Exclusive.com – and their near decade-long on-off affair began. After they presented their news site to Murdoch and senior management, Brooks was told there was a 'change of plan' and in 2000 she was made editor of the *News of the World*. As the youngest ever editor of the Sunday tabloid, Brooks was in charge of the hardened journalists like Greg Miskiw who had dissed her past work on features as 'fluffy.' She immediately brought Miskiw back from New York where he had opened an office, and made him head of a short-lived Investigations Unit. It was then that Miskiw drew up the 'research' contract for Glenn Mulcaire.

Throughout her editorship of the *News of the World*, Brooks claimed she had no idea about phone hacking. The Investigations Unit, she said, was expected to use legal subterfuge – with an especial reliance on Mazher Mahmood, the 'Fake Sheikh' who carried out expensive and elaborate stings. She listed some of Mahmood's scoops: a hospital throwing dead babies out with the rubbish, doctors who sold diet pills, and a breach of air force security. She cited a headline claiming the Fake Sheikh had 'collared' 105 crooks.

While editor she continued to oversee 'buy ups.' One article shown to the jury was about Siamese Twins: 'I remember it being Max because it was always expensive,' Brooks told the court. '£40,000 or £60,000 for a one-off payment… I often dealt with Max Clifford myself, so I might have negotiated directly with him.' To avoid the £50,000 limit an editor could authorise, Brooks said she might change the figures, so that £40,000 went to the parents and '£10k to Max.'

Brooks had given desk heads (news editor, features editor etc.) authority to run their own budgets 'like a small business,' with bonuses if they filled their pages and kept within their spending limits. Greg Miskiw's re-combined News and Investigations department had £25,000 per week for outside contributors and expenses, with authorisation to spend up to £5,000 on individual contributors without prior approval. Mulcaire was paid in weekly amounts which kept him under these limits.

(Later, in a memorable exchange with Edis, who said it was 'perfectly clear that the books were cooked to prevent anybody investigating or finding out what Mr Mulcaire was doing,' Brooks replied: 'I didn't cook any books.' Edis retorted; 'But the books were cooked.' Shaking her head, Brooks replied: 'I don't really know what you mean by book cooking.' The massaging of payments to Max Clifford over the Siamese Twins story suggested Edis had missed an open goal.)

Lest the jury become too bored with technicalities, Laidlaw asked Brooks about her affair with Coulson. She said: 'It wasn't until 1998 Andy and I became close,' saying she became 'intimate' with him again in 2003-2005, and again briefly in 2006. Exploring the unsent love letter, Laidlaw established it was written in February 2004, and pointed out that while the prosecutor Edis had drawn only on a brief passage, the jury had it all. Brooks now turned the prosecution case inside out, and transformed the letter into a weapon for the defence. 'I seem to remember sometimes I would write things down to myself,' she said, with insight into the unsent missives of a troubled lover. She laughed: 'In a time of hurt, after a few glasses of wine, you shouldn't get on the computer.' In the morning she thought better of it. 'I've read it a lot, since I knew this was to be used in evidence,' she added, making a reference to a line – 'waiting for six years' – that had not been said in open court before.

The jury were spellbound. Brooks, the prosecution's wicked witch, who had run a multi-million pound business and been friends of prime ministers, was vulnerable. She seemed to be speaking from the heart, but her words also bore the imprint of her years as a features writer. The spell was only broken by Laidlaw's clumsy formulation: 'You were describing a time there was intimacy upon you?'

Brooks, who knew both audience and confession better than any silk, got back to the heart of the matter. 'Any affair by its nature is dysfunctional,' she said. 'It added complexity to our friendship.' Sighs of recognition were almost audible through the speakers. She told the court: 'Everyone now knows my personal life has been a car crash for many years. It's probably easy to blame my work.' Before anyone could also process the fact Brooks was married to Ross Kemp during most of her affair with Coulson, she was ahead of them: 'Ross is a great man, but the two of us weren't meant to be'.

Then she met Charlie Brooks. Brooks smiled: 'I was happy for the first time. We knew quite quickly we wanted to be together.' For years Brooks had tried, but failed to start a family with Kemp, and now she warned Charlie of the situation. She told the jury: 'I told him of failed fertility trials. I told him that if he wanted kids I wasn't the right person. But Charlie said 'let's try anyway'.' (By this point most people in Court 12 probably wanted to have kids with Charlie). The couple tried IVF, then surrogacy was suggested. Brooks mother Deborah Weir, out in Warrington one day, had bumped into a cousin who then offered to be the surrogate. Brooks was with her cousin at a fertility clinic in July 2011 when the Milly Dowler story broke.

Quite what this had to do with the facts of the hacking trial was moot, but here was the erstwhile most powerful woman in British media speaking plainly and openly, without makeup – a modern day everywoman, the girl next door.

The approach was bold, but not without risks. By playing to her character and likeability, Brooks made assertions which, though good for reputation, could be problematic evidentially. Her affair with Coulson was one example. She kept on asserting it was based on closeness and trust. The intimacy was primarily emotional; they would share things. This was less than helpful when it came to the dozens of texts the night before Coulson confronted David Blunkett with his 'affair.' If they were sharing confidences, why not the name of Blunkett's lover published two days later in Brooks' *Sun*? Legally, it might have been better to say their relationship was just sexual.

Likewise, when in the second and third days of Brooks' evidence Laidlaw moved onto the Milly Dowler timeline, Brooks might have been well advised to play down her 'Sarah's Law' campaign in honour of the murdered Sarah Payne, who lived only a couple of streets away from the Dowlers. By stressing her activism over one murdered Surrey schoolgirl, it would be difficult to believe she wasn't all over the details of the Missing Milly story. But Brooks made the same decision as with Coulson's affair. Better to be a good person making a bad decision, that a bad one making a sensible one. Throughout her evidence, this was ultimately Brooks' message: 'I don't pretend to be perfect. I've done things wrong. But I'm a nice person. Forgive me.

That, at least, was the emotional tenor. When she actually discussed the Dowler or Blunkett stories in detail, the rationale was more brutal. Brooks said she wouldn't have sent a team of journalists up to Telford to look for Milly because she already had a 'steer' from the police that Milly's father was (erroneously) a suspect. On the Blunkett story, she said she didn't believe Coulson would have told her anything because she was editor of a rival newspaper and might have stolen the scoop.

Legally, it's better to be taken as a fool than a knave (as Charlie and Cheryl's defences would prove) but Brooks managed to maintain an air of both innocence and irony, and a compelling need to explain her career to the jury and the wider world.

The emphasis was on the personal confession (without any admission of any crimes). Covering the end of her career as a hands-on editor at the *Sun*, Brooks laid out her *mea culpas* in a separate bundle of articles she called her 'dossier of regrets.' She told the court: 'I personally made lots of mistakes during my 10-12 years as editor and deputy editor.' Foremost among these was a *Bonkers Bruno Locked Up* headline. 'A terrible mistake I made.' She also regretted an unpleasant article about Clare Short's attempt to ban the *Sun*'s topless Page Three girl, referring to the former Labour MP's appearance. She told the court: 'I went too far.'

Justice Saunders found this bit of Brooks' defence so unusual that he questioned Laidlaw about it during a break. Brooks' QC explained he'd only added this dossier of regrets under his client's instruction. Justice Saunders told Laidlaw he might explain that to the jury on their return, which he duly did. Once again, reputation had been put ahead of evidence, and given the ultimate result of the trial, rightly so.

◆ ◆ ◆

There was also a legal rationale behind Brooks' limited admissions of failure. Before long she was explaining that on a handful of occasions she had paid public officials – or wished she had. As deputy editor of the *Sun* she had paid a Ministry of Defence employee for a story that Saddam Hussein was trying to import anthrax into the UK. At a high level meeting with intelligence officials, Brooks gave up her source, who was duly arrested and tried under the Official Secrets Act. (It was unstated, but perhaps the lesson here was not to inquire too closely into a reporter's sources) She wished she had paid for the un-redacted data on MPs' expenses, which was eventually bought by the *Daily Telegraph*. To many in the annex, her admission of paying public officials seemed baffling. At least until at prolonged length Brooks went through the 11 emails which showed her approving a total of £38,000 cash to a military source who turned out to be the Ministry of Defence official Bettina Jordan-Barber.

Brooks' main argument over these requests for payment from a veteran *Sun* journalist was that she never 'policed' him because he was respected and trustworthy. If that stretched the credulity, Brooks and Laidlaw had a backup explanation. In a 'hypothetical exercise' on 27 February they went through every one of the

30 stories Brooks authorised, discussing whether Brooks would have published the story anyway had she known Jordan-Barber's identity, because of the 'public interest.' Legally there is no public interest defence for misconduct in a public office. Yet by going through this imaginary editorial process, Brooks was showing that she was a responsible, discerning editor who was determined to expose government cover-ups.

By now, we were into the second week of Brooks' defence. Though she hadn't put a foot wrong she was exhausted. Everyone was exhausted. The morning of her next day in the witness box, Laidlaw explained that he had received a call from Charlie Brooks. Laidlaw told the judge: 'Mrs Brooks is struggling. I was given permission to speak to her. She is exhausted and not sleeping. I have told her how important it is that she be able to focus and respond appropriately.' Ever understanding, Justice Saunders planned to let everyone off early that day. When the jurors came in, he told them how giving testimony was 'quite a tiring process... even more tiring for the witnesses.'

Even when exhausted, Brooks never lost her quick wits. As he closed his session, Laidlaw went through one of her desk diaries and noted: 'Friday 31st. The diary says you were with the 'Queen' in meetings.' He stopped, moved his glasses on his nose, and reconsidered. 'Oh, it says 'query' in meetings.' The court laughed, the laughter of relief mixed with weariness. Laidlaw explained: 'I thought it was the rock band.' Brooks chimed in with her perfect timing again: 'You really do need a break!' To peals of even louder laughter, Laidlaw looked like the straight guy in a double act: 'Oh dear all around,' is all he could say.

◆ ◆ ◆

While the first part of Brooks' story relied, to a certain extent, on her ingénue qualities with older reporters such as Greg Miskiw and Neville Thurlbeck (who had conveniently already pleaded guilty) the last phase, after the original phone hacking arrests in 2006 and then as chief executive from 2009, would be harder to explain. She was the boss.

Brooks had two defences for her failure to unearth the scale of hacking: uncertainty and loyalty. Of the arrests of Goodman and Mulcaire in 2006, she told the court: 'I think I remember hearing 'two people arrested' and thinking, 'that can't be right'.' There was 'uncertainty at the beginning to the veracity of the allegations' about hacking and her boss was away on holiday. She wasn't involved in any post-arrest discussions.

However, she did pass back information to News International in late 2006 after she met Detective Superintendent Keith Surtees at the RAC club, who told Brooks that her that her phone had been hacked. 'I was pretty shocked... certainly surprised. I had a personal PIN code,' she said: 'Your natural reaction would be 'how?' 'why?'.... I'd changed my PIN code years ago. I thought it would be secure.' She had met Surtees to discover the latest about the police inquiry 'from the horse's mouth.' For all the professional Chinese walls between her and the *News of the World* editor, Andy Coulson: 'It was a sister newspaper, they were close colleagues.' She declined to be a prosecution witness against Mulcaire, because it wouldn't have been good for the company.

A year later, Brooks had another meeting at the RAC club, this time with Clive Goodman, who had just come out of prison. Despite assurances to the PCC that anyone using phone hacking should be summarily dismissed, Brooks twice offered Goodman a job at the *Sun*. This wasn't just loyalty to an old colleague. She was reaching out to Goodman at the suggestion of a News International executive because 'the corporate side of the business had received this claim.' In an employment claim, Goodman was claiming unfair dismissal on the grounds that phone hacking had been rife at the *News of the World* – and sanctioned by Coulson. Brooks said she didn't believe the allegations, but she knew they were damaging to News International.

Then Brooks went on to her time as chief executive. She was appointed the same day that news broke of the £1 million pay-out to hacking victim Gordon Taylor. Brooks told the court she knew nothing of the settlement until Nick Davies exposed it in the *Guardian*. But soon she was dealing with a claim from another victim, her old associate Max Clifford. A public settlement would have only encouraged other claimants, Brooks said, so rather than pay Clifford off for phone hacking, she agreed a side deal whereby the publicist would be compensated up to a million pounds for his loss of earnings for the period when he had fallen out with News International. She accepted there was a much bigger threat. Clifford's lawyer was threatening to force Mulcaire to 'name names' in the courts. 'News International was facing an uncertain exposure,' Brooks explained, now shifting into impersonal management speak. 'The liability was huge. The best policy to protect the company was confidential settlements. This is pretty much the legal assessment… that was conveyed to me.'

On 14 January 2011, 11 days before Scotland Yard announced its new inquiry into hacking, Brooks emailed her PAs to set up a meeting with Coulson, still Director of Communications for the Prime Minister: 'Need to see Andy at 7.30am… somewhere discreet.' They met at the Halkin Hotel in Belgravia where she told him 'we found some pretty incriminating evidence.' Coulson resigned from Downing Street a few days later.

While on holiday in April 2011, Brooks heard through a conference call that James Weatherup had been arrested. Asked why News International lawyers cleared Weatherup's desk before the police arrived at Wapping, Brooks had been told the previous arrest of Neville Thurlbeck and search of his desk was 'not legal… not an approved search.' She told the court: 'I was told the police were incredibly angry at NI's actions. So angry they were going to consider their options: I was told they were going to take action…. against [law firm] Burton Copeland, [its partner] Ian Burton, for giving this advice.' Brooks was told she could be arrested soon.

On 23 June 2011, the day Levi Bellfield was convicted and sentenced for the murder of Milly Dowler, Brooks emailed her two PAs: 'I need my 2002/03 diaries.' Asked what prompted this, she told Laidlaw it was probably because Channel 4's *Dispatches* was doing a programme on a private detective who worked for papers including the *News of the World*. Later that night she emailed her ex-husband, Ross Kemp, who was holidaying with her in Dubai when the *News of the World* printed the Missing Milly story. She said this was because (she couldn't remember when), the police had informed her she appeared for a second tasking in Mulcaire's list, which included the numbers of Kemp and his friend AA Gill.

For every difficult question, Brooks had an answer. A message about email deletion that said 'Call Andy' meant the Andy in tech support. Another email to James Murdoch, in which Brooks was supposed to be talking to her husband about 'confiscations' wasn't about financial confiscations due to imminent arrest, but taking her Blackberry away because she was using it too much.

◆ ◆ ◆

After the Milly Dowler story broke on 4 July, 2011, Brooks had been hounded by paparazzi, subject to death threats and vilified by her own staff for closing the *News of the World*, even though she was trying to find them new jobs. As Charlie Brooks made clear in his evidence, she was sleepless with fear. She could be arrested at any moment and her career ended forever with a 'killer photo' of police leading her away.

Laidlaw turned to the messages and texts recovered from Brooks' Blackberry after the police seized it on her arrest. Piers Morgan joshed: 'You're trending worldwide on Twitter. Congrats.' Kath Raymond Hinton, a former adviser to David Blunkett who had married Les Hinton, Brooks' former boss, described a lot of the coverage as 'pretty misogynist, darling.' Brooks replied: 'Feeling slightly like a sexist witch-hunt.' To make sure this wasn't

overplayed, Laidlaw also cited a text from Brooks which said the
Dowler stuff was horrible and the reaction understandable. 'No
hint of self-pity,' the barrister remarked. Tom Newton Dunn,
the *Sun*'s political editor, emailed sarcastically 'incredibly objective reporting by our commercial rivals tonight' about the Milly
Dowler story. Brooks' reply suggested it was all about News Corp's
BSkyB bid.

Then the jury saw the comments of Tony Blair, her old friend.
'Let me know if there's anything I can help you with. Thinking of
you,' the former Prime Minister texted. Brooks' reply confirmed
another email, which talked of a '*Guardian*/BBC/Old Labour hit
job' and blamed friends of Gordon Brown for stoking the story:
'GB pals getting their own back.'

On the weekend of her arrest, Brooks explained she was given a
choice of police stations for her interview. 'You were given a choice?'
interjected Justice Saunders, surprised. She was arrested as soon as
her driver took her down to the underground car park, and spent a
few hours in the cell before she gave her 'no comment' interview. The
whole process lasted twelve and a half hours. When she returned to
Chelsea Harbour, exhausted, Charlie poured her a glass of wine. (In
cross examination Brooks said her husband was drunk – 'two sheets
to the wind.') The next day, Charlie told her 'a very odd story' about
how 'He'd hidden his rather large porn collection.' Brooks said: 'I
was quite exasperated. He'd hidden the bags. And now there was a
chance he would be arrested.' This was the 'final straw' in a rather
'cataclysmic few days' – and she hit the roof.

Not only did Brooks' narrative make sense, it would square
seamlessly with the narratives of the other defendants. There was
nary a contradiction in their versions, which fitted together like a
mortise and tenon joint, supporting each other in a strong bond.

Only at the end of her evidence in chief did Brooks make a slip
of judgement, which probably went unnoticed by the jury, but not
the judge. Talking of Cheryl Carter, and how 'scatty' her PA could
be (which might explain why she suddenly needed to do some filing

of beauty clippings on the day Andy Coulson was arrested and the *News of the World* closed) Brooks told an anecdote. She said: 'I once said to Cheryl I had to go out of the office for an important meeting, and if Mr Murdoch called she was to tell him I went to MI5.' On her return, she discovered that Murdoch had called and left an angry message. She couldn't understand why her boss was so furious, until Carter explained that she'd erroneously told Murdoch Brooks had been at MFI – a discount furniture warehouse. The jury enjoyed hearing this story. Brooks enjoyed telling it. But it was a very old joke. A quick Google search revealed dozens of versions going back years. Given its antecedents, was it credible? Indeed, how credible was Brooks' whole account? She didn't know about hacking while running the *News of the World*. She didn't know about paying public officials while running the *Sun*. When she was chief executive, she didn't know what her personal assistant was doing during the Milly Dowler crisis, or that her head of security and her husband were hiding stuff on her arrest. But it wasn't enough for the jury to believe 'she must have known.' To convict her, they would have to be sure she 'must have known.'

The defence had explained why crimes were hidden from this young, talented newspaper exec who, by her own admission, was promoted very rapidly. She also had a convincing explanation of why, when the *News of the World's* criminality was exposed, she was so shocked that all the mistakes that followed were due to exhaustion and distraction.

It was a masterpiece of narrative. The big question was, could Andrew 'The Cobra' Edis break it down?

◆ ◆ ◆

The short answer is no. During five days of cross examination, stretched over a weekend, Brooks rarely faltered and never cracked. She never lost her composure, and was nowhere near to losing her temper, the fatal moment any adversarial lawyer hopes for, when the mask slips to reveal another persona capable of the crime. Brooks never cracked, despite Edis' unpredictable moves, and differing tones and guises.

Edis opened his attack on her narrative in 2009 and asked Brooks if she was covering up. She denied it. He highlighted the anomaly between her agreeing the Clifford pay off, and earlier evidence that she hadn't believed Goodman's allegation of wider hacking. There was other evidence too. Detective Superintendent Surtees had told her about 100 hacking victims. The judge who sentenced Goodman and Mulcaire said other journalists must have been involved. Brooks offered Goodman a job on release from prison, despite his crimes in being in breach of the PCC code and his News International contract. (At the end of her evidence, Justice Saunders, the only person in the room who could out charm Brooks, casually asked Brooks about the job offer: 'There you are, a campaigning journalist at the *Sun*... you don't like cover-ups, damage limitations do you?' Brooks nodded. The judge asked: 'So why get involved at that stage? Why involve yourself as an editor of another newspaper?' All Brooks could say was: 'I was very loyal to the company.')

Edis pointed out that the phone hacking scandal had been important from the day she became chief executive in September 2009. He said: 'It was a big deal from day one of your new job.' Brooks agreed. He asked: 'What investigations did you carry out when you became CEO of News International into what was still on the *News of the World* servers?' he asked. She had to agree: 'None.'

Edis was on a roll. He said: 'Do you agree you settled with Max Clifford to stop Mulcaire naming names?' Brooks conceded again: 'Yes, in part.' And then to underline the *sub rosa* nature of the deal, the prosecutor pointed out the £1m contract for stories was never written down. 'So this £1 million was a gift,' he asked, 'and it had the desired effect of making sure that Mr Mulcaire didn't name the people who had tasked him.' Brooks nodded: 'Yes.' Edis pressed: 'Why wasn't it written down?' Brooks came up with one of her least convincing answers of the cross-examination: 'Well Max and I had worked together for a long time, he didn't feel it needed to be written down. I had been trustworthy so he didn't need it in writing.'

These were forced admissions. But they all related to Brooks' time as chief executive after the periods of Counts 1 and 5, and before Counts 6 and 7 on perverting the course of justice. (I was told email deletion was dropped as a third perverting the course of justice charge because most companies have a retention and deletion policy). So Brooks was on the back foot about phone hacking post the Goodman/Mulcaire arrest. It only made her an incurious editor, and a lackadaisical chief executive.

The only time where Brooks slipped, and it was a verbal slip, was on the second day of cross examination, when she was pressed about setting up Miskiw's Investigations Unit when she took over the *News of the World*. Adducing new evidence from Mulcaire that he was involved in tracking down alleged paedophiles for her Sarah's Law campaign, Edis directly asked Brooks how far she would go. 'When we did those campaigns we had to be above the law... I mean within the law,' she said. Edis immediately asked whether she took steps to ensure that going through bins, taping people, or voicemail interception, didn't happen. She did not, but it was all in the PCC editor's code, which had a 'public interest' defence for subterfuge. In exceptional circumstances, she might have agreed to intercept phone calls 'in principle.' But that hadn't happened.

Having failed to land a wounding blow, Edis changed to discreetness personified when he got to the 'sensitive matter' of the affair, perhaps wary of alienating the jurors. Describing the letter they had read, but which the public will never see, he said: 'It's your heartfelt anguish, which is absolutely genuine.' Brooks emphasised the emotional violation – just as she had of the dawn raid on her and her husband at Jubilee Barn in 2012: 'Police found this letter on my computer and served it as evidence.' Saying the letter was written in the 'emotion of the moment,' Brooks denied she had been 'sitting there like Miss Havisham waiting for six years.' Focusing on 2002 and the Milly Dowler story, Edis gently asked: 'At that time were you talking to him in that confidential way?' Brooks replied: 'I trusted him as a friend and my deputy editor.' 'Was it more than that?' Edis went on, drawing a parallel with an ordinary deputy who might have committed a crime: 'Was the relationship in April 2002 such that he would trust you with anything?' Brooks paused, and one sensed a fateful decision being made. Should I stick to what's best for me evidentially? Or what's best for my truthfulness and compassion? Brooks took the radical, personal and perhaps ultimately exonerating route. She whispered: 'Yes.'

On the Blunkett meeting with Coulson over allegations of an affair, Brooks turned the emotional entanglement with her successor as editor of *News of the World* to her advantage: 'Our relationship was complicated enough. I do not believe he would have told me in advance about meeting Blunkett.' 'Did he tell you the story was based on phone hacking,' Edis assayed, hardly expecting an answer which would suit him. 'No he did not,' Brooks replied.

And so it went on. Like jujitsu, Brooks converted the negative energy of the question into a more positive, self-affirming answer. Occasionally this backfired. Some of the prosecutor's more palpable hits were achieved through quick wittedness rather than probing questions. In an exchange about the cash payments to Bettina Jordan-Barber, Edis pointed out the accounting for them was ineffective. '[The payments] certainly happened a lot abroad, when *Sun* journalists were covering stories abroad,' Brooks told the court. 'Particularly in very difficult zones, if they were going into Afghanistan, Iraq.' In his most withering voice, Edis pointed out: 'This is Cirencester.' Pushing hard on her authorisation of the reporter's requests for payment to his top military source, Brooks was forced to admit she didn't really make any checks and was just acting as a 'rubber stamp.'

Having tried to break her down, or find a question she could not answer, Edis may have thought by the end of his cross-examination that this was a witness like no other. Going through Brooks' claims she had nothing to do with the missing boxes or Charlie's bags, he told her: 'You were running your world. Not much happened that you did not want to happen when you were at the top of the tree.' Edis ended his cross-examination on 12 March, memorably telling Brooks: 'Your evidence has been a carefully presented and prepared script and bears little relation to the truth of these offences.' She replied softly: 'No, it isn't.'

In his closing speech two months later, Laidlaw would make great play of this remark, suggesting it implied that he had coached his witness. Many have asked me since who prepped Brooks for her three weeks in the witness box. It's easy to credit someone else. She was protected and elevated by older men like Rupert Murdoch. Prime ministers were intoxicated by her charm. She was coached within an inch of her life. Senior lawyers from New York ran her multi-million pound defence. Top PR agencies cultivated her image. All these explanations avoid the obvious. Brooks had the money and power and influence from her own talents. She 'instructed' the eminent QC. And for all that legal and PR knowledge, who could possibly know more about the thoughts of the average man or woman in the street than the editor of Britain's two best-selling newspapers? Why invoke phalanxes of advisers or grey eminences pulling strings behind the scenes, when Brooks herself – over a 20-year career – had touched the pulse of a nation and shown time and again she knew its passions and prejudices?

# ROGUE MALE

*David Spens QC: We will be ready as we are under
considerably less pressure than Mr Langdale.*

*Timothy Langdale QC: Swot!*

Normally the defence cases proceed in the order of the indictment,
meaning Andy Coulson should have been next in the witness box,
but Coulson's QC wanted Clive Goodman to go next.

Goodman was described as a 'rogue reporter' after his conviction and imprisonment for phone hacking in 2007. But in the
preceding year, he had gone 'rogue' against his old employers,
waiving legal privilege on his previous conviction and alleging that
many others, including Coulson, knew about phone hacking at
the paper. In effect, as Timothy Langdale complained, Goodman
had become a 'proxy' witness for the prosecution, and for this
reason (over a few more days of legal argument) he applied to alter
the order of the indictment.

Langdale cited the principle that a defendant should know the
case against them before giving evidence. Goodman's defence statement had already asserted that Coulson knew about his hacking
and newly-released legal papers suggested that Coulson and other
News International executives had organised a cover-up after his
arrest. David Spens, Goodman's silk, applied to keep the order as
it was, so that his client could hear Coulson's allegations against

him and respond. The judge ruled in Coulson's favour, saying: 'It will be easier for the jury to follow Mr Coulson's response to Mr Goodman's case after they have heard what Mr Goodman's case is.' He noted that Goodman was almost as important a witness for the prosecution as Dan Evans.

◆ ◆ ◆

After Brooks, the arrival of Goodman in the witness box on 4 March was a change of tone and of tempo. Goodman had recently had an operation to correct an irregular heartbeat and still had hypertension. Yet he spoke so rapidly – as if years of bottled-up words were coming out – that his lawyer, Spens, had to tell him to slow down.

Spens took Goodman through his career from the Kentish Times newspaper group to Nigel Dempster's gossip diary on the *Daily Mail* in 1985 and eventually to the *News of the World* in 1986. After Princess Diana's death in 1997, Goodman explained, royal reporting became much harder and the press had 'almost instantly' agreed not to pursue William and Harry, her children, until they had completed their full time education. 'It had a very depressive effect on royal reporting,' Goodman told the court. 'All we were left to write about was Camilla and Charles.' The restriction held until Princes Harry and William went to Sandhurst in 2005 and 2006.

Before Goodman could continue his evidence, there was another hiatus – this time nothing to do with legal obstruction. On Friday 5 March everyone was mysteriously sent home for the weekend. As the press returned on the following Monday morning, there was an expectant but rather disturbed air. The jury didn't sit again and the court went into a private session without the press. Tongues wagged about the reason for the delay. Only later that day did it become apparent.

A female juror had witnessed a 'disturbing incident' the previous Friday which caused her to return home for the day. She had failed to come to court that Monday morning. After several inquiries with her doctor, the judge had decided she was 'unfit to continue' for reasons 'I can't explain.'

Having lost one defendant, the trial was down to 11 jurors, a perilous prospect given its expected length.

When Goodman finally returned to the witness box, he gave an insight into life at Andy Coulson's *News of the World*. Though he and Coulson had been fairly close and organised memorial services for their mutual friend Chris Blythe, the arrival of a new deputy editor, Neil Wallis, increased a hyper-competitive 'bullying' and 'toxic' atmosphere on the paper. Goodman, an assistant editor, was consistently demoted from the pecking order at news conferences and ordered to file his material through the news desk.

By the summer of 2005, Coulson was chastising him for being 'way off the pace' and telling him to 'find a means to get into the young royals.' By this time Princes William and Harry were 'coming into their own,' but following them into nightclubs was tricky for a middle-aged reporter whose face was well known. Under intense pressure, Goodman had responded to an idea from Mulcaire to hack the royals' phones. If Goodman provided the names of the targets, Mulcaire would supply PINs and direct dial numbers for £500 per week. 'If a PIN number went down,' Goodman said, Mulcaire could get a new one. But since Goodman no longer had a budget ('I was now effectively a foot soldier') he had to obtain his editor's approval. By this point, Goodman told the court, phone hacking was so rife at the *News of the World* that journalists were openly talking about it at editorial conferences.

Despite the copious evidence about call data, timelines, transcripts, invoices, and recordings, this was only the second time that the jury heard a witness describing hacking at the *News of the World*. (In his sentencing remarks for Dan Evans in July, Justice Saunders explicitly criticised this culture of *omertà*). To hear a second journalist confirm it in the flesh was strangely mesmerising, as if a taboo had been broken.

Yet Goodman would break an even bigger taboo, by discussing the corporate cover-up after his arrest in August 2006. Stuart Kuttner had driven him home from the police station and assured him he would be suspended on full pay and be represented by a company-funded lawyer. Kuttner returned with some cash the next day, but Goodman was still worried about the extent of hacking the police had shown him, and terrified he would be held responsible for it all. A few days later Goodman went to an internet café, logged onto his News International email account and downloaded incriminating messages from Coulson to 'show that Andy knew what was going on.'

Goodman said his News International-funded solicitor, Henri Brandman, raised the idea of him being a 'lone wolf' hacker. Goodman told the court he didn't feel comfortable with this, since his editor had signed off the budget for Mulcaire's royal hacking. Goodman complained: 'Andy had a lot of detail about the case… he could only have got from Henri Brandman.' Using the same terminology, Coulson told him: 'You've got to say you're a lone wolf.' Goodman said that Coulson's remark 'put the fear of god in me.' At one point he had insisted that his lawyer did not share his prosecution papers with News International. Yet emails shown to the jury suggested they were passed to executives, including Coulson. In the witness box, Goodman said he'd always suspected that this was happening but to see it in in emails was 'shocking.'

Goodman said messages came back from senior staff telling him: 'You're not going to be dismissed as long as you don't implicate other people.' A News International lawyer told him 'Andy would only take him back' if he didn't name 'others.' As drafts of Goodman's Proof of Evidence made clear, he eventually withdrew any suggestion other staff knew about his phone hacking. He became the lone wolf.

Preparing for his sentencing hearing, Goodman said he felt more 'threatened' by News International than the prosecution. Advised by his barrister (and later Rebekah Brooks' lawyer) John

Kelsey-Fry QC not to mention the involvement of others in his mitigation, Goodman decided to tell his probation officer, so that word would get back to the judge of the managerial approval for his law-breaking. He didn't even tell his own solicitor Henri Brandman about the meeting with the probation officer, because: 'Anything I told Henri would go back to the *News of the World*.'

As soon as Goodman and Mulcaire were safely in prison in February 2007, News International terminated their contracts. That spring Goodman launched an unfair dismissal case against News International, which had two hearings with the new *News of the World* editor, Colin Myler, and News International's head of human resources, Daniel Cloke. Though News International rejected his claim, Goodman was given a large cash payment.

(Several names have been redacted in this account of the post-arrest story at News International because at the time of writing police inquiries are still ongoing)

◆ ◆ ◆

Langdale's cross-examination of Goodman on 20 March 2014 was going to be crucial if his client, Coulson, expected any relief on the phone hacking charge. As he prepared to take on Goodman, Langdale, whose cross examination of Dan Evans had been described by Justice Saunders as 'very skilful,' looked and sounded confident. Legal argument and court gossip suggested he had something devastating up his sleeve.

In opening his evidence in chief, Goodman had acknowledged two extra hacks of royal aides which did not form part of his admissions in 2006, but said he couldn't remember any extra hacking activity. However call data disclosed by the prosecution to the defence told a different story.

As expected, Langdale crept up on Goodman slowly. He tried to undermine his credibility by showing that he exaggerated in emails. One concluded with the line that *News of the World* staff could end up wearing 'concrete wellies' for contempt of court. Goodman agreed it was over dramatic: 'I think I'm being dramatic for emphasis,' he said. Langdale smiled: 'You were rather inclined to use florid and over dramatic language, weren't you?' Goodman accepted 'reporters do exaggerate,' but the 'concrete wellies' had been a joke. To Langdale's barb that any editor would have to take what Goodman said with a 'large pinch of salt' Goodman came back smartly: 'You'll have to ask the editor.'

It was clear what Langdale was trying to do: sow doubts about the extent of Goodman's reliability. But now he had to turn to motive. And here Goodman's demotion in the *News of the World* pecking order could cut both ways. The former royal editor complained that things got 'very strange' in 2003 after Neil Wallis arrived as Coulson's deputy: 'He didn't like me, he didn't like my stories.' To the suggestion that his nickname at the paper was 'The Eternal Flame' 'because he never went out,' Goodman replied: 'You don't get stories in a small circle like the Royal Family.... by knocking on doors, because there were no doors to knock on.' He was steadily demoted in the conference order and told he wouldn't even be allowed to present his list. Goodman said: 'It was humiliating... and designed to be so.' Langdale pointed out that Goodman had direct access to the editor. 'On some matters,' Goodman acknowledged: 'But you can see from the tone of his emails he wasn't encouraging. One word, or two words, it was pretty dismissive.'

Towards the end of the first day of his cross examination, Langdale started skirting around the danger zone, asking Goodman about his Blackadder gossip columns about Princes William and Harry. Goodman, who had been robust and combative previously, now sounded edgy. Langdale purred with implied menace. As the day's session closed, he let Goodman know that the next day would be much more difficult: a tactic deployed by many interrogators to ensure a sleepless night.

The next morning, 21 March, Goodman was seen in the court canteen preparing for a tough day with two cups of espresso.

Minutes later, he was taken ill with an irregular heartbeat and, on the advice of the Old Bailey matron, taken by ambulance to St Thomas' hospital for a check-up. The court was adjourned to Monday in the hope he would be well. But he wasn't. Goodman was suffering from atrial fibrillation and a tachycardia and though not life threatening, he would need three weeks of a new drug regime and then an angiogram to check his fitness to continue his evidence.

After Ian Edmondson and the juror who were both deemed unfit to continue, Goodman had become the third casualty of the long trial. His absence created an almighty headache. Goodman, though, couldn't be severed as easily as Edmondson because he was mid-way through an important cross-examination. How could Coulson enter the witness box before his lawyer had finished challenging his assertions? If the judge forced him, Coulson, to give evidence, there might be strong grounds for a mistrial or appeal.

As Goodman's absence dragged on for days and then weeks, the whole trial was in danger of collapse. Langdale fought a bitter rearguard action to keep his client out of the witness box: 'We do not consider a follow on fair and would not do it voluntarily,' he protested: 'Your Lordship should rule on it.' He opposed Goodman's QC taking any instruction, but agreed he could be sent transcripts of the trial while he was recuperating. (Goodman later told me he found my tweets 'better than legal reports.') His lawyer, David Spens, argued Coulson could start in his client's absence because of his desire to hear Goodman's allegations had been achieved. Spens said that Langdale 'was simply taking advantage of your Lordship's original ruling.' Edis agreed: 'Mr Coulson can have a fair trial giving his evidence... sooner rather than later.'

But Justice Saunders was reluctant to go back on his original ruling – perhaps because he had ruled that Goodman's evidence should be scrutinised first. Overturning his own logic to hold the trial together might be pragmatic but would be inconsistent. The prosecution's hard fought-for coup in getting Goodman attached to the hacking trial was now becoming a curse. However, the Crown did make an important concession. After discussions with the Crown Prosecution Service, Edis told the court that Goodman would not be pursued for any further admissions of hacking he made in the witness box (though he would still be liable for any perjury). The booby trap that Langdale had so cunningly set, and which might have contributed to Goodman's stress and subsequent heart condition, was now partially defused. The worry was – would Goodman ever return?

# COMMEDIA DELL'ARTE

> **Andrew Edis QC:** *She went on and said*
> *you were scatty and forgetful.*

> **Cheryl Carter:** *I am sometimes. You*
> *saw me fall off the chair yesterday!*

> **Andrew Edis QC:** *You forgot it was there?*

With the main phone hacking element of the trial in abeyance due to Goodman's poor health, Justice Saunders called on the Operation Sacha defendants to fill the gap. Despite some grumbling that they were 'not ready' (which the judge had no truck with: they had had five months to prepare) Cheryl Carter, Charlie Brooks and Mark Hanna stepped forward to present their defences. After an intense few months with Edis, Laidlaw and Langdale, the jury were treated to a change of tone and presentation with three very different barristers; Trevor Burke for Carter, with his affable air and soft tones: Neil Saunders with his booming voice and rugby player frame: and William Clegg, a portly, almost Dickensian figure.

These three defendants had been charged with conspiracy to pervert the course of justice, which carried a maximum sentence of life imprisonment. But their cases appeared to have been composed as some light relief, especially given the 'scattiness' of

Carter and the buffoonery of Charlie Brooks. Combined with Hanna and then Kuttner, all five of the next defendants in the witness box resembled classic archetypes from the 15th Century theatre tradition of Commedia Dell'Arte: Cheryl the loyal servant girl; Charlie the rustic comic; Hanna the noble soldier; Kuttner the forgetful old man. These archetypes might be rooted in reality, but they were amplified in Court 12. That might have been part of the strategy. It's better to be a fool than a knave, and – it should go without saying – a good defence portrays the defendants as likeable, sympathetic people the jury would not want to jail.

As Burke pointed out, Carter, Rebekah Brooks' long-serving PA, was so petite her feet did not touch the ground when she sat in the witness box. Every time I bumped into Carter, she was smiley and chatty. One day I was waiting outside Starbucks for a shower to pass when I heard her voice behind me. She had a spare umbrella in her bag and said: 'Peter – don't get wet. Have this!' Towards the end of the trial, she came into the court sobbing after her father died. As the trial finally headed towards the judge's summing up, Carter felt so claustrophobic she was allowed to sit on a chair outside the dock.

Carter's character didn't obviate the charge against her that she conspired with Brooks to remove and destroy seven boxes of Brooks' notebooks when the phone hacking scandal was peaking in July 2011. Nevertheless, as the months passed and the evidence was beaten so thin by examination and re-examination, sympathy for many of the defendants rose. Mark Bryant-Heron described it as 'Long Trial Syndrome' – a kind of reverse Stockholm syndrome, in which the guards fall in love with their captives.

◆ ◆ ◆

Sensing that the jury were probably mystified by the abstruse process in which they had been incarcerated, Burke opened his case for Carter on 25 March with a helpful primer on court procedure to come: the defence cases, closing speeches and then the judge's 'route to verdict' and summing up. He outlined the nature of the charge faced by his client and her former boss, Rebekah Brooks. Since it was an alleged conspiracy, Burke told the jury: 'You cannot convict one of them and not the other. Carter and Brooks stand or fall together.' It was an interesting emphasis, and again underlined the intertwining of the private defences. Like climbers roped together, in court alleged conspirators can help each other up or drag each other down.

So Burke was making a joint defence here. What benefitted his client was advantageous for Brooks and *vice versa*. Carter's solicitor was none other than Henri Brandman, whom some of the defence barristers felt had been unfairly targeted by Goodman. Langdale would describe Goodman's testimony as a 'hit list' of vendettas. Yet at crucial moments, the carpentry joints locked. Cross-examined over an email during the Milly Dowler story, Carter told Edis how she had to book a helicopter to take Brooks back home to Oxfordshire. Lest the jury think Brooks was part of a privileged jet-set, in re-examination Burke made a point of establishing the helicopter was booked for James Murdoch and Brooks was merely 'piggy backing' off it. Fall together, stand together.

What was in no doubt was the longevity of the Brooks-Carter relationship, which had survived multiple office moves from the *Sun*, to the *News of the World*, back to the *Sun* as editor and then to the 'deepcarpetland' of the executive floor, where Carter said she wasn't so happy – and contemplated emigrating to Australia. After her resignation as chief executive in 2011, Brooks had paid for Carter and her family to fly to Australia where, thanks to the intervention of James Murdoch, Carter had an interview at a News Corp newspaper in Perth. She got the job. But her new life was put on hold when Scotland Yard discovered the notebooks were missing. Unlike most of her co-defendants, Carter answered police questions in interview, though she made a number of errors, including claiming that when she removed the boxes on 8 July 2011 her boss was at a personal training 'Boot Camp.'

Carter said the boxes had been filled with her own notes and clippings from her beauty column in the *Sun*. She had archived them in 2009 when clearing out Brooks' *Sun* office of 'old shit,' filing them under the name of her boss, because she didn't think she would be allowed to archive her own material. Carter claimed she only withdrew the boxes in July 2011 because the archivist, Nick Mays, had been chasing her up about Brooks' memorabilia stored elsewhere. The removal of the boxes wasn't urgent, and Carter didn't ask for the express delivery that took place. After getting the clippings of her *Sun* beauty column home, she put them in recycling bins and returned the few items that belonged to Brooks – a couple of Filofaxes and a desk diary. The following year, Kingsley Napley, Brooks' lawyers, delivered seven boxes of her belongings to Operation Weeting, and not long afterwards, Carter went with a solicitor to Putney police station to identity objects she might have returned. Another Rolls-Royce defence: all the gears meshed, everything cohered.

However, under cross-examination by the Crown, Carter's story began to shift a little. In one of the more visually dramatic moments of the trial, Edis took some of the cuttings books Carter had mocked up for evidence and tested her assertion that 30 of them would fill seven boxes. As he showed with a typical archive box, they would fit into four boxes. Edis mocked: 'Did you file three empty boxes?' 'No, I did not,' Carter said. The prosecutor sounded even more incredulous that the boxes had been removed on the day the closure of *News of the World* was announced. He asked Carter: 'Your first thought was to attend to a bit of filing?'

Carter's son Nick was working at the advertising section of News International and drove the boxes home. Burke had berated the prosecution for suggesting that Carter would ever involve her son in a criminal conspiracy to pervert the course of justice, but Edis pointed out that he wouldn't have been – because he didn't know what was in them.

Edis seized on other errors in Carter's original police statement, which stated she had reclaimed three pictures from storage for

Brooks. 'I got that wrong too,' Carter apologised. 'I was trying my very best.' Edis wasn't having it: 'Those boxes contained what it said on the tin, 'Rebekah's notebooks',' he continued. But Carter replied plaintively: 'Mr Edis, it's not an invention. I've tried my hardest to help the police.'

The anomalies began to grow as Edis probed further. Asked why the files from the chief executive's office were delivered to the garage of Carter's parents-in-law, Carter said it was because her garage was full of her husband's stuff, and Brooks' belongings would be safer at the parents-in-law, because they never went out. But she re really strained credulity when she maintained that the first she knew of the police inquiry into phone hacking, Operation Weeting, was when the Milly Dowler story broke on 4 July 2011. Edis seized on this. He pointed out that James Weatherup and Neville Thurlbeck had been arrested in April. Brooks' evidence was that she expected she could be arrested as early as them. Carter accepted her job was to assist her boss, but still said, 'I knew nothing…at all' until 4 July 2011. Carter conceded she knew about the company's Management and Standards Committee, set up to deal with phone hacking complaints and that requests for Brooks' bank statements meant 'something was going on.' My spy in the public gallery told me her counsel, Burke, looked grim at the end of the first day of cross-examination.

The next morning, Carter, who had been sparky, polite and smiling through much of her time in the witness box, was less confident. Edis kept pushing on this weak spot about her knowledge of phone hacking. He showed the jury emails Carter had received from News International's general manager, Will Lewis, in May 2011 about a 'mission critical' letter to Deputy Assistant Commissioner Sue Akers at Operation Weeting, mentioning the Commons media committee investigation. Carter answered that she would not have read the content, just printed it out and got Brooks to sign it. Edis pointed out, exasperated, that the last line read: 'Deliver to a police station.' 'You told us yesterday that you didn't know about the police investigation,' he continued, 'but that was simply untrue.' Carter tried to explain what she meant. 'That's when it first hit me on 4 July,' she said, 'how sad it was.' Looking at the evidence to the contrary Carter explained apologetically: 'Of course I can see I would have booked in meetings with lawyers and police but had no idea about it all.' Edis dismissed this as: 'Simply a lie.'

Finally Edis turned to a new document, a synopsis of a book Brooks was preparing when she was still Rebekah Wade, which spoke of her 'very close and trusting relationship' with her PA, and how 'whether I am having lunch with MI5 or the Beckhams' everybody loved and trusted Carter. This gave Edis the chance to dissect the MI5/MFI gag. 'I've lived with that story for years,' laughed Carter. In his most withering schoolmaster voice, Edis retorted: 'It's a very old joke.' But it was Justice Saunders who really deflated it. He pointed out that, in Carter's account her 'state of mind' was this: she told Rupert Murdoch that Brooks was at the furniture store, even though she knew her boss was at MI5. The smile left Carter's face. It was a funny anecdote, but as evidence it didn't make sense.

◆ ◆ ◆

It's better to be a fool than a knave, but Charlie Brooks' appearances in the witness box must be one of the most bizarre and comic performances in British legal history. Brooks and Carter had humorous anecdotes and well-timed asides, but apart from brief moments of anger or pathos over the dawn raids at his house and the death of his mentor Ian Wooldridge, Brooks was determined to live up to his name as a right Charlie as he explained how he made a fool of himself hiding his porn collection from the police when he was drunk ('two sheets to the wind') and even more so in his character witness statements, one of which spoke of him downing a bottle of *Fairy Liquid* detergent to cure a hangover.

After prolonged discussions of filing cabinets, dusty archives, call data and missing electronic devices, Charlie's account of his early adulthood, failing to get to university, becoming a stable lad and eventually a top trainer, was refreshing. He spoke of his failed business ventures like cryotherapy; a software horseracing game for the *Sun*; how he 'bought this pub' with a character called 'Johnny the Fish.' Charlie said: 'After a year I learned why he was called Johnny the Fish.' The court laughed.

Some of his ideas for novels sounded like a desperate Alan Partridge pitch of formats to a television commissioner: 'A Hooray Henry who had fallen in love with a Russian hooker… who had the temperament of a Roedean girl'; an updated Mrs Beeton-style household management book: 'I thought the perfect wife should know the offside and the LBW rule instead of knowing how to iron sheets and make flower arrangements.' Charlie began: 'The last book idea was a Bill Bryson type idea going round Britain… for horses,' before he was interrupted by the judge.

For all the comedy, this was deadly serious, because it explained the contents of an old laptop recovered by police after a cleaner found them hidden behind the bins at Chelsea Harbour: 'I was a bachelor when I owned this laptop, so there was quite a lot of smut on it.' It still seems unlikely to me that up to six drivers and security operatives would have organised a complex 'dead letter drop' in order to prevent the police finding some legal soft porn. But it was an explanation, and given there was very little if no evidence of anything incriminating being hidden, the absence of evidence remained just that. In the meantime, Charlie could attest to his wife's suffering during the hacking scandal.

Supported by his friend Jeremy Clarkson in the public gallery (who blew kisses to Charlie after the jury had left), his case was quite simple. He didn't deny trying to conceal his property from the police, but was in the final process of writing a novel for Harper Collins, who might drop him if the police seizure of his laptop caused any delay. He also feared what would happen if the police or his wife found out about his porn collection. Though he was 'stupid' and an 'idiot' for hiding his possessions from the police, he didn't think he was withholding any evidence bearing on the police investigation into hacking or corrupt payments. His greatest concern was his wife's reputation.

'I thought about my 'Jackie Smith' moment,' Charlie said, referring to the former Labour Home Secretary whose husband's purchase of some porn movies was exposed in the MPs expenses scandal: 'Ever since Operation Weeting had been in News International,' he told the jury, 'a lot of stuff had been leaked, particularly to the *Guardian*.' The Operation Kilo defence was in full swing again.

Charlie spoke of the extreme levels of 'paranoia' around his wife's movements after the arrest of James Weatherup in April 2011. On returning from their spring break, Charlie claimed his wife thought noise from the bin men was the police mounting a dawn raid. She especially feared the 'killer photo' of her arrest. When the Milly Dowler story broke, the couple were assigned a security detail code-named Blackhawk to deal with the ever-present 'rats' or 'paparazzi' that surrounded the couple's residences. Charlie said he feared the new surveillance team might leak their whereabouts to the press.

And he was at pains to talk of the 'political hit' behind the phone hacking scandal, telling the court 'Tom Watson hates my wife' and 'Chris Bryant had a grudge against the *Sun*.' In Charlie's version of that calamitous summer, the phone hacking allegations 'became pretty much all we talked about.' Despite reassuring Rupert Murdoch in person he would persuade Brooks to stay on in the weeks following the Milly Dowler exposé, he was called by James Murdoch at 6.30pm on 14 July and told she should resign. When Charlie broke the news her response was relief: 'Thank God for that!'

But there were cracks in Charlie's account which on cross examination the following Monday, Andrew Edis began to prise open. The most glaring was Charlie's insistence that he had wanted to explain the mix up with the computers to the police immediately – and yet he gave a no comment interview to the police when he was arrested eight months later.

Edis went line by line through Charlie's timeline of events, but the former horse trainer remained consistent in his account of the various calls and texts about the bag deliveries, pizza, and wine drinking. As the cross-examination looked set to continue unexpectedly for another day, the court broke off. And I had a drink with a contact who really landed me in it.

◆ ◆ ◆

An old friend was visiting from the US, who, I had quite forgotten, had worked briefly at News International's finance department before taking a job in Silicon Valley. We mainly talked about other things, but as I spoke of Charlie Brooks' comic turns in the witness box, this contact told me that because the lines of responsibility were so hazy at News International's subsidiaries, the only way to find out who really reported to whom was to check the budget approvals. And Charlie Brooks had appeared on the payroll as an employee and consultant to his wife. These spreadsheets rapidly disappeared. In parting, he said: 'Use this how you will.'

That night, I struggled with my conscience. I couldn't tweet what I'd been told, because it wasn't part of the trial – and I had no idea whether it was true. But it might be material to the case. I called a lawyer friend to discuss the implications. The next morning as I came into the annex to tweet the last part of Charlie Brooks' cross-examination, two Weeting police officers were waiting for me. My heart skipped several beats.

The detectives were polite but firm. They'd heard that I knew someone who had seen evidence Charlie was on the payroll. Would I reveal my source? I declined. They asked if my source would talk to them and give a statement. When did they want to talk to him? 'Now, before Charlie leaves the witness box.' Gulp.

That morning at the trial was probably my most stressful. While trying to record what was going on in the court, I emailed my contact. Meanwhile in court, Charlie – who had been funny and self-deprecating – showed a sharper edge when he remarked that three bottles of wine was a lot for him, 'unlike some people.' When he said he was talking about Edis, Justice Saunders reprimanded him for the jibe.

The banter had gone from the courtroom. Though I'm sure he wasn't, I wondered if Edis was prolonging Charlie's interrogation waiting for evidence from my source. He was gnawing away at the drinking and porn story, suggesting they were red herrings to conceal a plan to strip the Brooks' residences of incriminating electronic devices and papers. Charlie agreed it was 'one of the most telegraphed arrests in history.'

My source got back to me. He might go on the record, but needed longer to think about it. Such a decision would be life altering, perhaps career destroying. This was one of the most chilling messages I received during the trial. Here was someone in a completely different business, thousands of miles away, who was wary of coming forward as a witness. No wonder only two journalists, Evans and Goodman, had been willing to testify and their decisions were hardly voluntary.

Charlie's cross-examination was finishing now. It was all academic. He remained adamant that this was his 'stuff' and had nothing to do with his wife or the company. Though he did work on several projects for News International and several of the recovered electronic devices had NI stickers on them, he repeated several times: 'It was my property.' As he left the witness box, Charlie joked 'Better get out quick.' Whatever my contact told the police, no evidence that Charlie was a News International employee was adduced at the trial, so we must assume he was not.

♦ ♦ ♦

For a while, the appearance of Mark Hanna, the head of security for News International, was much anticipated. During the pre-trial hearings, his QC, William Clegg, was rumoured to have said that his client felt 'Brooks deserves all she gets.' But Hanna's evidence showed no sign of that sentiment. It was like the man himself: reserved, disciplined, and leaving no hostages to fortune. I'd often find myself walking behind him as he got the tube after court. At first he seemed a bit suspicious, and appeared to be talking on his phone, using the glass as a reflector to check me out (I was getting paranoid by now).

As it was, I was slightly distracted from his evidence by another medical emergency – in the annex. That afternoon James Doleman was uncharacteristically missing. It turned out he had filed his lunchtime report in agony and seen the Old Bailey's matron, who had dispatched him by taxi to St Thomas' hospital. The doctors there discovered he had a perforated appendix and, after getting him to sign a consent form which told him he might need a colostomy bag for life, performed an emergency appendectomy. Without it, he would have died. For the next few days, high on diamorphine, Doleman kept filing his pieces for *The Drum*: bold imaginative and unpublishable commentaries on the loveliness of the nurses and the sunsets over Westminster Bridge. He returned a week later, back to his no-nonsense self.

Back in court, Hanna's evidence was similar to Charlie's. He conceded he did take away some 'stuff' to conceal it from the police, but had not thought it pertained to Rebekah Brooks or the police investigation.

Then there was, though, one moment of drama. Clegg held one of Charlie's two hidden bags still in its evidence wrapper. 'It's not dangerous,' Clegg said jovially. 'No chemicals… the bag is safe.' With the prosecution's permission, the QC removed the brown bag and Hanna confirmed he had seen it on 17 July 2011. Clegg then withdrew the second bag, a black nylon computer bag, from its protective covering and passed it to Hanna. Hanna held it, looked at it, and said he hadn't seen that bag on 17 July 2011: 'It wasn't in the Range Rover.'

In his cross-examination, Edis was furious about Hanna's insistence three years on that he had not seen the black bag. The prosecution's case was that materials pertaining to Brooks had been hidden, and they were nearly all in the black bag. And there was now no way to check Hanna's contention – because any DNA of his found on the bag could be put down to contamination in the witness box.

The rest of Hanna's evidence went smoothly. He explained how he added a Jiffy bag of DVDs and a Sony Vaio laptop that Charlie had hidden behind the bins at Chelsea Harbour later that morning because there was 'smut' on them; though Hanna wasn't sure if he had been told this by Charlie or had just seen them. At News International's headquarters in Wapping he bagged up the items in a double bin bag with the help of another security operative, Marva Ingram, before returning home.

As for the 'Pizzagate' remarks by security staff who dropped the bags back behind the bin at Chelsea Harbour that night, Hanna confessed he didn't know where they got these terms from. Other references to 'a plan' merely referred to how Daryl Jorsling, working for a contractor ICP, was going to get into the underground car park without a key fob (though it turned out he had one). Hanna said he assumed the bags had been returned with the pizza delivery on the Sunday night and thought nothing more about it. He was as surprised as anyone when they were found by a cleaner and handed to the police.

Again, Hanna's account sounded coherent, and none of it crossed the threshold into a deliberate conspiracy to hide relevant evidence from the police. Like Charlie, he admitted hiding stuff, but didn't think it was illegal, and the whole incident had been a 'nuisance' to help out the husband of his former boss, rather than an elaborate conspiracy. A wild porn chase had now become a wild bag chase.

Again the judge was probably the best informed and most alert person in the room. We would soon get an expert witness, Will Smith, an 'excellence analyst' at Pizza Hut, explaining just when and how this pizza was bought and how many seconds it took to cook. But Justice Saunders had a simple question about the edible 'blotting paper' Charlie had asked the security operatives to provide for him and his friend Chris Palmer, after they had drunk six bottles of wine. Did Charlie ask for any specific kind of pizza? 'A Margherita perhaps? Or no almonds?' Everyone was stymied for a moment. Hanna said he did remember thinking it strange that Charlie hadn't specified the pizza he wanted.

◆ ◆ ◆

I couldn't believe it. The trial had by now gone on so long, even my 4G signal was faltering. At the beginning of the trial in October, there had been a building site opposite the main entrance. At that point it was surrounded by hoardings picturing a new steel and glass building. But over the months the central pillars of lifts and services of New Ludgate had risen to seven storeys and now the construction workers were noisily and rapidly filling the remaining floors with girders and reinforced concrete. The building had grown so tall that it was nearly blocking out my mobile signal. I got a new wireless attachment for my iPad, but that wasn't much better. Once again I tried to crowd-source my complaint to my mobile service provider on Twitter. Though they responded quickly, it was obvious they'd need to build a new mast and that would be weeks away.

So I found myself spending less time in the annex, and more time in Court 12, straining my ears to catch the voices. It was harder to hear, but I could see that many lawyers, defendants and police were following my tweets.

April is the cruellest month, and with spring came new problems: James Doleman was not the only one to suffer. Clive Goodman, who had generally been expected to return once new drugs had stabilised his heart condition was suddenly hospitalised with pneumonia. That meant he couldn't be hooked up to an angiogram until his chest infection cleared. That could be weeks away and the trial was already running way over time, and into that period when jurors had holidays booked. We were already down to 11 jurors: losing another would make life precarious and majority verdicts all but impossible. Having run out of Sacha defendants, the only defence case bar Coulson's yet to go was Kuttner, and even he was off ill for a while. If the defence tactic had been to delay and tarry until the trial ran into inevitable problems, then they had calculated well.

Hours of court time were spent assessing Goodman's fitness, both from the advice passed from his doctor and a specialist appointed by the court, Professor Hall, who was called to the witness box to talk about the timescale for new drugs to reach a 'therapeutic concentration.' Three days of monitoring would be needed before he could recommend Goodman return to the witness box. The trial itself could be partly responsible for the two abnormalities detected in Goodman's heart rhythms: 'Tiredness could be an exacerbating factor, as well as the tension and stress of being cross examined.'

The nightmare that Justice Saunders had done so much to avoid – the trial overrunning in a way that would jeopardise the jury – was becoming a reality. 'The acute problems start on 22 June,' the judge told the barristers. Clegg, for Hanna, complained that this shortened time frame could most impact most on his client, since he was the 'last defendant' and the jury needed to have sufficient time to consider his case. 'Most of us have known jurors in retirement for three or four weeks,' Clegg added. 'Absolutely,' Justice Saunders agreed, sounding grim: 'There's no way of predicting this.'

To ensure the show stayed on this rocky road, Jonathan Caplan QC agreed to open his case for Stuart Kuttner on 8 April, but with the warning his client would need many breaks because of his age and infirmity. 'Mr Kuttner does become extremely tired.' And so the veteran managing editor, one of Rupert Murdoch's longest-serving employees, stepped into the witness box.

Aged 73, and with an ascetic, almost professorial demeanour, Kuttner gave the court some sense of the history of the now defunct Sunday tabloid and its prominence in Fleet Street. He had reported on the Profumo affair and some of the top stories of the 60s and

70s, including the Moors Murders and the trial of Jeremy Thorpe. During his three decades at the *News of the World* until his retirement in 2009, he had served more than a dozen editors. He had liaised with the police over the Wapping dispute and become the main leader writer, main contact with the Press Complaints Commission (he helped write the editor's code) and a go-to guy for approaching senior politicians and police officers about stories and campaigns.

Despite having suffered two heart attacks and a brain stem stroke in recent years, Kuttner put up a robust and forceful defence. Time and again he stressed that voicemail hacking or bribing public officials were 'methodologies' that went against everything he stood for as a 'veteran newspaper man.' However, as his counsel Caplan explained more than once, his medical condition had affected his memory, and throughout his four days in the witness box Kuttner repeatedly explained he had 'no recollection' of certain events, at one point saying: 'I have no recollection of having a recollection.' A member of the prosecution team counted that Kuttner could not recollect events on 43 occasions, and 'could not recall' 17 times in a single day, 11 April.

But Kuttner did remember the basic procedures at the *News of the World* well, especially the payments system. He also emphatically denied that he ever signed off any payment to a false identity to protect a confidential source. When presented with the multiple payments to Glenn Mulcaire's company, he said he trusted other news editors who claimed the private investigator was a 'tracing and inquiry agent' who could save the paper money. When it came to many emails from Clive Goodman about police officers who had to be protected because of the illegality of payments, Kuttner talked about Goodman's disaffection with management, a 'bombardment of emails' and the former royal editor's habit of 'embellishment.' Kuttner was being used to undermine Goodman's evidence about phone hacking at the *News of the World*.

Goodman's lawyer, David Spens, emphasised Kuttner's animosity towards his client and detailed his meetings with Henri

Brandman, Coulson and a News International lawyer after Goodman's arrest. An alliance was being formed between the Crown and Goodman's defence. Spens was a useful ally; persistent and precise, he had a clear voice and lucid approach. As he said during one of the legal arguments: 'Small is beautiful and simplicity is what we should be aiming for.'

In the Crown's cross examination, Edis pointed out to the jury that the two neurological reports on Kuttner commissioned by his defence had not been adduced in evidence. Edis also leapt on other random details the 73-year-old did remember. Several times Justice Saunders had to intervene to check the nature of Kuttner's denials of hacking or corrupt payments: was he insisting that something hadn't happened – or was it just that he didn't remember it happening?

At the heart of Kuttner's argument was that because he was overseeing an editorial budget of £30 million, he couldn't investigate the hundreds of payments to contributors that went through the system monthly – and he had no reason to distrust the journalists who signed Mulcaire's contract or approved his payments.

But there were vulnerabilities. Kuttner's notebooks, diligently stored in News International archives, recorded his notes of his meetings with Goodman after his arrest in August 2006. Kuttner explained he was 'putting his arm around him for the company.' But Kuttner's contemporaneous note reiterated Goodman's assertion, made to the jury before he was taken ill, that Mulcaire was getting 'info' from the security services.

His other vulnerability was his involvement in the Missing Milly story. In evidence in chief Kuttner's barrister asked him 'mentally how is your memory?' Kuttner replied: 'It's piecemeal. The most outstanding example of memory loss I believe, was when the police were questioning me about the Milly Dowler affair and I had zero recollection.' Yet Kuttner had sent two emails to Surrey Police over the disappearance, on 12 April 2002 and again the following Saturday. The first, discussing a reward the weekend Andy Coulson was editing the paper, was sent around the same time five reporters were being dispatched to Telford to follow up a lead from a hacked voicemail. Kuttner signed their expenses when they returned.

The second email, written several days after Brooks had returned, referred to a 'hoax' call left on Dowler's voicemail. 'It seems to me,' Kuttner said in reply to Edis: 'I probably would have known where the information came from… that it was obtained from Milly's phone.' He was 'not disputing' that the *News of the World* had listened to Milly's voicemail messages. But he didn't accept he must have known 'someone illegally intercepted' them. When Edis insisted: 'Someone on behalf of *News of the World* must have hacked her phone,' Kuttner protested: 'I don't accept that.' Edis cited the expenses forms for the journalists at Telford. Kuttner said he couldn't remember. In the dock, Coulson looked concerned.

Kuttner's central role in the predominant newspaper of the era was underlined by his character witnesses. Lord George Carey, former Archbishop of Canterbury, explained how Kuttner and his wife had become good friends. The former head of the PCC, and chief executive of Telegraph Media Group, Lord Guy Black, said much the same thing. (At one point Kuttner was talking about payments to police and the proper guidance for journalists and Edis commented: 'Why didn't you get Lord Black in to come and give some tuition?') Sara Payne, the mother who campaigned for a public register of sex offenders, spoke of Kuttner's loyalty and honesty.

Whether co-incidence or out of a sense that the defence's case needed underpinning, the air campaign resumed soon after Kuttner left the witness box. Inspired by Kuttner's testimony that he had told the police immediately about the Dowler voicemail messages, an editorial in the Murdoch-owned *Wall Street Journal* was taken out from behind the paywall. It trumpeted: 'The death sentence meted out to the *News of the World* no longer smacks of justice' and went onto to describe a rather selective series of events. The phone hacking scandal came about because of 'actors

Hugh Grant and Jude Law complaining about their voice-mail messages being lifted.' It added: 'A profitable, 168-year-old tabloid was closed down in atonement by the *Wall Street Journal*'s then parent company,' claiming that was based on a 'false report' in the *Guardian* about the deletion of Milly Dowler's voicemails.

In some media versions of the trial, Nick Davies was in the dock again.

# LAST MAN STANDING

*Andy Coulson: This story was about someone's private life. Given what was going on in my own private life, the irony of it is not lost on me.*

*David Spens QC: Pure hypocrisy, isn't it?*

*Andy Coulson: The irony of it is not lost on me.*

However the *Wall Street Journal* wanted to spin it, Nick Davies wasn't in the witness box. The man who had called him 'traitor' in Glasgow in December 2010 was. Despite the protestations of his barrister about Goodman's continuing absence, the judge ordered Andy Coulson to face the jury in Court 12 before his royal reporter continued his cross-examination. Though he had a lower public profile than his former colleague and lover Rebekah Brooks, Coulson was perhaps the most significant defendant politically, because of his time as David Cameron's chief spokesman in Number 10.

Like Brooks, Coulson's evidence in chief and cross-examination, which began on 14 April 2014, would stretch over three weeks. Their defence strategies were similar. Like Brooks' lawyer before him, Coulson's, Langdale, started with a biographical sketch, then proceeded to go through every bit of the Crown's evidence and give a different account of it: to lay down his own explanation before the prosecution joined its dots. Coulson's testimony was more constrained than Brooks though, because there were many more smoking emails and smouldering events to deal with. Coulson also had to counter the testimonies of Dan Evans and Clive Goodman. That would need a careful balancing act – discrediting their accounts without being mean or overly aggressive.

Though their barristers' approach was similar, the two lead defendants had very different demeanours in court. While Brooks' engagement and humour often dominated the room, Coulson's ascetic approach meant that he was the most studious defendant in the dock. On dull days of legal argument, when his co-accused had gone home, Coulson would be sitting behind the Plexiglas, taking notes, watching the judge, barristers and journalists. You could see how he rose to the top of national newspapers and headed the Government's communications: his attention to detail was unflagging. He never lost his temper. But he looked grim.

In the obligatory opening *curriculum vitae,* Coulson related how he came to be Brooks' deputy in 2000 through his show-business connections. During the early noughties 'showbusiness became a much bigger deal.' 'Friends, relatives, celebrities, their agents… that bit I knew really well,' he said.

On Mulcaire's £105,000 salary during his editorship in 2005, he remarked: 'We paid double that to the astrologer.' Managerial checks on payments had passed him by. 'I was not involved in every payment for every story,' he said: 'You just can't run a newspaper that way.' Instead he had delegated the responsibility. 'Generally speaking I would rely on the judgement of the department head,' unless it was a story with a defamation risk, when 'the lawyers would be involved.' This was a new element beyond Brooks' defence that the desk heads were autonomous: blame the lawyers. This would be central to his explanation of the hacking of David Blunkett.

Defendants sometimes made limited admissions to defuse the charges against them. We'd already seen a classic case when

Charlie Brooks and Mark Hanna admitted hiding stuff from the police, while denying they were conspiring to pervert the course of justice. Now Coulson would try a similar tactic. He would confess to having heard the voicemails that Blunkett left for his lover in the summer of 2004. But while conceding he had 'knowledge' of phone hacking, Coulson denied being in 'agreement' with it. It was an important distinction, because the law of conspiracy requires spoken or tacit agreement, not merely knowledge.

Coulson's lead up to this admission was careful and detailed. He explained he was on holiday in Italy with his family in late July 2004 when he received a call from Neville Thurlbeck, the *News of the World*'s chief reporter. He told the court: 'Neville told me he had a tip David Blunkett was having an affair with Kimberly Fortier. He had heard voicemails.' Coulson was 'shocked,' partly because the information had been acquired through voicemail messages, but also because it was about David Blunkett, who was 'a very senior politician who happened to be a friend of the paper.' Coulson told Court 12: 'I used some colourful language, and asked him: 'What on earth do you think you're doing?' It was a very clear breach of privacy.'

When he returned to the UK, Coulson's mind was on winning a Max Clifford auction for Faria Alam's kiss and tell on the England football manager Sven Goran Eriksson: 'An expensive process which absorbed most of my time that week.' But then 'Neville came to my office to effectively re-pitch the Blunkett story.' Thurlbeck then played him some of the voicemails. 'I remember David Blunkett declaring his love,' Coulson said, but he also heard mention of 'terrorist arrests' and a 'reference to GCHQ' (Britain's signal intelligence headquarters). Thurlbeck also 'passed on other pieces of information' which Coulson 'assumed came from messages.'

'Neville was the chief reporter,' Coulson told the court. 'The more I listened to him the more I thought there was some public interest justification. David Blunkett was distracted by this affair… and sharing sensitive information. He was talking about his movements and security in a way he shouldn't be doing.' Coulson reconsidered the story and 'by the Monday I thought this was an investigation I should take further.' But it needed 'standing up' and he wanted 'another indication of proof.' So Coulson decided to confront the Home Secretary at his constituency home in Sheffield.

Before that fateful meeting, recorded by Blunkett and played to the court, Coulson pushed responsibility upstairs. In conversations with a News International lawyer, Coulson could not remember any 'mention of illegality' over the Blunkett voicemails; the privacy issues over Kimberly Quinn had been more salient. He had also informed a News International executive about the phone hacks. In retrospect 'it was clear the material was a product of an illegal act,' Coulson told the court. But, he added, at the time he didn't know phone hacking was illegal.

The next year, Coulson was involved in another story about a Home Secretary – false allegations that Blunkett's successor, Charles Clarke, was having an affair with his special adviser, Hannah Pawlby. Pawlby was hacked by Mulcaire so extensively that even Coulson's two voicemail messages to her were recorded on microcassettes recovered by the police. On Saturday 18 June 2005, Coulson called Pawlby and said: 'Hello Hannah… It's Andy Coulson here. I've got a story we're running tomorrow… It's quite a serious story.' Coulson told the jury this wasn't 'anything to do with an alleged affair.' Despite the fact that several other *News of the World* journalists, including Thurlbeck, were actively staking out Pawlby's apartment with the private detective Derek Webb, Coulson maintained that he probably wanted to speak to Clarke about a 'bullying story' (In his previous post as Education Secretary, Clarke had collaborated with the tabloid in running an anti-bullying campaign.) Other than that, it might have been for a response to a letter from Great Train Robber Ronald Biggs' solicitor, asking for him to be released from prison.

Coulson's explanation for the infamous 'Do his phone' command, revealed in a surviving internal memo, required the kind of stretch only trained Pilates teachers can do. As Langdale had indicated many times over, Coulson's concern at the time was that there had been a leak to Calum Best about Lorna Hogan's kiss and tell about him in the *News of the World*. Langdale now drew on previously unmentioned evidence that in March 2003, Rav Singh, showbiz correspondent for the paper, was being hacked by Mulcaire. For a moment this looked like a major coup. 'Do his phone' could mean hack Rav Singh's phone. Coulson said he had no knowledge of this, but confirmed that he had asked others to investigate Singh's billing to check whether he was leaking *News of the World* material to Best.

◆ ◆ ◆

Coulson's testimony was interrupted by the Easter break, but things didn't improve for him on his return. He had to wade into the morass of Dan Evans' testimony. Rather than an outright denial of talking about phone hacking during Evans' recruitment, Coulson reverted to the formula that he could not 'remember' it. (Around this time a journalist recorded that Coulson had used the formulation he could not recall matters 'from this distance' 34 times.) An email chain about 'special checks' Dan Evans had made on the Miller/Law/Craig triangle didn't mean anything to him either. 'All reporters think their checks are special,' he told the court. As for the allegations that Evans had played the Miller 'I love you' voicemail to Coulson and other senior *News of the World* staff, Coulson said he was at the Labour Party Conference in Brighton. Langdale showed the jury an email forwarded to his deputy Neil Wallis talking about being at 'Rebekah's table at the Press Ball.'

'At conference these parties are there for journalists and politicians to meet,' Coulson explained: 'It's a time-efficient way to meet lots of politicians and hear what they have to say.' Langdale then showed Coulson's 2005 work diary to the court referring to meetings with Alan Milburn, Charles Clarke, Tessa Jowell, John Reid, Jack Straw and Gordon Brown. Asked to detail which he actually attended,

Coulson admitted to a 'slight complication.' 'The Labour Party conference had also been in Brighton the previous year,' he said, 'so it's difficult to place these meetings in 2004 or 2005.'

Having tried to defuse Dan Evans' allegations, Coulson was now faced with the flanking attack of Goodman. As a royal reporter Goodman hadn't been 'firing on all cylinders,' Coulson told the jury. But he denied demoting his royal editor: 'If I did demean him it wasn't with intent.' 'I'm not a bully,' he protested, though he could be sharp 'if I was having a bad day.' The problem was Goodman. 'The more I worked with Clive,' Coulson said, 'it became a more frustrating process in terms of our professional dealings.' He was a 'tricky character' and 'prone to exaggeration' but, 'to be fair, the newspaper industry does attract that to a degree.'

All this preamble was a way of undermining Goodman's allegation that Coulson knew about and approved of his phone hacking. When it came to discussing Mulcaire's royal hacking in November 2005, the 'Alexander Project,' all Coulson could remember was a 'brief conversation' by the door of his office, and that 'Alexander' had been described to him as a royal source Goodman wanted to put on a retainer. 'I was minded to agree to it,' Coulson told the court: 'It was a trial.' When Goodman wrote about 'Matey's results' Coulson explained: 'Matey was a word Clive would use to describe his source.' Showing Coulson's attention to detail, he referred back to an email years before when Goodman had called another source 'matey.' It was a sharply observed point; perhaps a little too sharp.

After Goodman's arrest in August 2006, Coulson called Rupert Murdoch, who told him: 'The most valuable thing a newspaper has is the trust of its readers.' From then onwards Coulson was 'concerned about the paper and the company, and also – to be honest – concerned about me.' He added: 'But also concerned about Clive.' Legal advice from News International suggested that 'until that point nobody had any idea voicemail interception was illegal.' Though Coulson agreed he might have suggested to Goodman that he had 'gone off the reservation' in discussions after the arrests, he denied he used the phrase 'lone wolf.' 'I was feeling many things,' Coulson added, 'but I was not feeling influential.'

As for the alleged cover-up as Goodman prepared his plea, Coulson could not remember seeing the prosecution papers because 'I think Clive changed his mind.' By now Coulson was thinking on a wider corporate level. 'There were legal issues, but also media considerations,' he explained: 'My job was to ensure that the media coverage was as minimal as possible.'

When, in late November 2006, Coulson emailed his PA Belinda Sharrier to 'discreetly' store his draft emails he was already thinking of resigning. Though a News International lawyer thought Goodman's allegations 'make no sense at all' Coulson knew the 'PR fallout' from the sentencing in January 2007 would be 'pretty awful.' Coulson had handed in his resignation two weeks before sentencing because 'I was ultimately responsible.' On the day Goodman and Mulcaire were jailed, Coulson left the *News of the World* with the traditional ceremony of staff drumming on their desks with rulers: 'I did a short speech to the staff, and I left the building. They banged me out.'

◆ ◆ ◆

Defence cross-examinations of other defendants were usually tame, with the accused supporting each other, but David Spens' questioning of Coulson was perhaps the most devastating of the trial since Laidlaw destroyed Eimear Cook. Like an artillery bombardment before a full frontal assault, it would also pave the way for the prosecution.

Following his principle 'small is beautiful,' Spens began simply by asking Coulson about recruiting Neil Wallis, who was 15 years older than him, as his deputy. 'A great signing for me,' Coulson said. He agreed, however, that Wallis had come from the tabloid ethos of the 80s and 90s which was a 'different place.' 'There was a lot more shouting on the floor of the *Sun* when I was a reporter,' Coulson told the court. 'People were shouted at…. I was certainly shouted at.'

To counter Kuttner and Coulson's criticism of Goodman's performance, Spens produced a 22-page file of all the plaudits Goodman had received for his journalism, to give a more 'balanced picture.' And then he turned to Coulson's admission about knowing about the hacking of David Blunkett. Why hadn't he told the Home Secretary the source of his information for the affair – intercepted voicemails – rather than misleadingly referring to 'sources' plural? 'So David Blunkett, you agree, was a thoroughly decent man?' he asked. Coulson nodded: 'Yes.' Like a master confessor, Spens asked: 'Do you feel any shame about what you did?' to which Coulson replied: 'I regret the decision I made.' Then he paused a beat.

Spens was so open; perhaps this was Coulson's chance to add something? 'Sorry, can I add one other point?' Coulson said. 'This story was about someone's private life. Given what was going on in my own private life, the irony of it is not lost on me.' Spens retort was lethal: 'Pure hypocrisy, isn't it?' Coulson repeated that it was an 'irony.'

Spens alighted on the Alexander project, and emails about 'standing up' the Prince Harry Sandhurst exam story. 'You knew that source couldn't be revealed if it was a hacking source,' Spens said. Coulson denied it. 'But you knew about hacking didn't you?' Spens continued. 'I knew of one incident,' Coulson said. In another email exchange between Coulson and Goodman about Prince Harry, Coulson had asked: 'How do we know Harry true?' Goodman had replied 'same source we have on a retainer,' adding: 'We absolutely know it to be true.' Coulson really couldn't formulate a reply.

The rest of the session was equally bruising. Coulson dismissed Goodman's claim that the hacking details from the Royal Family came from an 'overspill' of information from the security services. If there were any truth in that, Coulson said, he would have told Goodman 'Clive, that's the best story you ever had.' He also denied that Goodman's possible return to the paper was dependent on him pleading guilty. But he did concede he didn't tell the police about the Thurlbeck hacking of Blunkett. 'I wasn't going to volunteer the information,' Coulson said, 'and the impact on me was a factor.'

Coulson explained that he only used the 'rogue reporter' line in the context of Goodman 'going behind my back.' But Spens wasn't dissuaded. The rogue reporter line was 'untrue for two reasons' because Coulson knew about the Thurlbeck hack in particular, and about hacking in general. Coulson denied the second half of the statement.

◆ ◆ ◆

The impression that Spens and Edis were tag teaming their attacks deepened as the prosecutor got to his feet, and immediately tackled the closeness between Coulson and Brooks. Asked about the 2004 love letter on Brooks' computer, Coulson said: 'I don't remember receiving it.' Edis homed in on the new phrase, revealed by Laidlaw's cross examination: 'Mrs Brooks wrote 'I've been waiting six years for you...'?' Coulson went through a roughly similar timescale to that outlined by Brooks: the on and off relationship began in 1998. But Coulson then added a new end-date; the affair only finally came to an end around the time he resigned from the *News of the World* in 2007.

Having roped Brooks into the crumbling case of Coulson, Edis then went to the *News of the World*'s investigation into Milly Dowler. He drew blood with a concession from Coulson: yes he was 'responsible' for moving the Missing Milly story in 2002 which quoted a hacked voicemail. Coulson had downgraded the story for later editions. 'The judgement wasn't just about the content of the story,' Coulson insisted, 'but about the mix of the paper.' (Previously he'd said the news pages of the first edition 'lacked glamour').

Playing to his forte as a great improviser, Edis shifted back to this episode several times. On the second, he got Coulson to concede the front page splash about 'Beppe' leaving *EastEnders* was 'not a particularly mind blowing story' and finding Milly Dowler would have been stronger. Coulson countered this by saying he thought the idea that a 13-year-old was being recruited to work at a factory was 'rubbish.' But Edis turned this denial to his advantage. A team of journalists would never have been sent to Telford on a wild goose chase for an incredible story, unless they had evidence. The article drew on 'accurate quotations' from voicemails. 'I think it's possible that I read it,' Coulson accepted, but he might have only have got to the fourth paragraph. Edis came back with a pretty devastating retort: 'If you can't be bothered to read it, there's not much chance of your readers reading it.'

Riffing his way through dates and emails, Edis segued quickly onto Coulson's arrest in July 2011: why did he give a no comment interview with police? Coulson explained that, even though he'd read about his imminent arrest in the *Guardian* the day before, it was still a 'traumatic event.' He'd not answered questions because there wasn't much disclosure from the police. Edis retorted: 'How much disclosure did you need to tell the truth?'

The only reason Coulson had made the recent admission over the Blunkett hack, Edis argued, was because the evidence was so 'overwhelming… you had to make the admission.' Coulson maintained: 'No, I made the admission honestly.' Edis wondered why he waited three years to come clean. Coulson said 2011 was a 'terrible time' and he was 'profoundly depressed' about the closure of the *News of the World*. Pressed on his contact with Brooks, he accepted it was 'possible' he talked to her around his arrest, but couldn't remember. Edis pointed out that though Stuart Kuttner had a medical condition affecting his memory, adding: 'There's nothing wrong with your memory, is there?'

After a break, Edis was back on the Thurlbeck hacking of Blunkett, and the alleged 'political justification' for revealing the affair. Coulson explained that there was a public interest in the Home Secretary sharing information of a 'sensitive nature' with

Quinn, and the relationship could have been 'distracting him from his job.' Justice Saunders noted that this concern was not voiced in the story that was published. 'Where's the public interest?' he asked. Coulson really didn't have an answer.

Edis went for the jugular over the Blunkett story. Coulson had confronted one of the senior ministers in the land and had told Blunkett he was sure about the affair. In the witness box, Coulson said he wasn't sure until he'd 'stood it up' with Blunkett's special adviser, Huw Evans. 'You said 'I know this is true',' Edis reminded him of the taped meeting: 'But your evidence here is you didn't know that. You were lying.' You could see Coulson wrestling with this. If he denied lying, and admitted he was already sure of the affair, then he'd be moving on from an admission of knowledge of Thurlbeck's hacking to an 'agreement' to use it – the criminal conspiracy. So he went for a half way option: 'I accept that I was being disingenuous,' he said.

But Edis wasn't having these half measures, saying: 'You were lying.' If Coulson agreed he had deceived the Home Secretary, what was to stop him lying to a jury? He had to make a stand. He came up with a half way solution: 'I prefer disingenuous,' he replied. But the judge wasn't going to let him haver over such an important issue either. 'Were you telling a deliberate untruth?' Justice Saunders asked, using slightly less emotive language. Coulson repeated: 'I prefer disingenuous.'

In one of his rare shifts from reason and charm to the full force of the law, Justice Saunders asked again in a voice that brooked no equivocation: 'You may do, but were you telling a deliberate untruth? Yes or No?' There was no ducking this. Making a quick evaluation that damaging his credibility would be better than admitting to a conspiracy, Coulson lowered his head, bit his lip and said: 'Yes.' By forcing Coulson into this admission of lying, and having to do so with a tone of exasperation after evasions, the judge's intervention shifted the mood of the court.

My friend in the public gallery noted this atmospheric change as he attended the next morning. A keen student of the barristers' demeanours, he noticed that Edis would lean back and play with his gown behind his back when he was uncertain, but would lean forward, his hands in front of him, when he felt confident. And that day Edis was always on the front foot, scoring points against Coulson every few minutes. When Ian Edmonson emailed, wanting to get rid of Mulcaire and the cost in 2005, Edis said: 'Somebody overruled him. Who was it?' Coulson tried to use jargon to get out of it – he was 'not party to the decision.' But now it was Edis' turn to use brutally plain English against one of the country's top tabloid editors: 'You must have done, who else?'

As Coulson started stumbling and repeating 'don't remember,' Langdale was looking wary, registering his client's disarray. Up in the public gallery my friend said Coulson's wife could see he was in trouble. Back on the Thurlbeck hack, Coulson was trying to downplay the significance of the story. Edis almost laughed: it was one of the biggest stories of the year. As Thurlbeck was tasked to check out another Home Secretary, Charles Clarke, Edis was almost cruel: 'Didn't you say to yourself 'Here's Neville doing that awful thing again'?'

Saved by the bell. As the jury got up and headed off for lunch, my friend in the gallery said the distress of Coulson's relatives was palpable. The court was suddenly very silent and still. Langdale sat there numb and unmoving, and in the witness box, Coulson sat looking abject and defeated.

After lunch, before the jury returned, Langdale told the court that his client had been unwell today, but still wanted to continue with the cross-examination. Langdale was clearly going to use this last little advantage by telling the jury about his client's condition himself. But Justice Saunders over-ruled him. He wouldn't allow that appeal to emotion. As the jury returned, Edis resumed his onslaught against Coulson…

Only to be slightly interrupted when a phone started ringing from behind the glass-fronted dock. 'I've a horrible feeling…. I think that's the phone in my bag,' Coulson said, recognising the ringtone. As he saw Brooks extract the phone from Coulson's bag,

Justice Saunders joked: 'Just put it on the floor and stamp on it.' He told Coulson: 'It's all right. Mrs Brooks is dealing with it.' With her perfect comic timing, and an ironic reference to the missing devices she claimed she never used, Brooks shouted out: 'Sorry. It's an iPhone. And I don't know how to work them.' Only Brooks could joke at this time. Coulson was beyond help or humour.

Coulson was going down. Everyone could sense it. Edis had left the most incriminating bit of evidence till last: the 'Do his phone' email about Calum Best. When Coulson explained this meant check the billing of his friend Rav Singh, Edis jibed: 'Not particularly friendly is it?' He also had evidence that Mulcaire hacked Singh at this time. Even if Coulson insisted the email was about Singh, it still led back to a potential hack. On re-examination by his counsel, Timothy Langdale, Coulson kept insisting 'Calum a Leak?' referred to a leak *about* him, not *from* him: hence 'Do his phone' meant target whoever was talking to Best. Justice Saunders waved this away as 'not natural English.'

It was nearly over. Edis ended on two points, probably the only two moments of pathos that Coulson had wrung out of the court, about having to resign from the profession he loved in 2007, and then again from Downing Street four years later. The first resignation was 'really quite dishonest,' Edis said, because 'you didn't bother to tell the truth about the Blunkett hack.' As for leaving his job as the Prime Minister's Director of Communications and Strategy, it was self-preservation. The prosecutor said: 'You knew the truth would come out and that's why you resigned from Number 10 just before the police inquiry opened.'

Edis sat down. Unlike after his cross-examination of Brooks, he looked not unhappy with himself.

# ROUTE TO VERDICT

*Mr Justice Saunders: Judges don't expect
compliments. They expect appeals.*

Coulson's cell door was closing. His predicament was obvious and it was worrying other defendants. One of the defence barristers, who'd previously offered a bet that Brooks would get off all the charges, now told me he thought he would have to pay me 20 quid. But Goodman's continuing absence had left Coulson's cell door ajar. Goodman had now been hospitalised for pneumonia, but the infection wasn't responding to antibiotics. He needed to be put on new effective treatment before he could be subject to an invasive angiogram to check if his heart had improved. That wouldn't happen for another 10 days, and by then 'we'll have finished all the evidence,' Justice Saunders told the jury, warning them: 'It could put the trial back a bit, but you're not unused to that.'

For all his good humour the judge was now deeply concerned. The trial was heading into the danger zone of June where the jury had holiday and work commitments. So that no time would be wasted, he asked the prosecution and defence to ready their closing speeches. Meanwhile in a departure from custom, the judge read out and distributed the legal issues facing the jury in considering the six remaining counts. This 'route to verdict' was essentially a flow diagram explaining the logical steps involved in assessing each count and defendant. A model of clarity, it showed the jury the hurdles they would have to clear to reach a guilty verdict.

First Justice Saunders outlined the nature of a conspiracy charge. 'Mere knowledge that others intend to commit an offence is not enough to prove a conspiracy. An agreement to commit an offence must be proved,' he wrote. The number of conspirators didn't matter; all it took was for one defendant to agree to commit a criminal offence with at least one other.

Oddly enough on this, Count 1 – that Brooks, Coulson and Kuttner conspired to unlawfully intercept communications – turned out to be the simplest. Since none of the phone hacking victims had given their consent for their voicemails to be accessed, the criminal act was easy to ascertain. All three defendants had to be considered separately, but Brooks, Coulson and Kuttner had all told the jury that they had not realised that accessing people's voicemails was a criminal offence. 'Ignorance of the law, however understandable and however widespread,' Justice Saunders told the jury, 'is not a defence.' Only the Crown Prosecution Service could consider the public interest when deciding whether to bring charges for hacking.

The simple route for the jury to consider was therefore: 'Are you sure that the defendant whose case you are considering agreed with at least one other person at some time during the period covered by the count to pursue a course of conduct which, if carried out in accordance with their intentions, would involve unlawfully accessing another person's mobile phone's voicemail? If you are sure your verdict is 'guilty.' If you are not sure then your verdict is 'not guilty'.'

The judge skipped over Counts 2 and 3 because of Goodman's illness. Count 4 had been dropped months ago. However, when Justice Saunders reached Count 5, misconduct by a public official, the logic of these multiple conspiracy charges became more problematic.

Since the charge involved a more complex crime, the prosecution had to prove that Bettina Jordan-Barber 'wilfully misconducted herself without reasonable excuse or justification in such a way as to amount to an abuse of the public's trust in the office holder.' Moreover, not only did the jury have to believe Brooks entered into an agreement with the *Sun* journalist to pay a public official, they had to believe that both Brooks and her journalist knew this – and the official herself was acting in such a way as to abuse public trust.

There was a further wrinkle, cleverly introduced by Laidlaw who went through his 'hypothetical, retrospective' public interest exercise with Brooks. Justice Saunders had to explain that although there was no 'public interest defence' for Brooks, there could be one for Jordan-Barber.

The net effect of this was that the jury had to go through four stages, each of which they had to be 'sure of,' before they could return a guilty verdict against Brooks on Count 5. First, the jury had to be sure Brooks knew she was approving payments through one of her journalists to a public official. Second, they had to be sure the information passed on by the public official was 'held in confidence by virtue of her employment.' Thirdly, they had to be sure this public official had no reasonable excuse for selling the information. Fourthly, they had to decide if the selling of information was serious misconduct, and that that was known to Brooks.

As soon as I read this, I thought the defence barrister would win his bet.

The charge against Carter and Brooks about the disappearance of seven archive boxes on the day of Andy Coulson's arrest was the only conspiracy charge faced by two people. Justice Saunders told the jury: 'Either they must both be guilty, or neither of them.'

The notebooks didn't have to contain anything incriminating to be subject to a search, only to have been of assistance to the police investigation. Yet there were still three hoops the jury had to jump through to reach a definitive conclusion of guilty. They'd have to be sure that the two defendants agreed with each other about the removal of the boxes. They would have to be sure what happened to the contents of the boxes had 'a tendency to pervert the course of justice.' And they had to be sure there was an intention by both defendants to pervert the course of justice.

Given the multiple innocent explanations Carter had for removing the boxes, plus the lack of any record of Carter talking to her boss about it, the prosecution had a mountain to climb. The Crown had only one thing in its favour. Count 6 was cross-admissible with Counts 1 and 5: in other words, if the jury thought Brooks was guilty of getting stories unlawfully by plotting to hack phones or pay public officials, then there was a motive for disposing of the boxes.

This element of cross admissibility was a factor in Count 7 too – the charges that Mark Hanna, Charlie Brooks and his wife conspired to hide material from the police. Yet the route to verdict here was so convoluted, with seven different options for Charlie and Hanna, you could see a conviction falling at one of the early fences. The jury had to be sure Charlie moved material prior to and during the police searches in July 2011. He had already admitted that, but the jury then had to be 'sure' this had a tendency to pervert the course of justice. Then they had to be sure Charlie intended to pervert the course of justice. If they had any doubts about any of these questions, the jury would need to find Charlie Brooks not guilty, and would have to find Hanna and Brooks not guilty too.

Only on finding Charlie guilty could the jury then consider Count 7 against Hanna. Did he remove the material? If so, did this have a tendency to pervert the course of justice? And if it did have this tendency, could the jury be sure he intended to pervert the course of justice?

After over six months of evidence, during which I was pretty sure something damn fishy was going on with Charlie's bags and his wife's missing electronic devices, I could easily see why, with all these variables, the verdict would be not guilty.

◆ ◆ ◆

Way back at the beginning of the trial (when was that? was Elvis still alive?) a lawyer had explained to me the aims of the barristers. Nothing really mattered – none of the hyperbole, emotions or shiny bright objects – other than the elements which spoke to the 'facts' of the case, the evidence or state of mind of the players around the allegations. These are the things no judge could ignore in his summing up. And it was all about the summing up.

At this point in the trial, Justice Saunders had circulated draft copies of the routes to verdict and his summing up, and there were hours of legal debate as the defence teams fought with the prosecution over various points. The simile with a script was increasingly apt, and it turned out the judge wrote the final summary – but like a scriptwriter on a Hollywood movie, he was faced with various demands and endless revisions from interested parties. When it arrived in written form, Justice Saunders' final document was 109,121 words.

Looking back on these closing phases of the trial, you could see neither side could claim outright victory. The defence had won many miles of ground since the phoney war of the pre-trial hearings, the opening salvoes of the autumn, and the attrition of winter. But the prosecution had not given up, and in their spring offensive had achieved some big hits and won some spectacular battles. Now all sides had one last push – their closing speeches.

Edis' closing speech (broken into two, as we shall see) was a tribute to his sense of history. Beyond all the details of timelines or budget approvals, he was now looking at the bigger picture. Many, especially among the police, credited Edis, more than Justice Saunders, with keeping the trial going, fighting day and night against overwhelming numbers (while also being willing to concede ground if it prevented the whole case collapsing). Throughout the trial, the chief prosecutor used an ink fountain pen to write his notes in a vellum notebook. As my friend in the gallery observed, he was more akin to scholar than schoolmaster.

Certainly he was one of the few barristers in the court to go beyond effective arguments, debating brilliance or humorous flourishes. The Cobra nickname was well earned, because though he could suddenly strike, his sinuous thinking could sometimes tie him up in knots. During his closing speech I once saw Laidlaw and his junior giggling and almost hugging themselves, as Edis got lost on the permutations of a particularly tangled piece of evidence on cash payments. While I heard some on the defence teams considered him a bit of a bully, I'd say – as a dramatist who has worked with many actors over the years – that he had something precious: a moral authority which, when ignited, few could match.

With his eye to history (or potential corporate charges) Edis drew on this wider moral vision in his closing speech on 7 May. 'This isn't an attack on freedom of the press or any tabloid press,' he said as if reprising the role of Robert Jay at the Leveson Inquiry: 'We accept a free press is an essential part of protection of democracy. But the ultimate protection of society is the rule of law.' He then went on to explain he had mentioned these concepts because 'other people have.' Without naming them, Edis implied the source: 'Who polices the journalists? Not Mrs Brooks it seems.'

Backing off from the philosophical question raised by Lord Justice Leveson, *Quis custodiet ipsos custodes?* (Who watches the watchmen?), Edis then reminded the jury, almost by way of disappointment, that all they had to do was consider the evidence and deal with the specific charges: 'If you're sure – guilty. If not sure – not guilty.' But still the sociological factors behind the *News of the World* fascinated him. Edis spoke of the protagonists – 'young, talented, ambitious, clever, charming people who have been placed in a position of great power' – and attributed the extensive illegal privacy intrusion to 'ambition, lack of experience perhaps,' adding that 'in the excitement of the chase, they thought [breaking the law] didn't matter.' And then asked, more in the manner of a professor or columnist than a prosecutor: 'Is that what happened?'

Edis knew he wasn't just dealing with a formidable and for-midably-funded defence team. He was combating some of the smartest people he'd encountered in the dock. 'You're dealing with an unusual collection of people on trial here at the Old Bailey,' he told the jury. 'Certainly an unusual group of suspected criminals, unusually talented, unusually articulate. These are people who held significant jobs. You don't get those jobs without decisiveness, toughness and ability.'

'We have suggested Mrs Brooks' was a carefully scripted and choreographed performance,' the prosecutor told the jury. 'Few people would have sustained that.' But the praise came attached with a warning. 'It might be harder to see behind the mask,' he added, saying that the defence cases had 'quite an amount of cho-reography.' He told the jurors: 'You have to be careful about clever little remarks about MI5/MFI and jokes about the Milibands... If these people wanted to spin you a line, they are quite capable.'

(At first I misheard 'spin you alive' and tweeted out 'skin you alive': blame Freud, or bad acoustics.)

For the rest of the day, Edis zoomed out to a big picture summary of phone hacking at the *News of the World*. '2005 is a big year,' he said, describing the arrival of Dan Evans and the hacking of royal aides. On 19 February 2005, Kuttner sent a 'very sig-nificant document' about 'cost cutting ideas' to Coulson, which mentioned Mulcaire's company. Another internal email said that payments to 'Greg's investigation man... has to stop.' There was a row going on in *News of the World* about Mulcaire's retainer,' Edis continued: 'Someone wins this argument.' The proposal to dispense with Mulcaire's services 'was over-ruled': only the editor could have made that decision.

Edis said 2006 was also 'a big year for phone hacking,' naming the new victims in the 'high season': Fred Windsor, Tessa Jowell, John Prescott's advisers, Calum Best (''Do his phone' and what that might mean.') Moreover, he added: 'Mr Mulcaire is now hacking the journalists at the *News of the World*,' including Andy Coulson,

Rav Singh and Neil Wallis. Edis told Court 12: 'That tells you what kind of place it was to work in.' After the arrest of Goodman and Mulcaire 'it appears the first instinct of Kuttner and Coulson was to cover up.' 'It all goes wrong in July 2009 when the *Guardian* writes a story,' said Edis, nodding to Nick Davies, 'and that was on any version absolutely true.' When Evans was caught trying to access Kelly Hoppen's voicemail later that year, Edis asked: 'What did you do about Dan Evans, Mrs Brooks?' Evans had been suspended on full pay until the *News of the World* closed in 2011

As for Cheryl Carter's defence, Edis waved it away: 'What was that performance about MI5 really about? It's quite a funny joke.' He paused. 'It always has been… But the story she tells is preposterous. It's inserted to suggest Mrs Carter is so scatty you can't trust her to go shopping.' He then spoke of Carter's loyalty to her boss, but wary of the jury's loyalties to the PA, he tried to mitigate the criticism: 'I'm not being unkind.' On the email deletion policy, Edis asked the jury to consider 'what Mrs Brooks was trying to achieve.' The policy explicitly talked of 'getting rid' of emails 'unhelpful in future litigation.' However, the company was supposed to retain correspondence related to 'actual or prospective litigation however compromising they would be.' By asking for a 'clean sweep' later that year Brooks, bypassed that preservation policy.

On the arrest of Brooks and search of her premises, Edis concluded that 'Jubilee Barn was cleared of anything connected with her work' and 'nothing relevant was found.' 'The police treated Mrs Brooks with particular sensitivity,' he pointed out, 'and gave her several days' notice, and a choice of police stations. Quite often in these courts none of that happens… People are simply arrested; it's called a dawn raid.'

Concluding that Brooks was 'treated pretty well' Edis went on to say 'she took advantage of that' with the disappearance of material, including Charlie's bags. Of the second dawn raid in 2012, Edis said: 'It's hardly surprising the police didn't accord her the same treatment. They didn't want anything to go missing.'

For his peroration, Edis turned back to the Count 5 allegations that Brooks approved payments to a public official, heightening the speculation that she was most in danger on this count. 'It never occurred to me this person was a public official,' Edis said, reprising her evidence that she 'wasn't policing' a senior *Sun* journalist over payments. 'What on earth was she doing?' he asked incredulously, dismissing the hypothetical public interest defence with a simple: 'It's not up to you to decide whether you've committed a crime. That's for the CPS.'

As ever with Edis, the instinctive nature of his speeches never came to a constructed climax, but tended to finish when he ran out of steam. Referring back to the 11 emails authorising payments to Jordan-Barber, Edis said: 'This is very simple. Very clear. In black and white. Over and over again. A military official being paid. That's all I have to say.'

# BACK IN THE BOX

*Andrew Edis QC: We have a timetable, ten days for closing speeches. It sounds horrific and it probably is but it's not as long as it might have been.*

It almost didn't happen. If Monday's Recruitment Agency hadn't dialled one digit wrong, the voicemail would not have been left on Milly Dowler's phone, and we wouldn't have had the *News of the World* article based on a hacked message which led to the paper closing. If News International hadn't tried to cover up in 2006, and instead immediately confessed to wider hacking by Mulcaire, none of this would have happened. If Nick Davies hadn't been contacted by his own Deep Throat, Mr Apollo, after an unpleasant interview with Stuart Kuttner on the BBC Radio Four *Today* programme, his 2009 article about wider hacking would never have been written. If Dan Evans hadn't decided to do one more clumsy hack of Kelly Hoppen's phone, the *New York Times* wouldn't have followed up with another article in 2010, which eventually led to the re-opening of the police inquiry. And had Clive Goodman not returned to the witness box, I might be still live-tweeting a second round of the phone hacking trial – because the first one had collapsed.

However, Clive Goodman did not return on time. Through clever scheduling, Justice Saunders and the prosecution had organised his return to the witness box in May 2014 to coincide with the end of Edis' closing speech. Even the defence teams obligingly readied their closing speeches. But it didn't happen. Though sufficiently recovered from his pneumonia to have an angiogram, Goodman told the doctor who was performing the procedure the circumstances of the trial. The doctor refused to perform the angiogram on the grounds his patient did not appear to have given his true consent. His patience snapping, Justice Saunders thought Goodman was being 'unreasonable.' He still had to answer bail conditions, and the judge wondered whether a prison hospital could perform the test. Goodman was told to return to the doctors to have the test. I'm told two police officers waited outside till the procedure was finished. Another detective told me he thought Goodman had been treated with kid gloves. He said: 'Imagine a 15-year-old kid from Hackney playing up like that?'

This was not the only variable that could have derailed the hacking trial in its closing stages. Langdale was the barrister with good cause to insist on Goodman's return because his evidence was so damning to his client, and 'fairness' could not be achieved for Andy Coulson until he had completed his cross-examination of Goodman. But even better for Langdale, and potentially disastrous for the prosecution, was the sudden revelation that the Weeting team had just discovered a DVD from the FBI with thousands of emails (estimates ranged from 48,000 to 80,000) the US authorities had subpoenaed from the News Corp in New York.

Horror was etched on Justice Saunders' face as Langdale complained about another 'systematic failure of disclosure.' It was a tremendous oversight, and if anything relevant to the facts of the trial had been overlooked at this stage, Coulson's team would have had a good reason to appeal, or even stay the prosecution. The prosecution disappeared that weekend looking grim, and I was told 30 Weeting detectives spent two nights and two days going through those emails, looking for material relevant to the facts of the trial. They came back empty handed – and judicial disaster was averted.

By the time Clive Goodman reappeared on 14 May, he'd been told a few days earlier of the CPS decision that they would not convict him on any new admissions of hacking, and strangely enough, he looked much perkier in the witness box, though he did describe, through his barrister, the pressure on him to take the angiogram as 'inhuman.' Since it was nine weeks since Goodman had been cross-examined, Spens asked for his client to be provided notes on his previous testimony to refresh his memory. Goodman's cross-examination by Langdale would be allowed to proceed in a way similar to Kuttner's evidence, with lots of breaks. For all his severity on insisting on Goodman's return, the judge added a note of pastoral care: 'I do hope he's all right… that's the most important thing.'

♦ ♦ ♦

You could tell it was a big day when Goodman finally made it back on 14 May, because the court began to fill up early. On that day I caught William Clegg QC coming in without his gown, in a suit, and I spotted his Garrick Club tie. By way of explanation, Clegg told me he was off to see the new play *Charles III* that night. It didn't surprise me that lawyers loved theatre. Courts and theatre had grown up together in the vicinity of the Old Bailey, even before their raucous cousin, the press, started touting its pamphlets on Fleet Street. Shakespeare so relied on the patronage of lawyers at the Inns of Court he wrote dedicated plays for them, including *A Comedy of Errors,* which effectively ends in a trial.

Watching a criminal court prepare for a full session is like watching a theatre prepare for a show. First the stage managers come in, the court clerks and ushers, moving files around and turning on computers. They are followed by the solicitors and the juniors, often without their wigs on at this point. The police file in – and there were a lot of them for Goodman's return – including the senior investigating officer of Operation Weeting, Detective Chief Superintendent Mark Ponting and Deputy Assistant Commissioner Neil Basu. Then come the lead players, the QCs and their defendants, pulling on costumes, straightening their faces. A new air of formality reigns when we're told 'All Rise,' for the judge. But this is still just a preparation. The judge is like a powerful director who can scorn one actor or cut the script. The curtain rises, and everything becomes still as the jury take their seats.

Though longer than the cross examination of Dan Evans, and almost as long as the Crown's cross-examination of Brooks and Coulson, Langdale's gruelling four days of cross examination of Goodman was not a dramatic highpoint. It was a low point. In the earlier phase, Laidlaw had won significant ground by grinding out hours of detail and questioning of data and provenance, but the jury was long past that now, and most of the evidence already adduced in email and verbal testimony was not particularly helpful to Langdale's client. In the end, all he could do was string things out in the hope that Goodman might collapse again (not through a heart condition, of course).

For all his medical setbacks, Goodman was hale and hearty. Langdale's first big hit should have been that Goodman lied about the hacking of Princes William and Harry and Kate Middleton. But knowing he wasn't in any further danger of conviction, Goodman could just parry the blame. 'You knew in 2006, after your arrest, you knew perfectly well you hacked Prince William and Prince Harry,' taunted Langdale, with his accusatorial rejoinder: 'What do you say to that?' Goodman barely batted an eyelid: 'I say I was never asked.' Langdale wasn't having it: 'Mr Goodman, please, just answer the question.' 'I was never asked about that,' Goodman replied. With nearly 50 years at the bar, Langdale tried to turn the tables one more time: 'Mr Goodman, can we make one more attempt to get an answer?' Goodman shrugged: 'You are getting an answer. You don't like it, but you're getting it. I can only answer the allegations put to me at the time. You are putting them to me now and I'm happy to answer.'

Coulson looked pale in the dock, while the prosecutors were all smiles and relaxation.

By this point, because of the bad 4G reception combined with terrible Court 12 acoustics, I was sitting near the witness box. Goodman smiled at me and thanked me for my Twitter feed. The court was becoming so familiar after seven months, everyone chatted to everyone.

Langdale then spent what seemed like a whole day going through every email which showed any kind of pleasant interaction among *News of the World* staff. The jurors looked bored rigid as Langdale pointed out 'Nothing angry here is there?' or 'Quite polite!' Even the dark-haired woman who acted as pro-tem foreman, who nearly always smiled at everyone, was pouting. Eventually Justice Saunders cracked under the tedium and said caustically: 'Yes: Everybody is reasonable at the *News of the World.*' Later he apologised for the interruption: 'I did not mean any disrespect to the *News of the World.*' To show his sense of fairness, the judge criticised Goodman too. As Langdale went through an email showing Coulson had replied 'fine' to the royal editor's request to miss a news conference, Goodman said bullishly: 'That's a typically curt, dismissive, Andy Coulson-ism. It's a dismissive, one word response. There's no 'well done, congratulations!' Exasperated, Justice Saunders exclaimed: 'What did you want him to say?'

However, as Langdale went on all day, and the jurors looked particularly restless and bored, Justice Saunders got irritated again, saying 'I think we've heard a lot about this' to the amusement of a juror, hoping Langdale would take the hint. But he didn't. One again, the judge inserted a sarcastic remark about 'perfect harmony' at the *News of the World.* Langdale ploughed on. Even my Twitter feed was getting bored. Coulson's counsel obviously hoped to sow doubts in the minds of the jury about the awfulness of the *News of the World* newsroom. Based on a sequence in *South Park*, it's what James Doleman described to me as the 'Chewbacca Defence':

> *Why would a Wookiee, an 8-foot-tall Wookiee, want to live on Endor, with a bunch of 2-foot-tall Ewoks? That does not make*

*sense! But more important, you have to ask yourself: What does*
*this have to do with this case? Nothing. Ladies and gentlemen,*
*it has nothing to do with this case! It does not make sense...*
*No! Ladies and gentlemen of this supposed jury, it does not*
*make sense! If Chewbacca lives on Endor, you must acquit!*
*The defence rests.*

When the jury left for a break, Justice Saunders sounded at the
end of his (long and silky) tether, complaining to Langdale about
the length of time the cross-examination was taking: 'I can't really
see where this is going,' the judge said, reminding Langdale it was
a criminal court, not an employment tribunal. In his humorous
way, Justice Saunders tried to warn Coulson's barrister about
exploiting his goodwill: 'I'm sure you've had more difficult judges
than me to deal with.' To which William Clegg could be heard to
mutter, hardly sotto voce: 'Quite a competition!'

With Langdale looking pained and going through the motions,
the judge shrugged. 'Well I may be wrong, you've been doing this
longer than I have. Who knows, maybe the jury are finding it absolutely fascinating.' Meanwhile, the Chewbacca defence ended up
in an own goal for Coulson when, under pressure from Langdale,
Goodman claimed that when he told his editor he might not be
able to go on a royal trip overseas because of family problems,
Coulson kicked the desk in anger. While appealing to the jury's
sympathy, Coulson's barrister may have alienated them.

On the alleged cover-up of the 'Rogue reporter' line after
Goodman's arrest, Langdale's main strategy seemed to be that
Goodman was an unreliable witness because he wasn't devious
enough. Going through the various conversations Goodman taped
between himself and Coulson post arrest, Langdale asked incredulously: 'Why didn't you get an admission from Mr Coulson that
he knew? It would have given you the most useful weapon you
could use: he was involved and approved of what you are doing.'
But Goodman had an answer for that: 'The evidence [against me]

was all there in black and white. It would have hurt him but it wouldn't have helped me. Are you suggesting I should have black-mailed your client?' The moral of the story? Journalists are tough witnesses for lawyers to crack. It's hard to spin a spinner.

And that was it. From its advance billing, everyone expected Langdale to destroy Goodman over new evidence that he hacked the royal princes and Kate Middleton. But once Goodman readily acknowledged these, they caused problems for his former editor. Goodman claimed that he showed Coulson a transcript of a voice-mail from Jamie Lowther-Pinkerton, and that the Prince William beagling story (about a clandestine meeting with his wife-to-be) also came from phone hacking. Perhaps the most memorable moment of the four-day cross-examination, apart from the judge losing his temper, was Goodman's line about 2007. There 'wasn't a significant story in the *News of the World* for the last two years that wasn't the result' of phone hacking.

However, Langdale's belaboured strategy may not have been completely fruitless. Though most of it probably didn't help his client on the hacking charge, the jury were so split they couldn't agree on a majority verdict on Counts 2 and 3 against Goodman and Coulson.

◆ ◆ ◆

With Goodman's cross-examination over, the trial was finally unlocked, and could proceed with closing speeches. Once again, they merely went over the ground covered before, but there were a few surprises.

Unlike Edis who – in breaks in his closing speeches – would sit at his bench pondering, Laidlaw prepared in the outer chambers by marking long sheets of foolscap paper and memorising everything. When Cheryl Carter was taken ill the same day, her barrister Trevor Burke joked: 'Matron has advised her to go home. She often swoons when Mr Laidlaw speaks.' But every joke tells a truth, and there was something very male and bullish about the delivery of Brooks' QC. When it came to his closing speech on 20 and 21 May he was fearsome. Head slightly bowed, looking at the jury as if they shared the same dour moral mission, his voice emphasised virtually every word. The variation came from his hands: he used those throughout, usually with a pen clenched between his fingers. Occasionally a finger would be pointed to jab up some egregious injustice. 'It is beyond ridiculous,' he said, summarising the eight months: 'The prosecution are trying to make you buy this fantastic tale of all that Mrs Brooks did and everyone she corrupted!' Then he'd raise his hands in protest, or clasp them to signify that there was only one conclusion to be drawn.

The theatrics of Laidlaw's closing were intensified by the presence of his client's mother and other, mainly female relatives. At the beginning of his speech, Laidlaw used the maternal presence to great effect (as he had in evidence). Gesturing up to the gallery, he asked the jury to imagine they were 'watching the trial of a member of your own family, a friend, a loved one. From up there you would be reassured by the care the jury have taken,' he said, 'and the commitment they have given.' But then he spoke of the 'attention from the media in all its modern forms,' with a particular swipe at social media and Twitter: 'Inaccuracy, bias, outright cruelty and vitriol.' He asked: 'Can anyone be strong enough to avoid being influenced by it? She is starting at a disadvantage, and cannot win.'

Of course prejudicial media coverage had always been Laidlaw's favourite theme – or, to be fair, the favourite theme of Brooks' solicitors from just after her arrest. In the culmination of his speech the next day, Laidlaw's accusation of prejudice reached its medieval apotheosis with the 'witch-hunt,' first introduced by Brooks in the acrimonious town-hall meeting with *News of the World* staff, and reiterated in a text to her friend Kath Raymond Hinton in a text around the same time. Laidlaw spoke of 'ducking stools' and continued the metaphor in a very personal attack on the lead prosecutor, casting him as the witch-finder general. 'If what Mr Edis claims you've seen is a mask, then Mrs Brooks must be a witch with supernatural powers,' he said. If Kath Raymond Hinton had found the tone of media coverage in 2011 sexist, 'What would she make of Edis' closing speech?'

No barrister I talked to could recall such a personal attack by a lead defence counsel on the Crown's lead counsel. It must have been calculated to win the jury over, rather than pursue any personal antagonism to a fellow member of his chambers. Laidlaw was also talking to an empty chair. Edis had excused himself the day before, telling the jury he had some electronic files to sort out. But he probably guessed what was coming.

However, for all the forceful, slightly scary invocations of witchcraft in Laidlaw's closing speech, it must not be forgotten that his client was perhaps the best storyteller. Brooks was understandably fiercely protective of her case. I felt her controlling eye on me during those closing speeches. During a break, she asked the *Independent*'s Jim Cusick who I was (which was odd, since she had been following me on Twitter for months). But the next day she smiled again and came up to me: 'I'm sorry. Of course I recognise you…' In a way I felt the gaze of her and the other defendants more intently now than the lawyers, CPS, Attorney General's office or police. I now understood an anecdote that a friend of mine, a former TV executive, told me about joining Brooks on the floor of the *Sun* as the daily tabloid was put to bed one evening. Brooks was over everything, he said, publicly upbraiding some journalists, praising others. And for a while the court felt like another of Brooks' newsrooms. Only on this occasion she was the headline. The story was her own.

Underneath the passionate claims of persecution and protestations of innocence, there were two important concessions in Laidlaw's closing speech. The first could have long-term consequences for potential corporate charges against News International and News Corp. For all her campaigning against injustice (and Laidlaw framed the leaks of a public official against the government of the day trying to 'put a lid on bad news') Laidlaw admitted that as soon as Brooks became chief executive she 'did nothing to investigate' phone hacking, and was eventually only 'forced to do so by civil litigation.' Though the cover-up, eventually exposed by the *Guardian*, may 'not to you be very attractive, and we are the first to accept that,' Brooks only did this 'to protect the reputation' of her company. It was nothing to do with 'covering up her own involvement in phone hacking, but was to protect the company.'

The second important element of Laidlaw's closing was to say that 'hacking only really started in earnest' when Brooks left the *News of the World,* and it's possible staff hid the Milly Dowler hacking from her when she was on holiday in Dubai. Referring to Coulson's editorship, Laidlaw added: 'If there had been as much hacking when Rebekah Brooks was editor as there was subsequently, there would be good grounds for convicting her.'

This was almost a replay of the prisoner's dilemma: he was using Coulson's apparent guilt to make his client look more honest. The difference between the evidence against the lead defendants had been glaring since the start of the trial, but never expressed so openly as in Laidlaw's closing, perhaps because by this point the prosecution had so effectively harried Brooks.

But it meant Langdale, in his closing speech on 28 and 29 May, had to push back on behalf of Coulson. Langdale said: 'You've heard a powerful and compelling speech from Mr Laidlaw on behalf of Mrs Brooks.' But he took exception Laidlaw's line that 'they' at the *News of the World* 'wouldn't have told Brooks about voicemail messages.' Batting back the suggestion that Coulson would have hidden such a thing from his boss, Langdale said: 'How on earth would he take such a risk?'

Otherwise, Langdale's closing speech went over much of the same ground he had covered in his cross-examination of Goodman a week or so before, though referring back to Spens' closing remarks, he stressed the point: 'It's unusual, to say the least, to face two prosecution speeches.' He called Goodman a 'surrogate prosecutor,' a gun that Edis could train on Coulson, without any 'comeback against him.' In his final words about the cover-up, Langdale tried to turn the whole case around, and claimed it was 'ironic' that the prosecution and Goodman alleged a cover-up at News International when police and CPS had their own 'cover-up' in 2006. But if irony was a crime, Britain would be a nation of lawbreakers

The other closing speeches held few surprises. Goodman's QC had hit his high point with his cross examination of Coulson, and beyond his proxy prosecutor's role, was largely a spent force. He made a good point that while others 'had been struck down by collective amnesia in the last few years' his client, despite his poor health, had a good memory. He also made a lawyer's point against Goodman's solicitor in 2006. 'Make no mistake about it,' he said, 'though News International were footing the legal bill, Goodman was Brandman's client,' and the alleged breach of privilege 'was not something we should accept.' But these good points were slightly undermined by the sophistry of his argument about emails: because most *News of the World* journalists hid their criminality in coded words, the jury should consider 'if a crime is actually mentioned in an email it probably didn't happen.' Immediately he tried to backtrack and say this 'wasn't just a clever lawyer's point' – but it was hard to think of it any other way. Journalists joked that, if you went into a bank with a shotgun and balaclava, you would be innocent, because it would be too blatant.

The real revelation was Stuart Kuttner's barrister, Jonathan Caplan QC, who proved 'less is more' even more effectively than Spens. We'd hardly heard from him during the trial. His closing speech showed why he was considered such an effective QC for the media. In a beautifully presented speech, which like Clegg's comments about *Charles III* showed Caplan was another keen theatre-goer, he pointed out that 'trials, like West End plays, don't usually last seven to eight months... the impression is no resource was spared by CPS and police.' He pithily summed up the trial as 'a heady mix of royalty, celebrities and politicians' and used the space dramatically.

Gesturing to the ceremonial sword installed above Justice Saunders, he spoke about 'the traditional symbols in this court-room.' Then he pointed out the glass barrier to the dock was to 'prevent defendants jumping the dock and attacking the judge.' He questioned why such a minor issue should be tried in the Central Criminal Courts. (Justice Saunders had to explain later the case was only in the Old Bailey because of the large legal and media demands). All this Caplan used to highlight the potential abuses of the CPS, and to downplay the significance of the trial: 'There are no dangerous people in this dock. No one has been killed and no physical bombs have been detonated. Feelings may have been hurt, but no one has been injured.' Hidden in this succinct prose poem of innocence and experience however, was the line that Kuttner would have immediately contacted police when he heard of Milly Dowler's alleged Telford visit. The clear evidence that Justice Saunders pointed out in his summing up, is that the call came at least 24 hours after the *News of the World* learnt of the story.

Then came Trevor Burke QC, with his affable man-of-the-people style. Cheryl Carter was the perfect client for him, as he pointed out her height ('she nearly fell off the stool because her feet didn't touch the floor') and polite 'Thank you, Mr Edis' after a day of cross-examination. Burke asked: 'Has there ever been a more unlikely character to stand in the dock of the Old Bailey than Cheryl Carter?' To Edis' point that she wouldn't have involved her son Nick in a criminal conspiracy by helping to remove the boxes 'because he didn't know,' Burke mocked the 'preposterous' and 'sophisticated suggestion.' It was pure character stuff. Cheryl was a 'good person… with a very big heart, which she wears on her sleeve.' Her only fault was loyalty. Burke also scored a laugh when he pointed out the quality of Carter's character witnesses:

'Can I confess that in 30 years of practice at the Bar, I have always wanted to call an archdeacon in support of a defendant I represent? How rare in this court. Imagine my disappointment then when Mr Caplan calls the Archbishop of Canterbury in support of his client.'

But for all the confidence and humour, Burke acknowledged it could go the other way, and made a special pleading for his client at the end of the speech. Using the reality of the 'long trial syndrome' Burke told the jury 'not to be timid' in speaking up for Cheryl no matter what happened with other defendants on other charges. 'You are not relative strangers after seven months,' he said. He begged the jurors to speak up for Cheryl in their deliberations: 'and you'll get the right verdict.'

Looking back on all the closing speeches now, they all address different constituencies and sensibilities, and track them so closely I cannot help but wonder if the jurors' demographic, professional and cultural backgrounds were skilfully profiled by the defence teams. Call me a conspiracy theorist, but if I were running a defence team with almost limitless resources that is what I would do.

The last two closing speeches clearly reflected this pattern. Neil Saunders, for Charlie Brooks, did exactly what was expected. (He never mentioned once that Charlie went to Eton and his older brother was a close friend of David Cameron). He appealed instead to the country pub bravado epitomised by the leader of UKIP, Nigel Farage. (Charlie has since been reported to be standing for Farage's party at the next election). So he had business failures, liked a glass or four of wine, but he gave 'lovely support' to his wife. He also made a telling point that a Weeting officer left one of her bags behind after searching Jubilee Barn; that was just one of 'two forgetful bag episodes' that day. After a brief résumé of Charlie's apologies for stashing away his porn ('ashamed… furious…. mortified…. horrified'), he described the 'gratuitous' and 'aggressive' second dawn raid of the Brooks' Oxfordshire home in 2012, when there was a young baby and 82-year-old mother on the premises. Saunders still ended with the comedy routine, though. Of Charlie, he concluded: 'He is a man capable of drinking a bottle of Fairy Liquid, but not this crime.'

What did this leave for William Clegg, representing Mark Hanna? Well, Clegg's love of acting was amply displayed at this point, as he took over the front bench previously occupied by Laidlaw: 'I feel like the chap who has travelled all the way to Sydney in tourist class and been upgraded for the short hop to Melbourne.' The laughs started and never really stopped. Clegg brilliantly painted his client as a middle ranking soldier and member of middle management who found himself caught up in this strange world: 'There were no archbishops and lords of the realm speaking for him,' he pointed out: 'The only time he saw Tony Blair was on TV.' Pointing to Mr and Mrs Brooks, Clegg said: 'While they're dining in style… he's walking the perimeter of Enstone Manor.' And then he focused on the legal point: Hanna could only be found guilty if Charlie Brooks was found guilty. In one of the best riffs of the trial Clegg went through Charlie's actions on the days leading up to his wife's arrest: Thursday: reading copies of the *Racing Post*, another gin and tonic. Friday more copies of the *Racing Post*, more gin and tonics. Saturday the same. Then Sunday 'panic… I've got to get rid of incriminating material.'

Clegg ended with one of the most memorable sections of any closing speech – and it was all about Charlie: 'If he had been minded for one reason or another to set himself up as some master criminal, the Moriarty of the Chipping Norton set, to hide all this incriminating property, it might have crossed Charlie's mind on Thursday, Friday or Saturday to pop down to the council tip, drop anything there, to drive down to the reservoir, rivers, to dump anything he liked in there.'

In his summing up, which began on 4 June, Justice Saunders awarded Clegg an Oscar for comedy. There was more than a hint of irony, perhaps envy. Justice Saunders would spend the next week scrupulously going through every argument from all sides of the hacking trial, about all bits of evidence. It was so long, repetitive, and even-handed that even he wondered if it was appropriate in such a long trial. But finish it he did – and distributed it in a 140-page document to the court. As it is now published and summarised facts we had already heard the summing up hardly needs to be reiterated here. Justice Saunders made a point of detailing the 12 confirmed hacks during Brooks' era at the *News of the World*. (In the end, the only question the jury asked in retirement was if there was a newspaper piece about one of these targets, Charlotte Church, but there was none in evidence.) And he defended Nick Davies' original 4 July 2011 Milly Dowler piece, against some of the things said about the 'false hope' subheading, and the new evidence since then that Milly's voicemails hadn't been deliberately deleted. They may not have been, Justice Saunders pointed out, but the mere fact of listening to them may have caused automatic deletion.

My last breaking news of the trial was Justice Saunders' remark to the jury on 11 June 2014 as they retired to consider their verdicts: 'It's been a privilege to work with you.'

# TRUTH'S BOOTS

*Operation Weeting Detective: I'm a small man.
But I want to believe we all live in the same
system, and that no one is beyond justice.*

Waiting in the Old Bailey for a jury to return with a verdict is like waiting for a flight from a remote 1970s airport when some conflict has grounded all the planes. Journalists, lawyers and defendants hang around in a state of abject boredom, ready at any minute (there's only a 15-minute warning) for the adrenalin-pumping call for a potential escape. Whenever the announcement went out on the Tannoy: 'All parties in Brooks and others to Court 12,' there would be a scramble to pack computers and run up the stairs to the court. If this was around 4pm, the movement would be more leisurely – after all it was just the jury being sworn out for the day. Journalists would scrutinise the 11 remaining jurors for any signs: were they happy and united? Were they red-faced after arguing? We weren't the only ones.

A week into retirement, Justice Saunders noticed what many journalists had spotted months ago and which Trevor Burke had referred to in his closing speeches: after seven months, none of us were strangers. And though it's forbidden for journalists, witnesses or defendants to approach a juror, after so long in one small room the sense of familiarity was overwhelming. Smiles, nods and long glances of recognition had been shared by defendants and jurors. In a written and verbal warning after the jury left, Justice Saunders had to tell the defendants to stop making eye contact with the jury. It was hard to see if he was looking at any defendant in particular, but Rebekah Brooks was the most engaged of all those in in the court. Even after the judge's warning, Charlie Brooks continued to stare at the jurors.

While the hours passed in the canteen, most journalists compiled 'backgrounders' for publication after the verdicts. A key issue was the cost of the trial. I had long conversations with reporters from *The Times, Daily Mail, Telegraph*, and *Financial Times* trying to work it out. To me, the most extraordinary aspect was the discovery that the length of proceedings and the number of privately-paid defences did indeed make this the trial of the century. The prosecution barristers and their one solicitor earned less in a day (around £1,200) than just one of the leading QCs and juniors did in an hour, perhaps explaining the relative deficiency of the Crown's case. Multiply that by six, and it was easy to see how the defence had spent more than £10 million on barristers alone. Meanwhile, the official court and prosecution costs were £1.2 million.

In a briefing embargoed until the verdicts, the Metropolitan Police had revealed the total cost of the three police operations arising out of the phone hacking scandal – £32 million. In a previous annual report, News UK (News International re-branded name) had put a figure on the civil hacking claims and its Management and Standards Committee, but there were no costs for the trial. All we knew for sure was that the £10 million on silks would be a fraction of the total: there were as many as 30 solicitors and barristers in court most days, and some of them had been on the case for two years. News UK's expenditure on the trial could have easily been several times as much as the £13 million Scotland Yard spent on the phone hacking inquiry, Operation Weeting.

All this was a jolly way to keep us out of mischief. James Doleman managed to program his phone and get his heavily American accented text to speech program to say: 'Brooks and others to Court 12.' Most of us laughed, but a serious print journalist had started packing away his computer and contacted his news desk. There were sweepstakes on when the jury would return (I never got to bet). I wish I had, because it seemed to me that after such a long trial jurors would have made up their minds. I estimated a day for each count, meaning they'd come back with a verdict on Tuesday 22 June.

On Monday 21 June, as I began to pull together the legal judgements for this book, there was a call on the Tannoy: 'Mark Bryant-Heron to reception, please.' From some of the previous public address announcements I'd noticed that this call to Bryant-Heron almost always preceded a call to the court. I'd told James Doleman that it looked like the court was being called back in. But it was only around 3.30 pm – too early for the jury to go home. Sure enough, a few minutes later the Tannoy announced: 'All parties in Brooks and others.' I grabbed my iPad for live-tweeting. This could be it. As we all rushed upstairs, I felt my heart pounding with anticipation. The end of the longest concluded criminal trial in history was imminent. There were 40 or so people in the court, but hundreds of thousands watching as I tweeted the court was back in session.

As it was, the jury just wanted to go home early. They looked bored. They looked like they had just been going through the formalities. False alert. But as I wandered home that evening, I felt sick. The surge of excitement had left my flight or fight response with nowhere to go. I learned that evening that red wine is the only antidote to an adrenaline overdose.

The next day, 22 June, the call to Bryant-Heron went out well before lunch. I knew this was it, but because my adrenal glands had been depleted, I was fairly calm as the court assembled. Most the defendants were hanging out nearby – Brooks had rented a house in Bloomsbury. I could tell from the seriousness of the judge when he came in that verdicts were imminent. My fingers were ready to type out the most important tweets of the entire eight months. And then we were all told we couldn't report anything.

The problem, as Justice Saunders explained, was the jury had reached partial verdicts. They'd spent a day locked in debate about some counts but couldn't agree. Rather than hold up the whole process for those outstanding charges, the jury wanted to return with their agreed verdicts: Justice Saunders didn't know which charges they were. He wanted to discuss what to do about reporting restrictions, given the impact the explosion of media coverage might have on the jury's deliberations on the remaining counts (whatever they were). The judge and barristers decided to hear the verdicts, then discuss whether they could be reported. All the journalists looked confused, if not mortified. I'd already tweeted that court was sitting. Twitter followers were asking: 'Is this it?' It looked like I wouldn't be able to tell them.

The jury came back in and the forewoman read out her verdicts; it was quite simple to remember. Rebekah Brooks not guilty on all charges. Kuttner, Carter, Charlie and Hanna not guilty. Coulson guilty of conspiracy to hack phones. No verdict on the Counts 2 and 3 corruption charges against Coulson and Goodman. The judge sent away the jurors to have another go at reaching verdicts on those. A tense debate ensued among barristers and journalists over what could be reported. Everyone knew that private communications of the verdicts would spread like wildfire and Coulson's conviction would reverberate through Westminster. Though Langdale objected to any reporting, Nick Davies stood up and spoke for the press. 'We have held back from publishing relevant material,' he told the judge. 'But if the Prime Minister goes public, it becomes ludicrous we can't report what we know. As soon as the partial verdicts were announced, I spoke to counsel and said this would happen.' Justice Saunders took these words seriously. He asked Langdale to contact the Attorney General, Dominic Grieve, and ensure the Prime Minister made no comment until the other verdicts against Coulson had been decided. Justice Saunders agreed the verdicts so far could be reported. I sent out my tweets:

> BREAKING: Jury find Brooks NOT Guilty on all counts at Hacking Trial: Coulson guilty on Count One.

Another reporter asked for confirmation that this could also be live-tweeted. 'Yes,' said the judge. But by that time I was on to my second:

> BREAKING; #hackingtrial jury not able to bring in a verdict on Coulson Goodman Counts 2 & 3 - jury discharged: decision about retrial Monday

I barely looked at my Twitter feed, as the legal arguments raged. I knew there would be a large volume of anger and disappointment about the verdict on Brooks. It was no surprise to me, but unless people had been following the case in detail, they might have presumed that the evidence was overwhelming, or that, as editor, Brooks was morally responsible for the hacking of Milly Dowler. In the court of public opinion, yes. In the hard clarity of a criminal court where the punishment is loss of liberty, no.

Among those reacting was Louise Mensch, who was claiming that all my tweets from the court had been biased – an odd allegation because she had retweeted me several times. (The next day I happened to pass Laidlaw and Brooks' solicitor, Angus McBride, who thanked me for my coverage and told me they found it impartial.) The Twitter storm was tiny compared to the bigger political storm. Nick Davies' warning had been prophetic and within minutes of the verdicts the Shadow Chancellor, Ed Balls, raised Coulson's record on the floor of the House of Commons. Shortly after the Prime Minister had publicly apologised for appointing Coulson and said Coulson had lied. This had drawn a response from the Labour Party leader Ed Miliband, who questioned Cameron's judgement.

Soon everyone was piling in. The chair of the Commons media committee, John Whittingdale MP, was on TV saying that Coulson had lied to Parliament. As Court 12 convened again, it emerged that minutes after the verdict when Langdale had spoken to the Attorney General, the law officer had been with David Cameron. The cameras had just left after filming the Prime Minister's apology statement. With the jury still deadlocked over the remaining charges against Coulson and Goodman, Langdale was going to apply to have the jury discharged from returning a verdict on the remaining counts. Justice Saunders said he would write to the Prime Minister and ask for an explanation, and the court rose till the next morning. At the last pass, part of the trial could be derailed by prejudicial comment – from the leader of the country.

Meanwhile, the dock was empty, bar one person. All the other defendants had left Court 12 for good and were passing through massed TV crews and photographers outside. Coulson remained to sit through yet another hearing about releasing to the press the full contents of the love letter Brooks wrote to him. For all the rights and wrongs, it was mournful and instructive to see Coulson alone in the glass box when his companions had been set free. I felt some pity. According to Nick Davies, Coulson had been appointed the fall guy back in 2007. And yet here he was, watching us all, listening to Langdale, making notes, trying to determine what could be in the press. Right up to the last moment he was still editing the papers.

◆ ◆ ◆

I really can't remember much about the night of the partial verdicts: the publicity was intense and I had to give interviews, file a report to the *Daily Beast* and get on with this book. The next morning I missed some of the defence's opening arguments, but Langdale's point was fairly clear. Because both the Prime Minister and the chair of a Commons committee had accused his client of lying, over matters which had never been tested in court (and which could not be tested in court, because of parliamentary privilege) the publicity could sway the jury on the remaining counts. He had a good point. If the jury returned with a guilty verdict on those counts now, the conviction could be unsafe and an appeal launched.

Opposing the motion to discharge the jury, Edis argued that the jury were now immune to adverse press and social media comment. Taking a sneaky swipe at Laidlaw for his 'indefatigable searches of remote parts of the internet' for prejudicial coverage to prove Brooks could not have a fair trial, Edis pointed out: 'but she did…. that was all wrong.' In another wry moment, he said, 'I can rely on high authority' that the jury was not swayed by 'hysterical clamour on social media.' The words were taken from a *Sun* editorial about the verdict on Brooks, which maintained the prosecution was a waste of taxpayer's money and precious police resources. By taking sides in an ongoing trial, Edis also observed, Britain's bestselling tabloid had broken the strict liability contempt rule.

Ruling against discharging the jury, Justice Saunders explained that he had received an explanation from the Prime Minister's parliamentary secretary stating David Cameron had explicitly steered clear of any mention of 'any matters that might still be before the court.' But the judge protested that the explanation 'misses the point' because of the accusation of lying, followed by the remarks by John Whittingdale. 'The chairman of the parliamentary committee which investigated phone hacking has told the public that Mr Coulson lied to them in the evidence that he gave,' Justice Saunders. He added: 'Evidence of what Mr Coulson said before the committee could not be given in court as it would amount to a breach of parliamentary privilege.' For the same reason Brooks' statement to the committee in 2003 that she paid police had been inadmissible.

Justice Saunders continued: 'Whether the political imperative was such that statements could not await all the verdicts, I leave to others to judge. I consider that what has happened is unsatisfactory so far as justice and the rule of law are concerned. The press in court have been extremely responsible in their reporting of this case but when politicians regard it as open season, one cannot expect the press to remain silent.' Though the jury were still 'deep into analytical discussion of the evidence on counts 2 and 3,' the judge was sure they would 'continue to try Mr Coulson and Mr Goodman on the evidence that they have heard in court and solely on that evidence.'

Later that afternoon, the jury returned and said that despite prolonged discussions they still could not reach verdicts on the remaining counts. They were discharged, and the Crown Prosecution Service said it would decide whether it would press for a re-trial against Coulson and Goodman on Counts 2 and 3.

The trial was over, but another was beginning in the court of public opinion, and it would have both a defence and prosecution.

◆ ◆ ◆

For eight months I'd counted myself lucky to mix with some of the best court reporters around. In person, they'd been unfailingly helpful, polite and friendly. My respect for their hard work, caution, and analytical skills had increased inestimably. Without them, I probably would have made even more errors. But regardless of their personal qualities, their employers participated in what can only be described as calculated propaganda in the days following the verdict.

It's very rare to have the three major newspaper groups agree on one headline. But *The Times*, *Daily Mail,* and *Daily Telegraph* (and to a certain extent the *Financial Times*) had one common take on the phone hacking trial after the verdicts – £100 million had been wasted on one guilty verdict. It was so loudly trumpeted and so ubiquitous that even the BBC promulgated this figure for days, with the presenters on the BBC Radio Four Today programme asking what all the money was for. The figure was plucked out of thin air. Most newspapers had tossed in all the Metropolitan Police costs for its Operations Weeting, Tuleta and Elveden into phone hacking, corruption and other illegal breaches of privacy respectively. Those operations were responsible for at least another 10 forthcoming trials. Most of the £100 million figure accrued to News UK, in legal bills. When the CPS and the police tried to correct it, *The Times'* headline was Met Have to Explain Hacking Trial Costs. I wasn't surprised to see *The Times* bury Coulson's conviction on page 36. A line had been drawn, probably connected to the Leveson recommendations for stronger press regulation – and editorialising overwhelmed reporting.

Nate Silver's FiveThirtyEight blog put the cost of the trial to taxpayers at £25 million. Rebekah Brooks and three other defendants put in a claim for a similar amount for their legal fees. Rupert Murdoch's business has to shoulder some blame for that. Had it come clean about the true extent of hacking in 2006, much of the expense would have been spared.

The issue of finances became, briefly, a personal issue for me the weekend after the verdict. The Indiegogo site published all the money supporters had donated to crowd-fund my live-tweeting. Louise Mensch had discovered that, in the initial wave of funding in November 2013, the phone hacking victims' group *Hacked Off* had donated £500. To Mensch, this was confirmation I must have been partisan. Of course, I didn't have any control who contributed, and 95% of the funds had come from members of the public. Besides, I could no more express my personal opinion live-tweeting a criminal trial than a brain surgeon could inquire into a patient's politics.

Yet this mini campaign to discredit me attracted the usual online suspects, and Dennis Rice inserted himself into the situation, referring back to the blog in January and agreeing with

Mensch. While out of phone range for a while that Sunday night, I discovered a new interlocutor, Matthew Drake, was asking me persistently whether *Hacked Off* were sponsoring this book. I knew *Hacked Off* had sent an email commending my reporting. I wondered why this issue was so pressing to Drake, when someone emailed me to tell me he was a former investigations reporter for the *News of the World* who had worked with its private investigator Derek Webb. I asked Drake about this and he fell silent. Now there was no danger of contempt, I tweeted out that this book would contain some of the background stories about pressure during the trial.

Soon, TabloidTroll was back on Twitter, writing: 'If @Peter-Jukes writes any shit on me in his book the gloves will really come off. Newsnight ex wife, business failures.' The fact the mother of my two children had been made a target was pretty disturbing. As for 'business failures,' I crowd-funded my tweets because my earnings from freelance journalism were insupportably low (though I love the job.)

A week or so later I received some anonymous texts mentioning vague legal threats and hoping I would 'enjoy the weekend.' Some other Twitter accounts (which I didn't see at the time) also wished me well for the weekend, and suggested some kind of 'Daily Mail Tuesday.' On Monday morning I received a call from Richard Marsden, a *Daily Mail* reporter, demanding to know about my mortgage payments. A little taken aback, I asked what business it was of his. He reminded me of my original crowd-funding blog, when I said I had been so broke I missed a mortgage payment. I told him this was entirely true and wondered why I should lie about such an embarrassing personal disclosure. He said I could have been raising money under 'false pretences' and, having confirmed my address, asked me why I didn't have a mortgage.

Marsden later told me that he'd been handed an anonymised email with personal financial details and a separate piece of paper with my email address and mobile phone number. I explained to him calmly that there was no mortgage on my property because I had sold it two weeks previously. I could easily prove I had quite a sizeable mortgage until then. Marsden then started asking why I didn't rent out the property to avoid being short of money.

Minutes later, when I tweeted the approach, Media Guido (another *Sun* employee, who had called my coverage 'boringly partisan' earlier in the year) was on at me, confirming my apartment address and asking if I had a mortgage. He'd clearly been handed the same information. It was an embarrassing mistake for them: it was a false, non-story. Soon afterwards TabloidTroll closed down and deleted his account.

My minor brush with press 'investigations' has made me more attuned to the acute and systematic intrusions into personal privacy by the *News of the World*. The threat to me was minor and nothing was published. But thousands of people were targeted by Mulcaire's hacking, and hundreds of relationships, friendships and marriages, were badly damaged by the cruel publication of private secrets. This has nothing to do with a free press or exposing public interest scandals. It's a display of power designed to intimidate and silence.

Yet, thanks to interactive media, we're no longer passive consumers of news, entertainment and opinion but can share countervailing information – and answer back. The press had tried to shape public opinion with its take on the hacking trial, but other forces are now in play.

◆ ◆ ◆

At the beginning of July, five of the six convicted of phone hacking returned to Court 12 to plead their mitigation. Andrew Edis QC (at the end of the month to become a High Court judge) argued that hacking was not only industrial at the *News of the World*, on occasion it was used 'in pursuit of a political agenda' and was highly lucrative. The *News of the World* had been named Newspaper of the

Year in 2005 for three stories, at least two of which – Blunkett and Goran Eriksson – had been based on hacking. Edis announced he'd also made an application for costs against the defendants, and told the judge that the total prosecution costs for the trial and two years preparation were £1.7 million for the entire trial, including £1.1m for the phone hacking element. He wanted to recover £750,000 from the guilty defendants.

Gavin Millar QC, for Glenn Mulcaire, revealed that creditors were trying to force the sale of the family home. Mulcaire had no other assets. In hacking Milly Dowler in 2002 he claimed he had acted 'with lawful authority by police.' He also maintained pages in his notes had never been disclosed at the trial, to the Leveson Inquiry or in civil proceedings.

Trevor Burke QC, who returned to the court representing Greg Miskiw, also talked about his client's parlous financial and personal health. Miskiw was not in good health, was sole carer for an elderly relative, and made bankrupt in 2010.

The most interesting mitigation came from Neville Thurlbeck. Of phone hacking, his barrister, Hugh Davis QC, told the judge: 'The intention was not to cause distress but to… increase circulation in a highly competitive industry.' Through his counsel, Thurlbeck claimed that voicemail hackings 'were a corporate practice' known to Stuart Kuttner, Andy Coulson, another senior *News of the World* executive and a News International lawyer.

He also said he was just one of a substantial team working on the Milly Dowler story in 2002 and that Kuttner and Coulson had been running that operation. He said it was their decision not to inform Surrey police immediately of Dowler's presumed whereabouts.

Davis added that Coulson set the editorial line on the Blunkett story, and the hacking of the Home Secretary was known to both a senior News International executive and a company lawyer. As Thurlbeck's QC described how his client had pleaded guilty to help the court, Justice Saunders observed: 'It's slightly sad that capable investigative journalists have not come forward to reveal what was going on.'

Representing Weatherup, Charles Bott QC pointed out that his client only re-joined the *News of the World* in 2004, when he was instructed to use Mulcaire. 'It was standard policy at the *News of the World*, Bott said. 'He [Weatherup] was required to follow that policy. At odds with Coulson and other executives at the paper, he asked to return to reporting.'

On 1 July, the court heard Coulson's mitigation. Would he be admitting his role in the greatest scandal to afflict the newspaper industry in decades? No. Timothy Langdale, for Coulson seemed to be re-fighting the whole trial, and (very unusually) called a live witness, the *Spectator* journalist Mathew d'Ancona, who said Coulson had played a highly significant role in Cameron's inner circle and helped on matters other than journalism.

On July 4 2014, the five men – Coulson, Miskiw, Weatherup, Thurlbeck and Mulcaire – returned to the Old Bailey for sentencing. In his remarks, Justice Saunders explained the statutory requirements, imposed on him by Parliament over intercepting voicemails – a maximum two-year sentence. He said: 'There will be those who will be outraged that I haven't passed sentences well in excess of the permitted maximum and there will be those that think that it shouldn't be a crime for the press to intrude into the lives of the famous.' He remarked how stories from hacking caused 'upset and distress' and created 'an undercurrent of distrust' between friends and family.

Justice Saunders said Mulcaire's claim that he was working for the police on the Milly Dowler story was 'incapable of belief.' Justice Saunders told the court: 'The *News of the World* were using their resources to try to find Milly Dowler. The fact that they delayed telling the police of the contents of the voicemail demonstrates that their true motivation was not to act in the best interests of the child but to get credit for finding her and thereby sell the maximum number of newspapers.'

Of the 'rogue reporter' line after Goodman's arrest, Justice Saunders said there had clearly been a cover-up: 'Mr Coulson was not the only person at the *News of the World* who knew that this activity extended beyond Goodman.' Of Mr Justice Gross' remarks during the sentencing of Mulcaire and Goodman in 2007: 'Anyone who read the transcript of the proceedings in front of Gross J would have been put on enquiry that others at the *News of the World* were involved.'

In passing sentence on Coulson, Justice Saunders accepted two points of mitigation to reduce the maximum sentence– his good character in helping others in times of distress, and the long wait till the trial. He jailed Coulson for 18 months.

For Miskiw and Thurlbeck, the maximum sentence for their offences was 12 months. Justice Saunders reduced this by a third for their guilty pleas and another two months for their delay till trial. Each was sentenced to six months in prison, with qualifying curfew reducing the final amount by 53 days.

Weatherup would have received a sentence of eight months, but two months were removed for pleading guilty and another two months for delay. Given the qualifying curfew, Weatherup was ordered to perform 200 hours unpaid community service and given a four-month sentence, suspended for 12 months

To Mulcaire, the judge said: 'Mr Mulcaire: you are the lucky one. It would in my judgment be wrong to send you back to prison today when you have already served a prison sentence, although one that was too short to reflect the full extent of your phone hacking activities. If a full investigation had been carried out in 2007 then all those matters could have been dealt with at the same time. It is not your fault that they were not.' Mulcaire received a six-month sentence, suspended for a year, and was ordered to do 200 hours community service.

I watched as Mulcaire and Weatherup exited through the normal entrance to the dock to go home. Court guards led Miskiw, Thurlbeck and Coulson to the right, down to the Old Bailey cells and a waiting prison van.

I felt no satisfaction about this result. From the beginning of the trial, I was more interested in transparency than incarceration, and for the truth to come out. Most of these convicted phone hackers now were broken men, financially and professionally. Meanwhile, in three years, partly as a result of the split of News Corp from 21st Century Fox, Rupert Murdoch's personal wealth had surged by $3 billion. If there was something to hold on to, it was one of the closing remarks of Justice Saunders, who by praising these men's initial aims, also gave hope for better to come: 'There is a certain irony in seeing men who pride themselves on being distinguished investigative journalists, who have shed light in dark corners and forced others to reveal the truth, being unprepared to do the same for their own profession.' He added: 'I accept that that would require great courage, but the best investigative journalists have never been short of courage.'

I looked around to see if Nick Davies was still in court.

◆ ◆ ◆

The weekend after sentencing, I went to the Cornbury Music Festival on the Great Tew Estate near Chipping Norton. I knew Rebekah Brooks had been there the previous two years: in 2012 she just missed meeting both Cameron and Coulson. Last year I saw her by the VIP enclosure (where she was also snapped by *Tatler*), smoking a cigarette and chatting to Jeremy Clarkson. To the surprise of many, she didn't show up this year. Locals felt a bit let down; they'd supported her during the tough years and now she'd abandoned them. But virtually everyone I met, and those who attended a talk on the hacking trial had one simple question: how did she get away with it?

I heard that on a train soon after the verdicts the MP Tom Watson was asked by passengers: how did she get away with it? He told them that there were two sides of the story and people had to accept that a jury found no evidence of guilt. The crowded carriage erupted in laughter.

I hope this book has provided some kind of answer as to why Rebekah Brooks was acquitted, while Andy Coulson was found guilty. There was insufficient evidence to convince the jury she must have known about illegal hacking or payments to public officials. But the burden of proof in the court of public opinion is much lower and – apart from a handful of News International journalists – I have not met one person who thinks the police or the CPS were wrong to bring this case, or that Brooks was victimised by the authorities. Meanwhile, though 11 men and women were not persuaded she must have known about hacking, she stands in many other journalists' eyes convicted of incompetence. Her former deputy and two of her desk heads are currently in jail. Another *News of the World* news editor, Ian Edmondson, still awaits trial, as does the former deputy editor Neil Wallis, and head of features, Jules Stenson. All were senior executives.

The fact that both Brooks and Coulson, as part of their defence, pushed some of the responsibility for the decisions about phone hacking and the cover-up upstairs, makes a corporate prosecution more likely. *Regina v News UK* could be a landmark case. It would be a tricky prosecution, though. If the hacking trial taught me anything beyond some redtop practices, it was the power of a corporate defence.

At the end of July I returned to the Old Bailey for the last act of this drama: the sentencing of Dan Evans. He had his overnight bag with him, ready for prison, and though he looked nervous in the dark wood dock of Court 2, he also looked relieved, blinking in the summer light, like a long nightmare was over. He had pleaded guilty to four counts: two of phone hacking at the *Sunday Mirror* and the *News of the World*, one of paying a prison officer for information on the Soham murderer Ian Huntley, and a fourth of lying in a court document over his hacking of Kelly Hoppen. Because Evans had been recruited to hack, pleaded guilty and entered into a deal to become a prosecution witness, he was given a 10 month sentence, suspended for a year. Justice Saunders made an additional point: 'Why so few people have been prepared to give evidence in court about what went on is not for me to say, but it makes Mr Evans' position unique.' He could go home.

Outside, the building that had ruined my phone reception was nearly complete. Eight months before, New Ludgate, a massive bright new glass complex, had been a hole in the ground. Now this brand new corporate headquarters dwarfed the Central Criminal Court and, in its shadow, the bastion of British justice looked almost puny and irrelevant.

# ACKNOWLEDGEMENTS

My presence at Court 12 at the Old Bailey for 8 months was only made possible by hundreds of individual and often anonymous donors who paid for me to live-tweet the whole trial. My first debt is to them. Thanks for taking a chance on me. I hope I repaid your trust.

Beyond those who provided financial support, there were hundreds more people I've never met, who provided moral support by engaging with me on Twitter, and watching my back when things got a little tense. I've explained in the text the phenomenal work of Jon Lippitt and Claire Pollard on my live-tweeting blog, and Gabrielle Laine Peters in fundraising and publicity. Many others provided links, fact checks and copy editing services for free, and in real time: so cheers to Rosie Robertson, Bilbocroft, Mr Ceebs, Mrs T, and Joe Public for your continuous support.

It would be churlish not to thank some of my trolls, too, for keeping me honest.

As I've said several times in this book, I've been the beneficiary of the experience and camaraderie of dozens of journalists throughout the last eight months. Many are already named, and their kindness and probity recorded. Those I haven't mentioned in the text include David Hencke, Dominic Ponsford, Meirion Jones, Paul Cheston, Eliot Higgins, Nico Hines, Harry Evans, Brian Cathcart, Tom Latchem, Mike Giglio, Marian Wilkinson, Helen Lewis, Louise Roug, Stefan Stern, Angela Haggerty, David Donovan, Jeremy Vine, and Mark Williams Thomas. Thanks.

I've also been lucky enough to meet some great lawyers. Most of those who advised on this book, or helped me in court, cannot be named. But David Allen Green and Vanessa Saxton provided me with a clear idiot proof outsiders guide to both the civil and criminal law. Polly Sprenger, Counsel at Eversheds Fraud and Investigations Group, kindly shared her great record of court quotations. David Pirie, with his keen dramatist's eye, also shared many insights.

Given the tight deadlines, I've had some amazing assistance from complete strangers providing copy proofing and corrections between the first issued e-books, and the final printed copy. Three people stand out of the crowd for their stunning attention to detail: Steve Phillips, Jane Owen and Jake Alston.

Special thanks to Tamsin Allen at Bindmans for being so brilliant under pressure. For the same reasons, under even more pressure, Martin Hickman has been the ideal editor, tightening up my loose dramatist's prose, and rooting everything in the factual. Maybe he'll teach me to be a journalist one day.

# INDEX

# SUPPORTERS

By taking a gamble and buying the book in advance, these people made it happen. Thanks again. I hope you thought it was worth it.

A Leslie Haynes ◆ Adam ◆ Adam Fronteras ◆ Adam Macqueen ◆ Adele Jolliffe ◆ Aidan Cadden ◆ Alan Jackson ◆ Alan McPherson ◆ Alan Stanford ◆ Alan Wheeler ◆ Alan's Kindle ◆ Alastair Ray ◆ Alison Alexander ◆ Amanda Wayling-Yates ◆ Andrew Barker ◆ Andrew Briggs ◆ Andrew Forbes ◆ Andrew Hill ◆ Andrew Holt ◆ Andrew Howson ◆ Andrew Kelly ◆ Andrew Oliver ◆ Andrew Sadler ◆ Andrew Wiggins ◆ Andrew Wilson ◆ Andy Bravery ◆ Andy Rogers ◆ Ann Adair ◆ Ann McMorrow ◆ Anna Jolley ◆ Anthony Midgley ◆ Apartment 207 ◆ Archie Harris ◆ Arlene ◆ Ashley ◆ Ashley Mitchell ◆ B L G Breton ◆ Barbara ◆ Barbara Hughes ◆ Bernie Ursell ◆ Bigflannel ◆ Bill Brooks ◆ Bob Digby ◆ Bob Eggington ◆ BobRoyMiller ◆ Brian Connolly ◆ Brian Hughes ◆ Brian Jacobs ◆ Brian Mitchell ◆ Brian Richardson ◆ Bryan Tookey ◆ C J Whitmey ◆ Cameron Low ◆ Cameron MacLean ◆ Carol Croft ◆ Carol Reid ◆ Carol Ward ◆ Catherine Hoskyns ◆ Catia Galatariotou ◆ Ceri Williams ◆ Charles O'Kane ◆ Charles Thomson ◆ Charlie Petherbridge ◆ Chris Anderton ◆ Chris Eccles ◆ Chris Llewellyn ◆ Chris Novakovic ◆ Chris Smith ◆ Chris Walker ◆ Christian Angelsen ◆ Christiane Link Christopher Wilson ◆ Claire ◆ Claude Green ◆ Clive Milner ◆ Colin Butler ◆ Colin Hall ◆ Colin Richdale ◆ Craig Harrison ◆ Craig Innes ◆ Dalekpete ◆ Dameo ◆ Damien Saunders ◆ Dan Rebellato ◆ Dan Tyrrell ◆ Dan Waddell ◆ Daniel Green ◆ Daniel Kleeman ◆ Dave Adams ◆ David Boardman ◆

David Burnley ◆ David Eddietorrent ◆ David Firman ◆David Isaacs ◆ David Gerow ◆ David Jones ◆ David Keir ◆ David Mills ◆ David Pirie ◆ David Pollock ◆ David Puckridge ◆ David Renwick ◆ David Sell ◆ David Shackleton ◆ David Stuart ◆ David Symes ◆ Dean Humphreys ◆ Debbie Wheawall ◆ Dennis North ◆ Derek Wilson ◆ Derek Wyatt ◆ Dermot Smith ◆ Des Hanlon ◆ Diane Ellis ◆ Dianne Desmulie ◆ Dominic Gallacher ◆ Donal Young ◆ Donald Simpson ◆ Donk Dawson ◆ Dr Natalie Martin ◆ Dr P Willetts ◆ Duncan Nimmo ◆ Dylan Williams ◆ Edward Williams ◆ Ed Wilson ◆ Einar Torbjørnsen ◆ Elaine Decoulos ◆ ElementaryForce ◆ Emer O'Farrell ◆ Fiona McD ◆ Fiona Stanier ◆ Frank Lawson ◆ Frank McNamee ◆ Frederick G E Irwin ◆ Front ◆ Gabriel Webber ◆ Gail Tuft ◆ Gareth Lane ◆ Gareth Milner ◆ Gavin Dutton ◆ Gavin Freeguard ◆ Gavin O'Farrell ◆ Geoff ◆ Geoff Cox ◆ Geoffrey Buckingham ◆ George Mckenzie ◆ Gerard O'Brien ◆ Gerard van Tonder ◆ Gian-Paul Tracey ◆ Gina M. Briggs ◆ Gordon Dangerfield ◆ Graeme McFadden ◆ Graham Bean ◆ Graham Harper ◆ Graham Smith ◆ Grant McKenna ◆ Greg Davies ◆ Greg Hocking ◆ Hannah Dadd ◆ Heather Smart ◆ Henry Fox ◆ Horatio ◆ Hugh ◆ Huseyin ◆ Ian Batten ◆ Ian Clarkson ◆ Ian F. Bray ◆ Ian Hadingham ◆ Ian Henderson (ForensicGod) ◆ Ian Reeve ◆ Ian Volans ◆ Ian Winkworth ◆ Jackie ◆ Jacob Alston ◆ Jacqueline ◆ James Aylett ◆ James Grant ◆ James Inman ◆ James Price ◆ James Tweddle ◆ Jamie Anderson ◆ Jane Cook ◆ Jane Owen ◆ Jane Winter ◆ Janet Seeley ◆ Janet Tice ◆ Jeane ◆ Jennifer Keohane ◆ Jennifer Short ◆ Jerry & Joan Bishop ◆ Jim Pailing ◆ Jo Tritton ◆ Joan Addison ◆ Joe Aspinall ◆ Joe Oliver ◆ John ◆ John Dady ◆ John Dale ◆ John Davies ◆ John Flood ◆ John Ferguson ◆ John George ◆ John Johnson ◆ John Keenan ◆ John Kellett ◆ John Lunn ◆ John Macdonald ◆ John Porter ◆ John Saunders ◆John Stovin ◆ Jon Dalladay ◆ Jon Matthews ◆ Jonathan Bruce ◆ Jonathan McCully ◆ Joseph Bulat ◆ Joyce Quarrie ◆ JP Blackband ◆ JPG Hamilton ◆ Judith Ann ◆ Judy Tomlinson ◆ Julia D. Byers. ◆ Julia Gurney ◆ Julian McElhatton ◆ Julian Petley ◆

Julian Randall ◆ Karen Darnton ◆ Karl Coverdale ◆ Karyn Reid Bliss ◆ Kate Harmond Allan ◆ Katherine Stewart Phillips ◆ Kathleen ◆ Kay ◆ ◆ KDOD ◆ Keith ◆ Keith James Raison ◆ Keith Grafton ◆ Keith Hunt ◆ Keith Severs ◆ Ken Houston ◆ Kevin Lyons ◆ Kevin Maxwell ◆ Kevin Walsh ◆ Kevin Wilson ◆ Kirstie MacGillivray ◆ Lawrence Jenkins ◆ Leo Watkins ◆ Leslie R. Woodhouse ◆ Lisa Quattromini ◆ Lisa R. Cohen ◆ Liz Gerard ◆ Liz Luder ◆ Liz Whitelam ◆ Lord Birt ◆ Lord Martin of Springburn ◆ Louise Burton ◆ Louise Jallow ◆ Louise McKenna ◆ Lucie Grant ◆ Lucy ◆ Lucy Flannery ◆ Lucy Proctor ◆ Lydia Willgress ◆ M Risbridger ◆ Mal Warwick ◆ Mal Woolford ◆ Mal Young ◆ Malcolm Allard ◆ Malcolm MacIntyre-Read ◆ Manny ◆ Marcus Carty ◆ Mark Cornwall ◆ Maria Fifield ◆ Maria O'Connor ◆ Marilyn Thorpe ◆ Máire Davies ◆ Mark ◆ Mark Baldwin ◆ Mark Eltringham ◆ Mark Reed ◆ Mark Turner ◆ Mark Walker ◆ Mark Wallace ◆ Mark Wilson ◆ Martha ◆ Martin ◆ Martin Baker ◆ Martin Jonsson ◆ Martin Kemp ◆ Mary Durcan ◆ Mary Hoffman ◆ Mary Jane Mulqueen ◆ Mary Peate ◆ Mary Williams ◆ Matthew Darroch-Thompson ◆ Matthew Taylor ◆ Matthew Willis ◆ Maureen Eddershaw ◆ Maurice ◆ Meirion ◆ Mervyn Deem ◆ Michael ◆ Michael Cadoux ◆ Michael Dolan ◆ Michael Duncan ◆ Michael Green ◆ Michael Green & Family ◆ Michael Harcup ◆ Michael Jennings ◆ Michael Moore ◆ Mike Clark ◆ Mike Fisher ◆ Mike Grace ◆ Mike Jempson ◆ Mike Pennell ◆ Mike Ward ◆ MikeH ◆ Miles Kirke ◆ Mordechai Cohen ◆ Mr Alan R Wilkinson ◆ Mr D Maskill / Mrs A Maskill ◆ Mr D R Harding ◆ Mr D Kenihan ◆ Mr Frank Dee ◆ Mr GT Hardy ◆ Mrs J E Davies ◆ Ms Kate Mariat ◆ Ms M E Preston ◆ Natalie ◆ Nicholas Jackson ◆ Nicholas Witcher ◆ ◆ Nick Davies admirer ◆ Nick Fitzsimons ◆ Nick Richards ◆ Nick Whitehurst ◆ Nico Gubbins ◆ Nicola Wortelhock ◆ Nigel Barrow ◆ Nigel D Baynham ◆ Nigel Doe ◆ Nigel Pauley ◆ Nigel Robertson ◆ Outside Influence Garden Design ◆ Owen Kane ◆ P McBride ◆ P. M. Goodman ◆ Pam Todd ◆ Pamela Smith ◆ Pat Maguire ◆ Patricia Tierney ◆ Patrick Hall ◆

Patrick Maw ◆ Paul Denvir ◆ Paul Dodd ◆ Paul Hutchinson ◆ Peta Barker ◆ Pete Morgan ◆ Peter Brooker ◆ Peter Conmy ◆ Peter D Cox ◆ Peter Huw Jenkins ◆ Peter Kerry ◆ Peter Weightman ◆ Peter Zaduk ◆ Phil Bowes ◆ Phil Cooper ◆ Philip Matthew ◆ Philip Ralph ◆ Portia Kamons ◆ Raj ◆ Ralph Douglas ◆ Ralph Milne ◆ Reg Megeney ◆ Rhoda Macdonald ◆ Richard ◆ Richard Bartholomew ◆ Richard Bonshek ◆ Richard Thomas ◆ Richard W H Bray ◆ Rob Boney ◆ Rob Harries-Harris ◆ Rob Willans ◆ Robert Payne ◆ Robert Sprackling ◆ Robert Wilson ◆ Robin Hay ◆ Rocket Roy ◆ Roddy Ashworth ◆ Roderick Fisher ◆ Roger Brown ◆ Roger Calvert ◆ Roger Palmer ◆ Ron Spencer ◆ Rowland Gwynne ◆ Rric Jinks ◆ Ruairi McAleese ◆ Russell Worsley ◆ Ruth Andrews ◆ Ruth Kennedy ◆ Sallie ◆ Sam L-B ◆ Sandra Black ◆ Sandy Roberts ◆ Sarah Cheverton ◆ Sasha Bates ◆ Sean ◆ Shaun Tinsley ◆ Shaun Williams ◆ Simon ◆ Simon Butt ◆ Simon C Shaw ◆ Simon Chapman ◆ Simon L Jones ◆ Simon Longley ◆ Simon Whittaker ◆ Simon Wood ◆ Sir Wynn N Hugh-Jones ◆ Sonya Douglas ◆ Spocko ◆ Start Space ◆ Stefan Laros ◆ Stefan Stern ◆ Stephen Barber ◆ Stephen Cropper ◆ Stephen Hayes ◆ Stephen Laffey ◆ Stephen Mennell ◆ Stephen Thompson ◆ Stephen Watson ◆ Steve Goodey ◆ Stuart C Wurtman ◆ Tim Coleman ◆ Stuart Coles ◆ Sue Cracknell ◆ Sue Young ◆ Ted Bailey ◆ Terence & Elizabeth Eden ◆ Teresa Durran ◆ Theresa Musgrove ◆ Thom Dyke ◆ Tina Kulski ◆ Tom ◆ Tony Watson ◆ Tony Beamish ◆ Tony Hatfield ◆ Tracy Amos ◆ Trevor Arrowsmith ◆ Trevor Earthy ◆ Trevor Williams ◆ Trevor M. Williams ◆ Trevor Maggs ◆ Val Fletcher ◆ Valerie Bainbridge ◆ Valerie McEvoy ◆ Valerie Mortlock ◆ Vanessa Jane Saxton ◆ William Astout ◆ William Crossland ◆ William George Smith ◆ William Fowler ◆ Zappafreak

# REVIEWS

Top court reporting – NICK DAVIES, REPORTER, GUARDIAN

Written in a chatty, gossipy style that brings the courtroom drama alive. Peter's marathon tweeting effort earned respect from all but his bitterest foes. A vital and essential read for everyone who cares about journalism and justice – NIGEL PAULEY, JOURNALIST, DAILY STAR

A great account – DOMINIC PONSFORD, PRESS GAZETTE

An absorbing and highly revealing account of the trial, with masses of new information, even for obsessives like me who followed every tweet. What's striking is how the mass of cash Rupert Murdoch threw at the defence disrupted, disturbed and thwarted the prosecution and its narrative – DAN WADDELL, AUTHOR AND FORMER TABLOID JOURNALIST

I walked the dog, brewed a large pot of coffee, made a sandwich and sat down to read. It's gripping…Hours later, I had a cold pot of coffee, a half eaten bacon butty and a reproachful dog pawing to be fed and walked again – BROWN MOSES' 'REGULAR CONTRIBUTOR'

Utterly compelling – EMER O'FARRELL, READER

Peter Jukes is the Mo Farah of citizen journalism, extraordinary endurance topped by a medal-winning flourish. A thorough, forensic and fascinating read. A must for every media professor's book shelf, and required reading for journalism students everywhere – PAUL CONNEW, FORMER DEPUTY EDITOR, NEWS OF THE WORLD

Peter paints a picture so vivid of the places, people and processes involved in the 'trial of the century' that those who were there or have been there will instantly connect, and those who've only seen the Old Bailey on television will get a feel for what it's like to spend days within its walls – JIM QUINS, READER

Peter is such a pioneer: without his absolute professionalism this experiment could have failed – MARK COLVIN, ABC PRESENTER

With sharp minds sparring to uncover or hide motives and intents, Peter's insightful commentary shows how slender, yet how vital, is the rule of law defending the people against corporate power. Who won? The legal process coped – just. The reader will have to judge for herself whether justice was done. But the innovation of crowd-funded live tweeting of the trial and the rapid publication of this book must be judged an outstanding success – CHRIS HAYNES, READER

Peter Jukes is a genuine media pioneer, the citizen journalist personified, exposing one of the greatest Establishment scandals of our time like no other journalist. This is the definitive account and is a must read for anyone who wants to understand not only our media, but power in Britain – OWEN JONES, AUTHOR AND COMMENTATOR

Quite remarkable. As a reader I feel I now know all the key players in the trial and their tactics, why some defendants were found guilty and some not, all this despite me never having spent a minute at the trial – PROFESSOR STEWART PURVIS, FORMER ITN EDITOR IN CHIEF

# ABOUT

## PETER JUKES

Peter Jukes is a British writer and journalist, who live-tweeted all 130 days of the phone hacking trial. His 2012 book, *The Fall of the House of Murdoch*, was described by the former *Sunday Times* editor Sir Harold Evans as 'a roaring great read.' He is also a dramatist for radio and television, whose credits include *In Deep*, *Bad Faith*, *Waking the Dead* and *Sea of Souls*. His account of living in the modern city, *A Shout in the Street* (Faber & Faber, 1990), was called 'a dream of a book' by John Berger. He lives in London.

*Contact*
Email: peter@peterjukes.com
Twitter: @peterjukes

## CANBURY PRESS

Canbury Press was founded in 2013 by Martin Hickman, formerly a reporter at *The Independent* and co-author of *Dial M for Murdoch*. It is exploring new ways of publishing long-form journalism.

*Contact:*
Email: canburypress@gmail.com
Twitter: @martin_hickman